Intermediate GNVQ
Information and Communication Technology

Intermediate GNVQ Information and Communication Technology

Jenny Lawson

In this book you will find helpful icons showing which Key Skills the Activities can be used for:

Communication

Application of number

Working with others

Problem solving

Improving own learning and performance

Pearson Education Limited
Edinburgh Gate
Harlow
Essex CM20 2JE, England
and Associated Companies throughout the world

ISBN 0 582 41878 X

British Library Cataloguing-in-Publication Data

A catalogue record for this book is available from the British Library.

Set by 3 in Humanist, Rotis Serif, Caslon
Produced by Pearson Education Limited
Printed in the United Kingdom by Henry Ling Ltd, at the Dorset Press, Dorchester, Dorset

Contents

		Page number
	Introduction	vi
	Acknowledgements	xiv
	The Case Studies	xvi
CHAPTER 1	**Presenting Information**	**1**
	Standard documents and their purpose	3
	Styles of writing	52
	Accuracy and readability of information	56
	Presentation	66
	Organisations and their use of information	72
	Revision questions	77
CHAPTER 2	**Handling Information**	**79**
	Information handling and handling techniques	80
	Design of information handling systems	100
	Database methods	103
	Spreadsheet methods	125
	Revision questions	153
CHAPTER 3	**Hardware and Software**	**155**
	Hardware	156
	Software	193
	Computer programming	209
	Revision questions	220
	Good Working Practice Guide	**221**
	Portfolio Guide	**241**
	Key Skills Guide	**249**
	Examination Guide	**257**
	Abbreviations	**261**
	Index	**263**

Introduction

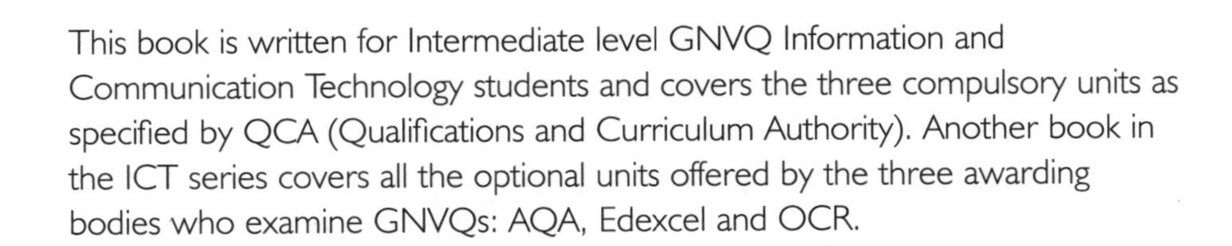

This book is written for Intermediate level GNVQ Information and Communication Technology students and covers the three compulsory units as specified by QCA (Qualifications and Curriculum Authority). Another book in the ICT series covers all the optional units offered by the three awarding bodies who examine GNVQs: AQA, Edexcel and OCR.

This book is also suitable for Intermediate level Part One students of GNVQ Information and Communication Technology.

What is Intermediate GNVQ Information and Communication Technology?

GNVQs were designed to offer students a one- or two-year full-time course as an alternative to GCSEs. There are two qualifications at Intermediate level GNVQ:

- **The 6-unit GNVQ qualification is equivalent to four GSCEs at grades A* to C or NVQ level 2**
- **The 3-unit Part One GNVQ qualification is broadly equivalent to two GCSE grades A* to C**

GNVQs are vocational qualifications, related to broad areas of the world of work, such as information and communication technology (ICT). A GNVQ qualification in Information and Communication Technology helps you to develop an understanding of ICT and introduces you to some of the skills and knowledge you will need to go on to work or further study.

For Intermediate GNVQ Information and Communication Technology, there are three **compulsory units**:

- **Presenting information**
- **Handling information**
- **IT systems**

Together, these three units cover all the material you will need to understand how ICT is used at work.

Each awarding body then offers more units, called **optional units**. The optional units give you the opportunity to choose areas that you find particularly interesting. You can broaden your experience, or you can specialise in particular areas of ICT, whichever you prefer.

How do you achieve an award in GNVQ Information and Communication Technology at Intermediate level?

The 3-unit Part One GNVQ in ICT involves about half the work of the full award, but you are tested on each unit.

For the 6-unit award of an Intermediate GNVQ in ICT, you must complete six units:

- **3 compulsory units**
- **3 optional units**

You will be tested on two units: one compulsory unit and one other chosen from the optional unit suite. This means that two-thirds of your work will be assessed as you work through the course (continual assessment), and one-third will be tested at set times of the year (January or June), after you have worked on a particular unit.

These two methods of assessment appeal to different types of students. Some students do not like tests; for them continual assessment seems less stressful.

Others quite like tests, perhaps because they think they can leave all the learning until just before the exam. Having both methods of assessment within the one course, students are encouraged not to leave things to the last minute, and, although there are exams to face, your work is assessed in the least stressful way.

For Part One students, all your work will be assessed, and all three units will be tested.

For both awards – the 6-unit award and the 3-unit Part One award – evidence of your work will be kept in a portfolio.

While studying for your GNVQ course, you will also have the opportunity to gain the Key Skills qualifications. As far as is possible, evidence of Key Skills may be seen within your portfolio of work, and your teacher will advise you on how you can build evidence of Key Skills into your assignments. The Key Skills Guide on page 249 also provides useful information about Key Skills.

What is a unit?

A unit covers one area of study. Intermediate GNVQ ICT Unit 1, for example, concentrates on 'Presenting Information'.

Each unit specification has four main headings:

- **About this unit**
- **What you need to learn**
- **Assessment evidence**
- **Guidance for teachers (including guidance on delivery, guidance on assessment, resources and Key Skills guidance)**

The final section is written for teachers, but since your success on this course depends on you, rather than your teacher, you should find it quite useful. It explains how you can work hard to achieve a good grade for the unit, and what Key Skills you might achieve while doing the unit. With GNVQs, you are expected to take responsibility for your own learning, so it makes sense to make time to read this section very carefully.

How to 'read' a unit

The **title** of the unit gives a broad description of what the unit covers e.g. Handling Information.

The **About this unit** section introduces the unit. It explains what benefits you may expect from completing the unit, and gives a broad description of what you will do. It also tells you about any links between this unit and other units.

The **What you need to learn** section is the longest section. It lists all the topics you should cover for this unit, though not necessarily in the order you will learn about them. Notice that this section is called 'What you need to learn' rather than 'What you will be taught'. This is because it is quite possible that your teacher will do very little 'teaching'! GNVQ students are expected to take control of their own learning, and it is your teacher's job to guide you towards this independent approach to learning. At first, you may find this a strange and difficult experience. You will have more freedom to decide what to do, but also need to make decisions for yourself. It is very important that you meet deadlines set, and put in the hours expected on your course. Otherwise, you may be given poor assessment grades for your portfolio material. However, your teacher will help you to learn how to work responsibly. One of the objectives of a vocational course like a GNVQ course is to prepare you for a job, and this teaching style is an important part of the GNVQ process.

How will your understanding be tested? If you are on a 6-unit Intermediate GNVQ course:

- **for two-thirds of the units, you will demonstrate your understanding by your portfolio material**
- **for one-third of the units, there are 90-minute written tests, one per unit**

If you are on a 3-unit Part One Intermediate GNVQ course:

- **for all three units, you will demonstrate your understanding by your portfolio material, and**
- **for all three units, there are 90-minute written tests, one per unit**

The obvious way to learn about work is through your work experience placement or a part-time job. However, your course should also offer you the opportunity to try out a variety of work experiences:

- **Working on your own as well as with others in a team**
- **Doing short projects and completing long assignments**
- **Visiting local firms and businesses, and interviewing people such as the employers, their staff and their customers**
- **Designing products and services**
- **Organising events**

The **Assessment evidence** section is given as a chart with four columns.

- The top section lists what evidence you need to produce for the unit. There may be one large piece of evidence, or the task may be broken down into a number of smaller tasks for you to complete. You will need to have covered the unit and developed an understanding of the topics in the 'What you need to learn section' to produce your portfolio evidence, but not all topics need be evidenced. This will also specify how many examples you need to produce for your evidence.
- The first column in the lower section of the table explains what is expected for a pass. When producing your evidence, you should use this first column to check that your work is at the required standard for a pass.
- The second and third columns explain what is expected of a merit and distinction student. For a merit, you must do the things in the pass column as well as those in the merit column. For a distinction, you must do the things in the pass column, and the things in the merit column, as well as those in the distinction column!

The things listed in merit and distinction columns are not extra tasks for you to complete; instead, they show what extra qualities you are expected to demonstrate in your evidence:

- How good you are at planning and organising your work
- How independent you are when carrying out your work – whether you can cope without a lot of help
- How much the quality of the work you are producing is improving
- How much you show a greater understanding of what you have learnt

It is important that you read this chart very carefully.

The portfolio

Your portfolio contains all the evidence collected as you work through the units. It must contain at least the minimum stated in the pass column of the Assessment Evidence section of each unit.

Mostly, this will be evidence of your work on a computer system and so will be printouts, annotated to explain what you have done. Some units may ask for a special form of evidence to be produced by you:

- **Unit 1 asks for a portfolio of six original documents, notes and an evaluation of your work**
- **Unit 2 asks for a relational database and a spreadsheet to meet user needs**
- **Unit 3 asks for screen prints and printouts**

When assessing your work, your teacher is looking for the right quality and quantity of work. He or she will first look to see that you have covered everything by checking all the items listed on the Assessment Evidence chart. However, work of a high quality may earn you a merit or distinction award, so your teacher will be looking at the last two columns of the chart in particular.

Before handing in your work to your teacher for assessment, you should check exactly what is required for each unit, and make sure that your portfolio holds all this information in an easily accessible way. Guidance on how to present your portfolio is given in the Portfolio Guide section of this book on page 241.

Grading

By the end of your course, your portfolio will contain a great deal of evidence. In deciding what grade to award (pass, merit, or distinction), your teacher will consider a number of things:

- **Your approach to learning and how you tackled your work**
- **How much responsibility you took for planning your work**
- **How you decided what information you needed**
- **How well you reviewed and evaluated your own progress**
- **The quality of your evidence**

It is important, therefore, to aim high.

During your course, you should receive feedback from your teacher giving you a clear picture of how you are doing, and how you might improve your performance.

The external tests

For the 6-unit Intermediate GNVQ ICT award, there are two tests: one compulsory unit and one optional unit.

Each examination board offers different tested units so, depending on which board your school or college uses, you will have to choose at least one optional unit that involves an external test.

- **For OCR and AQA centres, the tested compulsory unit is Unit 3: Hardware and Software, and the optional choice is between Unit 6: Graphics and DTP and Unit 9: Monitoring and Control Systems**
- **For Edexcel centres, the tested compulsory unit is Unit 1: Presenting Information and their only tested optional unit is Unit 5: Information Resources**

When you have completed the work for a single unit, you should be ready to sit the external test. This comprises a written test, lasting 90 minutes, in which you write your answers within a booklet in the spaces provided. Sample papers that you can use as 'mock' examinations, are available from the websites of the examination boards.

Some guidance about how to prepare for these tests is given in the Examination Guide on page 257.

How should you use this book?

This introductory chapter explains how GNVQs work. The main part of this book is then divided into three chapters, which match the three compulsory units in Intermediate GNVQ Information and Communication Technology.

- **Unit 1: Presenting Information**
- **Unit 2: Handling Information**
- **Unit 3: Hardware and Software**

There are many features within each chapter:

- **Notes on what you need to know, with plenty of diagrams and examples, mostly based on case studies**
- **Stopping points with questions and exercises to check you have understood what you have been reading about**
- **Activities to test your understanding and to help you to produce portfolio evidence**
- **Sets of revision questions**

Towards the end of the book, there are four guides:

- **The Good Working Practice Guide provides useful information about Health and Safety issues and other good working practice expected of you during your practical work**
- **The Portfolio Guide explains how you might present your portfolio material plus some help in gaining merit and distinction grades**
- **The Key Skills Guide explains what you have to do to demonstrate your Key Skills in Communication and Application of Number. Key Skills in IT at level 2 are automatically covered within the GNVQ ICT course.**
- **The Examinations Guide offers useful advice about preparation for the written examinations**

There is also a list of abbreviations and a comprehensive index. The index lists all important words used in the book. Indexed words appear in **bold** within the text, or within headings. The index also includes cross references, to help you find what you are looking for.

What else do you need?

As well as this book, you need a copy of the unit specifications for Intermediate GNVQ Information and Communication Technology, plus sample papers and past papers for the written examinations. All the information is available on the Internet and can be downloaded free of charge.

The compulsory unit specifications are available on the QCA site and also on the sites of the three awarding bodies. Access to all these sites and other useful sites for GNVQ and NVQ resources is available through Pearson Education's website: http://www.longman-fe.com

You are also recommended to visit the website of the British Computer Society (BCS) and to obtain a copy of the glossary published by Pearson Education, which explains all the terms used for this GNVQ course and in this book. Two versions are available:

- **A Glossary of Computing Terms, ISBN: 0582369673**
- **IT Glossary for Schools, ISBN: 0582312558**

Acknowledgements

I am very grateful to all those who provided material for the many examples and case studies in the book:

- Alan and Maxine Wade, Penhaven Country House Hotel
- The Green Team at Chris Lane Family Leisure Club, especially Tim Lane, Andy Harris, Simon Thorpe and David Gabb
- Peter Hawkes of Hawkes Design
- John Hore, Sailing Breaks
- Red Letter Days
- Sarah Armstrong and her contacts at Lush
- Toby Bishop, The Candle Shop, Bodmin
- Richard Haslam-Hopwood, St Breock Gallery, Cornwall
- The Press Office staff at the Met Office
- Sailing friends who suggested ideas for the fictitious case study in Chapter 2, too many to list by name
- Peter Pitchforth, Midland Bank Pensioners' Association, for the poem on page 62

Thanks are also due to my colleagues of many years: the principal examiners (Graham Redfern, Geoff Brignell and David Bittlestone) and the many assistant examiners who offered advice, or who, during discussion at our many examination meetings, raised questions that I have tried to answer in this book.

Special thanks go to my colleagues at the examination boards – everyone in the GNVQ units, the teams of setters, pre-moderators and moderators involved in the preparation of external test papers.

Finally, the team at Pearson Education deserve a mention for their encouragement and support – Sonia Wilson, Eva Martinez and Kay Spragg – and my family, who were very patient during the preparation of this book.

The Case Studies

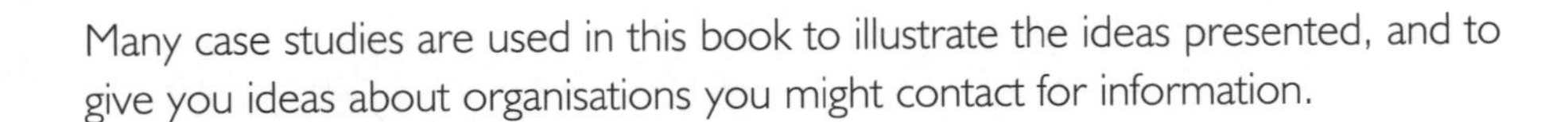

Many case studies are used in this book to illustrate the ideas presented, and to give you ideas about organisations you might contact for information.

- The Candle Shop
- Chris Lane Family Leisure Club
- Hawkes Design
- Lush International
- The Met Office
- Online Cruising Club (OCC)
- Penhaven Country House Hotel
- Sailing Breaks
- St Breock Gallery

In this section, each one is introduced, in alphabetical order, so that you have some background information on each organisation:

- Who is involved
- What product or service the organisation provides
- How ICT systems are used in the organisation

When you are trying to find users for whom you can develop projects, think about similar organisations to these case studies.

The Candle Shop

The Candle Shop in Bodmin, Cornwall, is a business owned and run by the Bishop family. They make many different kinds of candles on the premises. They welcome all visitors, especially coach parties, to see their candles and hopefully to buy some!

Chris Lane Family Leisure Club

Chris Lane opened his club 15 years ago, initially as a tennis club with 150 members and four staff. Since then the club has grown dramatically and now has thousands of members enjoying facilities which include indoor and outdoor tennis courts, a fully equipped gym, therapy rooms, beauty treatment rooms, studio, pool, crèche, bar and restaurant. Recently, the clubhouse has been redeveloped to incorporate KidSports, a facility for children to learn through organised activities.

The staff at Chris Lane, called the Green Team, are committed to customer care. The aim of the Green Team is to make each visit to the club a positive experience for every member, every time they visit the club.

The club keeps in touch with members using the club magazine, leaflets and posters which are displayed around the clubhouse. Producing posters is a full-time job; over 250 new posters are needed each year to advertise the many events on offer to members.

ICT is used in a number of ways within the club. Many of the Green Team work in the gym, in the dance studio, the pool, or on the tennis courts, so their use of ICT is limited. For the rest, there are about 30 computers in use daily, all networked and providing information to the various departments: Accounts, Membership, Reception and the Management Team.

When members enter the club, they swipe their membership card through a sensor which releases a turnstile and lets them into the clubhouse. The system records that they are present, which is useful in case of fire or if someone rings the club trying to contact a member. This record also allows the club to monitor which members use the club more regularly and, most important, which members have not been to the club for a while. These members can be contacted by telephone to see if they need some encouragement to return to their training schedule or to check that nothing untoward has discouraged them from using club facilities.

Members can also put money onto their membership cards for use in the bar and restaurant. Members are given a 10% discount on any purchase made with the card. The club benefits from this positive cash flow – but it does offer the opportunity for members to leave valuables at home and to visit the club to train, carrying only their membership card.

There are many similar clubs in the UK, and it would be worthwhile visiting one near you to find out how ICT is used by their staff and how it affects their members.

Hawkes Design

Peter Hawkes is a graphic designer. His clients include educational publishers, environmental organisations and local organisations. For his clients, Peter designs and produces logos, magazines, theatre brochures and programmes, advertisements and publicity flyers.

Each year, Peter creates a one-page calendar which includes samples of his work. He sends a copy to his clients and contacts within the publishing industry, to remind them of the services he offers.

Peter is one of the many freelancers that publishers use to produce their books, and my first contact with Peter was in producing a series of Maths books. Artwork briefs were sent to Peter. He drew the artwork using his software and not inconsiderable artistic talent, and then these final drawings were placed within the text of the book. His work is time-consuming and requires a great deal of patience. He checks his work very carefully before sending it back to his client for approval.

The hardware and software used by Peter is explained in Chapter 3.

The publishing industry relies on freelancers like Peter. You may find details of local people with similar skills by looking in your Yellow Pages.

Lush International

Lush produce fresh handmade products which are sold mainly through mail order. They produce a newspaper called *Lush Times* which is sent to all customers four times a year.

They also have shops in Australia, Canada, Croatia, Sweden, Scotland and England.

Many organisations produce newsletters and magazines, either for staff or clients. Lots of design ideas can be seen if you look at a variety of magazines.

The Met Office

The Met Office use ICT in a big way! The computers used to process weather data are huge, and their use of telecommunications spans the world. Like other governmental organisations they have a website on which you can find out how they work: http://www.meto.gov.uk

It is possible to arrange a visit to the Bracknell headquarters, but since this is so popular it may not be feasible within the time span of your course. However, a visit to their website will give you lots of information. You can also ask to be sent a copy of their annual report – one copy for the whole class should be enough!

Online Cruising Club (OCC)

The Online Cruising Club case study is loosely based on a sailing club of which I am a member. For confidentiality reasons, none of the data given in the examples is real.

This case study was devised because it is similar to any sports club:

- **Members' details need to be kept so that newsletters can be sent to them with details of club fixtures and social events**
- **Subscriptions will be paid and recorded by a treasurer**
- **Meetings will be held and minutes taken**
- **The club will be run by a committee – usually volunteers. The committee changes each year although some members may remain on the committee for a few years**

It is quite likely that such a club would provide opportunities for projects. Most committee members are busy with daytime jobs and work done for the club is fitted into spare time in the evenings and at weekends. Any suggestions that will reduce their workload would be warmly welcomed.

Penhaven Country House Hotel

The level of detail given here is an indication of how much information you should try to get from users that you hope to help with your project.

Penhaven Country House Hotel was opened by Maxine and Alan Wade, who retired from the music trade before they reached the age of 40. Their lounge bar is decorated with trophies of their musical past: gold and platinum discs from groups such as the Thompson Twins, Men at Work and Musical Youth.

Penhaven Country House Hotel is situated in Penhaven, a village in North Devon, quite close to the sea, and is set in 11 acres. There are 12 bedrooms – all en-suite, with tea-making facilities, remote control television and telephone. Some bedrooms have extra facilities like an extra lounge, or a four-poster bed. There are also six cottage suites in the grounds which can house a family of guests.

Maxine and Alan have created a peaceful atmosphere with excellent accommodation, food and wines, and want their guests to relax and enjoy themselves during their stay at Penhaven. The hotel is open seven days a week, 52 weeks of the year, with a break each January, when the hotel is redecorated and Alan and Maxine go in search of the next year's wine list.

Penhaven attracts the older visitor. Children under ten are not accepted, although pets are. The atmosphere is very peaceful, perfect for a stress-free break. In the grounds there is a nature trail, useful for walking off the excellent meals. There are badgers in the grounds and these are encouraged and protected by Alan and Maxine. A parking space is left clear in an area where the badgers are likely to appear, and their nightly visit can be watched from the lounge. Badgers are included in the graphics of several pieces of stationery: the breakfast menu and special weekend menus.

Maxine is responsible for the administration side of things.

Booking enquiries, usually in response to an advertisement, are mostly received by telephone. Maxine, or one of her staff, takes down the name and address and any special requirements. On the same day, she sends a letter (on headed notepaper) thanking the caller for the enquiry and enclosing a copy of the Penhaven brochure, the tariff, a booking form and copies of any 'special' weekends in the near future.

The letter heading includes the country house motif. The brochure is in full colour and includes both the country house motif and one of the badgers, as well as a map to show how to find the hotel and several photographs of the restaurant, bar and grounds. The tariff is A4 folded to A5 and includes the AA 3-star and RAC 3-star symbols. All these documents go in an envelope which bears the Penhaven Country House logo, and are posted first class.

When the caller receives the mail the next day, this envelope will announce that Maxine has dealt with the enquiry immediately, as promised. This is the first indication of the level of service to be expected from Penhaven.

Confirmations of bookings may be by telephone, on a booking form in the post, or by fax. Recently, Maxine and Alan have arranged for Penhaven to have a website at http://www.penhaven.co.uk on the Internet, so they may also soon be receiving bookings by e-mail. The details are recorded in the bookings diary and a letter confirming the booking (and the deposit taken) is sent in the mail.

Each day, Maxine prepares the 'welcome pack' for the arrivals the following day:

- **A personally addressed brochure of guest information, such as meal times**
- **A card which is handed to the guest with the room key, which shows the name of the guest, the room number, the cost of the room and the leaving date**

When guests arrive, they are asked to complete a registration form. This includes extra details such as car registration number, whether newspapers are required and how the guest intends to pay for the stay. This information is used to update the customer record file, and is used for future mail shots.

Great care is taken to produce promotional material which reinforces the impression that guests are given the 'red carpet' treatment and will enjoy their stay at Penhaven.

- **The headed stationery has the country house motif**
- **The compliments slip has the badger motif, including a red carpet**
- **When guests arrive in their room, more small touches are evident: the notepad beside the phone, the complimentary toiletries all bearing the Penhaven logo and the freshly made biscuits**
- **At reception, postcards with a colour photograph of the gardens at Penhaven are on sale**
- **At breakfast, special menus are on display, depending on the type of breakfast available: full English or continental**
- **Menus for lunch and evening meals are displayed in the lounge/bar area and orders taken before guests go through to the restaurant**
- **At the dinner table complimentary matchboxes bear the country house motif**
- **When orders are taken, these are written on pre-printed pads, which have the country house logo**
- **In the restaurant and bar area, drinks mats bear the Penhaven logo**

Alan is responsible for the food and wine. Penhaven offers an excellent menu and has an extensive list of fine wines to match the food. Menus are planned the evening before – a lot depends on what local butchers and fishmongers have available – and individual menus are printed during each morning.

Penhaven advertises in national newspapers. The hotel is in an excellent position for anyone wanting to explore Devon, so guests could come from anywhere in the UK. Another way of attracting guests is to offer special weekends at special prices and these are held several times a year: Christmas, St George's Day, May Bank Holiday, Midsummer's Day, and so on.

The menus for these special weekends have to be decided months in advance, to allow Maxine time to send out a mailshot of 400 menus to past guests. For this, Maxine keeps records of all past guests: their name, address and telephone number. With the advertising and the mailshots, enough enquiries should result in a 'full house' for each special weekend.

Penhaven's home-made marmalade is served at breakfast and is so popular that it is bottled and sold to guests. The label stresses that the marmalade is home-made and that it is produced at Penhaven.

At the end of dinner, coffee is served at the table or can be taken in the lounge – a comfortable room with a huge log fire. With the coffee, Penhaven's home-made fudge is served. It too is delicious and many guests asked if they could buy some. Now it is sold at Reception.

When guests are due to leave, an invoice is prepared, showing their room charges plus any extra charges such as telephone calls or drinks. The invoice has room for details of seven days' stay, although most guests stay for a few days only.

Hotels, even those that appear to be small, require levels of administration that can be made very efficient by introducing ICT. Wherever you live in the UK, there will be a hotel near you that you may be able to visit to find out how they use ICT. You do not need to stay in the hotel to find out how they take bookings, confirm bookings, prepare advertising material and other information such as menus.

Sailing Breaks

I first met John Hore when I attended a course run at the local Adult Education centre. John is a RYA Instructor and gives courses to those interested in learning about sailing. His course notes were excellent. They were produced using a word processor and included diagrams which John had drawn or scanned in. Because they are word processed, John can easily amend them. So, each year his course notes improve – an enormous help to his students.

John's company is called Sailing Breaks. He has a yacht called *Half Nelson* and he takes groups out for sailing days. Apart from courses arranged to provide RYA practical qualifications, Sailing Breaks provides fun sailing for anyone keen to try it, and the opportunity to take part in races. Full information about Sailing

Breaks and a photo of John, looking rather windswept, can be seen on his website: http://www.sailingbreaks.co.uk

Some of his trips are organised through a company called Red Letter Days. You can visit their web site too: http://www.redletterdays.co.uk

All teachers in schools or at Adult Education centres are faced with preparing class notes to give to their students. Looking at how teachers produce this material can teach you a lot about the ICT they are using. You may also be able to suggest improvements for those teachers who are not as familiar with ICT as you are. If you help them, you will also be helping their students.

St Breock Gallery

Richard Haslam-Hopwood's gallery at St Breock in Cornwall is a centre for fine reproduction furniture. His leaflet may be found in Tourist Information Offices around the west country.

Presenting Information

1

- Write original documents in styles that suit your readers
- Improve the accuracy and readability of documents that you create
- Improve the quality of presentation in documents you create
- Choose and apply standard document layouts

This chapter also offers the opportunity to develop good working practices. Details about these, which apply to all units in this course, are on page 221 in the Good Working Practice Guide.

This chapter looks in detail at five topics:

- Standard documents and their purpose
- Styles of writing
- Accuracy and readability of information
- Presentation
- Organisations and their use of information

Several case studies are used to introduce and illustrate the ideas of this chapter:

- Chris Lane Family Leisure Club
- Lush International

- **Penhaven Country House Hotel**

Background information about these organisations is given in the Case Studies section of this book, starting on page xvi.

You will look at many sample documents supplied by these organisations. You will see the writing style used and the way information is presented to their clients.

For your portfolio you will need to present a similar collection of sample documents. These documents must have been designed for different purposes. You will have to judge their quality and produce a guide on effective presentations based on your experience.

You should try to identify some local organisations, like the ones used in the case studies, that might be willing to show you examples of the documents they use. You could also collect any letters or leaflets received at your home. This will give you some examples, without your having to contact the organisations concerned.

Finally, you will then need to produce your own documents, showing that you understand the topics covered in this chapter.

Standard documents and their purpose

Here are some examples of documents:

- A formal letter to an organisation in reply to a job advertisement
- A brief newspaper advertisement for something second-hand
- A note explaining a child's absence from school
- A formal invitation to a party or special event
- A single-page advertisement for a new car
- An order form for mail-order goods
- A letter to a newspaper
- A table of results for a sports league
- A draft of the results of a survey
- A report of a local council planning meeting

Exercise 1.1

Write down four more examples of documents.

Think about the **writing style** and presentation of some of these documents. This will help you to recognise that different writing styles and **presentation techniques** are used to meet different needs. Here are some examples of needs:

- Attracting attention and creating interest
- Setting out facts clearly
- Reminding colleagues about something
- Explaining details
- Summarising information

Exercise 1.2

Look at your four example documents. Which need do they meet? (Some documents may meet several needs.)

A brief newspaper advertisement for something second-hand needs to attract your attention and set out the facts clearly (that is, what is for sale, how much it costs and who to contact).

Activity 1.1

Copy and complete Table 1.1, adding more rows for the extra documents you have thought of. Then, tick two boxes for each document listed in the table, by deciding which two needs are the most important. Are any other needs met by these documents?

To include a good variety of documents, you might concentrate on the needs and think of documents that meet those needs, rather than the other way round.

	Needs				
Documents	**Attracting attention**	**Setting out facts clearly**	**Reminding colleagues**	**Explaining details**	**Summarising information**
A formal letter					
A note					
A formal invitation					
An advert	✓	✓			
A table of results					

Table 1.1 *The needs met by documents*

Organisations design their own documents to suit their own needs, but some documents are used by most organisations. These are called **standard documents**.

- Business letters and business cards
- Invoices, orders and delivery notes
- Memos, e-mails and faxes
- Publicity flyers
- Newsletters
- Drafts
- Reports
- Agendas and minutes
- Itineraries and programmes

Each of these standard documents meets a particular need and has its own writing style and presentation technique.

A screen – the last item listed – is not a 'document' in that it does not appear on paper. However, nowadays organisations may decide to present information about their products and services by having a website. The site is made up from several screens, each one called a **web page**.

Penhaven Country House Hotel

Maxine and Alan decided to advertise their country house hotel and have a website which gives all the details that prospective guests might need. You can visit their website at http://www.penhaven.co.uk

The first screen you will see – called the **home page** – is shown in Figure 1.1. You can then visit other pages on their website by double clicking on 'Penhaven', 'Directions', 'Tariff' or 'Specials'. From each of these pages you can skip directly to any of the other pages, or return to the home page.

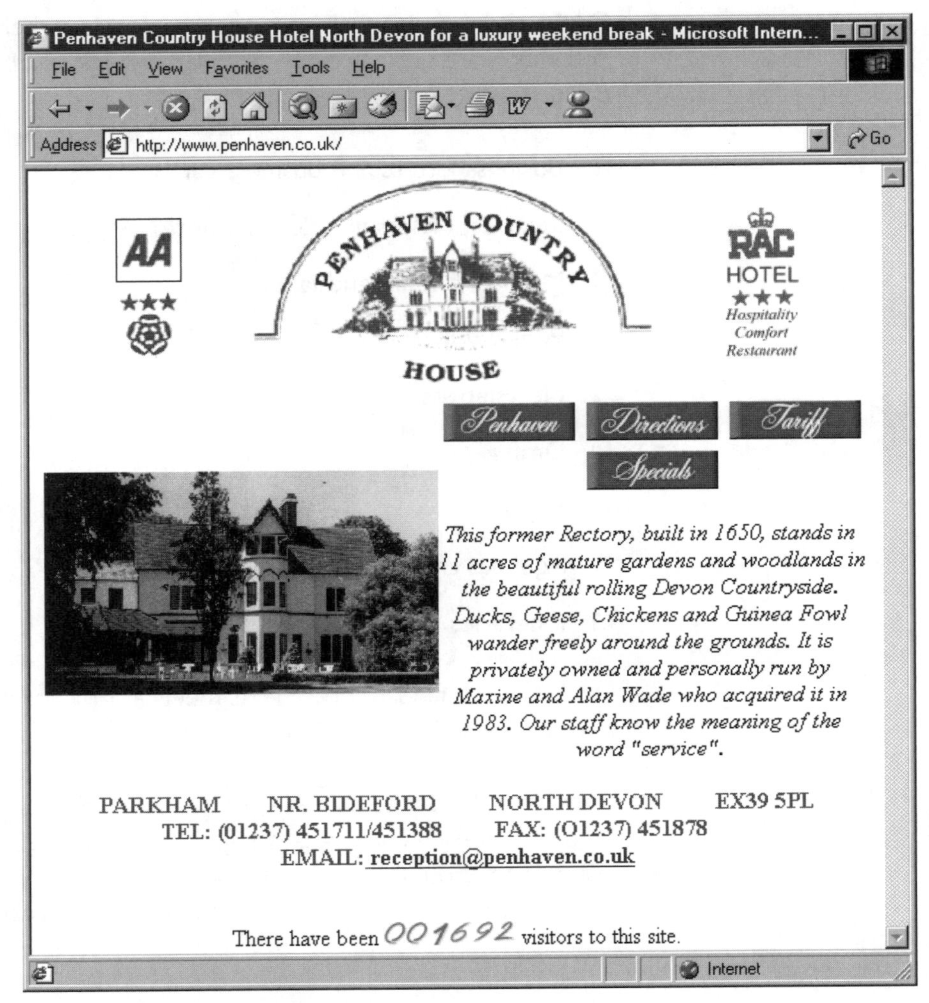

Figure 1.1 *Penhaven's home page*
Courtesy of Penhaven Country House Hotel

For those customers with access to the Internet, a website can provide an easy way to find out about a company and to buy from them. **E-commerce** is buying through the Internet. All purchases are made using credit or debit cards.

To buy a copy of this book, or any other book, you could visit the Amazon website at www.amazon.co.uk. If you order today, the book could be with you in 24 hours.

The design of web pages needs to be good enough to attract the viewer but not so complicated that the loading time leaves the user bored. There is no 'standard' for web page design, but some features will become standard over time.

Exercise 1.3

For one particular website, look at all the pages that are available. Is there a common format to each web page? If so, sketch it.

Compare the layouts used on three or four websites. What 'standard' features do you recognise that they all share?

You can create web pages from most DTP software, and on the latest versions of word-processing software. Web page design is part of the Graphics and DTP unit, so if you choose that unit you will have the opportunity to design your own web pages. (The companion to this book – *Intermediate GNVQ Information and Communication Technology Options* – includes web page design.)

Business letters and business cards

External communications are those that an organisation makes with people outside the organisation, e.g. with other organisations, or with the public.

Business letters are used for **external communications**.

All organisations write business letters to clients, suppliers and other external organisations, such as the bank, their auditors or the Inland Revenue. The business letter is an important document, not only because of the information it contains, but because of the impression it gives of the organisation.

Chris Lane

Figure 1.2 shows an example of a business letter written by the Customer Care Supervisor at Chris Lane's in reply to a letter received from one of the members. Notice that Chris Lane's logo is similar to his signature. This conveys the very personal attention Chris pays to all members of his club.

continued

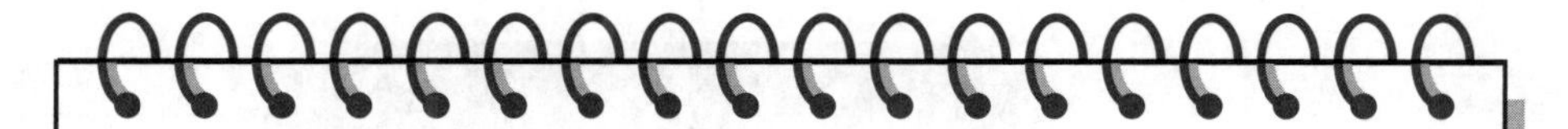

continued

July 12, 2000

Joan Turnbull
14 Acacia Drive
West Hill
Surrey
GU21 4RZ

Dear Joan

Thank you for the suggestions outlined in your letter dated 3 July 2000.

Your ideas for improving the timetable of events were well thought out and clearly stated. I have forwarded them to the Events Organiser for consideration.

As I'm sure you know, many factors affect which events appeal to members – and sometimes it is very difficult to please all of our members all of the time!

So, although we can't promise that we will implement your suggestions, we appreciate them and will give them the serious consideration they deserve.

Thank you again for taking the time to share your ideas with us.

Yours sincerely,

Jeremy White

Jeremy White
Customer Care Supervisor

CLUB OF THE YEAR AWARDS:
R.O.L.I.A. Award Winner,
Outstanding U.K. Sport, Health And Fitness Club of the Year
Award Winner of Schweppes/Coca Cola Club of the Year
Award Winner of Girobank/LTA Tennis Club of the Year

Grasspost Ltd, trading as Chris Lane Tennis & Health. Registered in England No: 1584666
Registered Office: Ashcombe Court, Woolsack Way, Godalming, Surrey GU7 1LQ
VAT Registration No: GB413393865

***Figure 1.2** Chris Lane business letter*
Courtesy of Chris Lane Family Leisure Club

Penhaven Country House Hotel

Figure 1.3 shows an example of a business letter written to confirm a booking.

PARKHAM · Nr. BIDEFORD · N. DEVON · EX39 5PL ☎ (01237) 451711/451388 Fax: (01237) 451878

31st March 2000

Mr and Mrs Lawson,
12 Ravens Close,
Knaphill,
Woking,
Surrey,
GU21 2LD

Dear Mr and Mrs Lawson,

Thank you for faxing through the booking form and we are pleased to confirm the reservation of our double bedded mini-suite on the second floor for a three night May Day break at a rate of £183.85 per person.

The rooms are available from 2.30 pm.

We look forward to seeing you both again soon.

Yours sincerely,

Maxine Wade

MAXINE and ALAN WADE

Figure 1.3 *Penhaven's letter of confirmation*
Courtesy of Penhaven Country House Hotel

At the top of a business letter the organisation's logo and contact details are shown. This will include the name, address, telephone number and any other important information. This information may also be preprinted on the **envelopes** used by an organisation. Figure 1.4 shows some examples.

Figure 1.4 *Envelopes with logos*
Courtesy of Penhaven Country House Hotel and Lush

Exercise 1.4

Using envelopes with a logo is more expensive than using a plain envelope.

- ★ **What effect do you think the logo has?**
- ★ **Have you ever received a letter in an envelope with a logo on it? If so, what was your reaction when you saw the envelope?**
- ★ **In what other ways can an organisation advertise their name on the outside of an envelope?**

Lush International

Lush have their logo printed on the envelopes used to mail out their newspaper. Then, when their customers receive this, they know it is not 'junk mail' (see Figure 1.4).

Penhaven Country House Hotel

Maxine and Alan have a drawing of their hotel as their logo. Their website and business letters have the Penhaven Country House logo and contact details, as well as the AA and RAC logos (see Figures 1.1 and 1.3). The same logo appears on their envelopes (see Figure 1.4).

Exercise 1.5

For your portfolio you need to collect example documents from at least three different organisations. Start to think about the types of organisations you will approach.

- Do you know anyone who works for a large organisation?
- Do you know anyone who works in a hotel, a sports club or a shop?
- Do you know anyone who works for themselves, e.g. as a book-keeper?
- Do you have a Saturday job?

Look through the advertisements in your local paper. You may notice an organisation that you would like to contact.

When choosing which organisations to approach, look for those whose logo impresses you. Try to decide what it is about a logo that is eye-catching. What does this tell you about the organisation?

What is written in a business letter is obviously important. It should meet any legal requirements and convey its message clearly and briefly.

Activity 1.2

Compose one letter to send to organisations. In the letter, ask whether they will help you with your GNVQ ICT course by allowing you to meet with one of their staff to discuss the standard documents used by the organisation. Include your own contact details, so they can write back to you. Keep a copy of the letter in your portfolio.

Send the letter to ten different organisations – with luck you will get a positive response from at least three of them. When you receive the replies, do not throw away the envelopes.

Try to choose organisations that none of the other students on your course have chosen. Also, if you have personal contacts within local organisations, write your letter to them.

Paper size
Stationers use a coding system – A0, A1, A2, A3, A4, A5 etc. – to label different sizes of paper.

Orientation
is the direction of the print on a page: **portrait** orientation prints across the width of the paper; **landscape** orientation prints across the length of the paper. The paper is fed into the printer in the normal way for both; with landscape orientation the printing appears 'sideways'.

There is a variety of **paper sizes** (see Figure 1.5). Most business letters are produced on A4 size paper, used in portrait **orientation**.

Most office IT systems have printers that accept A4 or smaller paper. For larger documents (e.g. plans) special plotters are needed.

The layout of the information on a business letter, the typeface used and the point size all have an effect on the impression the letter gives.

The quality of the paper on which a business letter is written is also important. High-quality paper may give the impression of a high-quality company; low-quality paper will not.

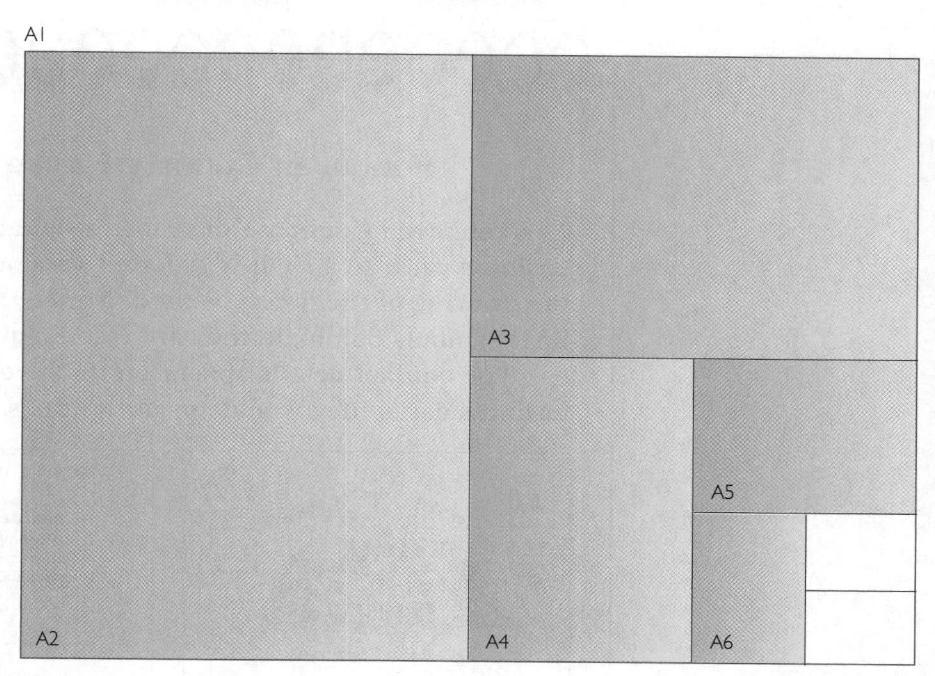

Figure 1.5 *Paper sizes*

Typeface
There are two 'families' of typeface: those with **serifs** and those without (known as **sans serif**). Sans serif looks 'cleaner' and is often used for headlines. Serif fonts are used for normal reading text.

Point size
is a measure of the vertical height of a font. **Pitch** refers to the number of characters printed in a horizontal inch.

Font
is a typeface of a particular **size** and **attribute**. For example, 12pt Times Roman is one font. 8pt Times Roman is another. The abbreviation 'pt' stands for 'point'.

The term **type** describes all the printed letters (a–z, A–Z), numbers (0–9) and other characters and symbols (!, ", £, $, % etc.). The **typeface** and **point size** define a **font**.

Chris Lane

Chris Lane's letter is set in a **sans serif font** and uses minimal punctuation (see Figure 1.2).

Penhaven Country House Hotel

Maxine uses an italic **serif font** when writing to confirm bookings (see Figure 1.3).

Business cards are used by people in organisations to pass their contact details to people they meet. The organisation's logo and all contact details are usually printed on a card small enough to fit into a wallet. Business cards are usually made from heavy card to make them more durable, i.e. to last longer.

Penhaven Country House Hotel

The Penhaven Country House logo would not fit on a business card, so a slightly different version, still including the drawing of the house, is used. Notice that the AA and RAC symbols dominate the card (see Figure 1.6).

The contact details appear on the reverse side. On most business cards they would appear on the same side.

Maxine and Alan Wade
Penhaven Country House
Parkham, N. Devon EX39 5PL
Telephone (01237) 451711/451388
Fax: (01237) 451878

Figure 1.6 *Penhaven business card*
Courtesy of Penhaven Country House Hotel

Activity 1.3

You have been asked to design a logo for Pam Turner, who is setting up in business to provide a catering service for children's parties. Pam has not yet decided on a name for her service but has a couple of ideas: Kids' Catering, Pam's Party Food. Pam will need her logo to appear on business letters, quotations and invoices, business cards and publicity flyers.

- ★ Decide on a name and design the logo.
- ★ Present the logo as it would appear on a business card.
- ★ Choose a size of card that would match a credit card and draw your design actual size.

Pam's contact details are: Longfield Farm, Newbridge, Devon EX25 1PL Telephone: 01237 114567.

Keep a copy of the business card for your portfolio.

If you are using Microsoft software you could use WordArt to design the name.

Collect together the replies received from the organisations contacted in Activity 1.2.

For now, try to ignore the message given in the letter. Instead, concentrate on your impressions of the organisation, based on the overall look of the letter and the feel of the paper.

- ★ Make notes about their logos. Which ones impress you the most? What is it that impresses you?
- ★ Compare the amount of information shown in the letter headings. Is it clear how you could contact the person who wrote to you?
- ★ Look at the layout of the letters. What do you notice?
- ★ Look at the fonts used. Can you recognise the typefaces? What point sizes are used?
- ★ Look at the quality of the paper used. Are you particularly impressed with the choice of paper?

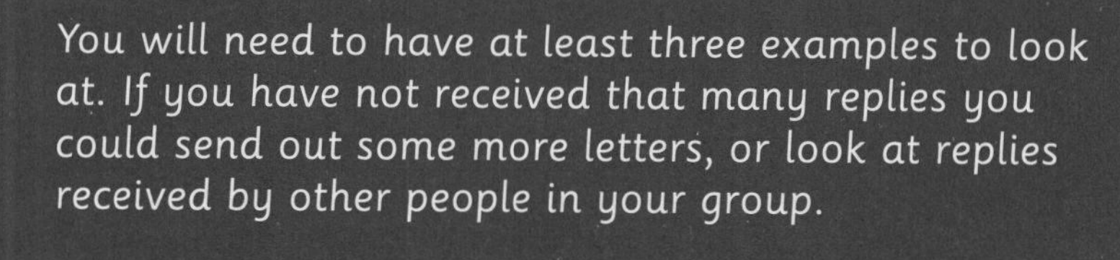

Invoices, orders and delivery notes

An **invoice** is a legal document sent by companies to their customers confirming the prices of goods or services provided and stating the terms of the sale. Every invoice must include some essential information:

- The name and address of the seller
- For limited companies, the company number and registered address
- The name and address of the buyer
- The date of the invoice (called the **tax point**)

- How much the goods or services provided cost (usually broken down into the number of units and the cost per unit)
- For companies which are registered for VAT, their VAT registration number and the amount of VAT charged on the invoice

Penhaven Country House Hotel

While guests stay at Penhaven they can be served drinks at the bar and use the telephone in their room, and the costs of these are added to the final bill. When a guest is about to depart an invoice is prepared which shows how much expense has been incurred during a stay. It shows daily expenses, broken down into the various services available and a total amount due for payment.

The invoice is multipart (Figure 1.7) so that when it has been paid the guest can be given one copy, and another can be placed in the accounts file.

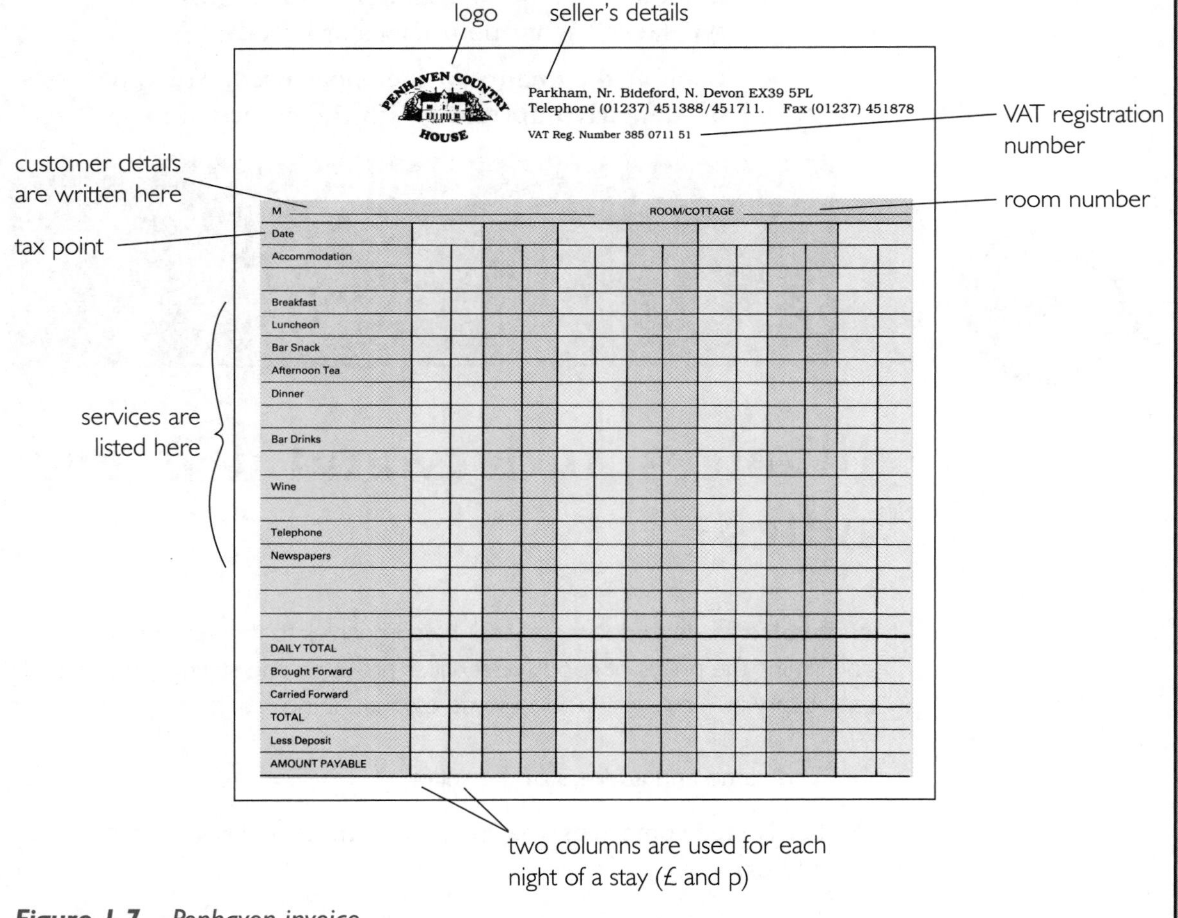

PENHAVEN COUNTRY HOUSE

Parkham, Nr. Bideford, N. Devon EX39 5PL
Telephone (01237) 451388/451711. Fax (01237) 451878
VAT Reg. Number 385 0711 51

M ______ ROOM/COTTAGE ______

Date
Accommodation

Breakfast
Luncheon
Bar Snack
Afternoon Tea
Dinner

Bar Drinks

Wine

Telephone
Newspapers

DAILY TOTAL
Brought Forward
Carried Forward
TOTAL
Less Deposit
AMOUNT PAYABLE

Figure 1.7 *Penhaven invoice*
Courtesy of Penhaven Country House Hotel

Because invoices are legal documents it is especially important that all relevant information is entered correctly. However, at the bottom of an invoice companies often include – written very small – '**E&OE**' which stands for 'errors and omissions excepted'. This means that any mistakes made by the supplier are not binding.

If a company produces more than a few invoices each day, and especially if the accounts information is processed on an ICT system, each one is usually identified by a unique number (the **invoice number**) rather than using the date to trace an invoice. It is also helpful to include any original order number. 'Terms' should always be included, to show how many days before payment must be received, and also if there is any discount for prompt payment.

To save printing separate labels, because invoices always show the customer's address they are often sent in **window envelopes**. Figure 1.8 shows how important the positioning of the address details on the invoice is, and how the page must be folded and placed inside the envelope; otherwise the address will not show through the window!

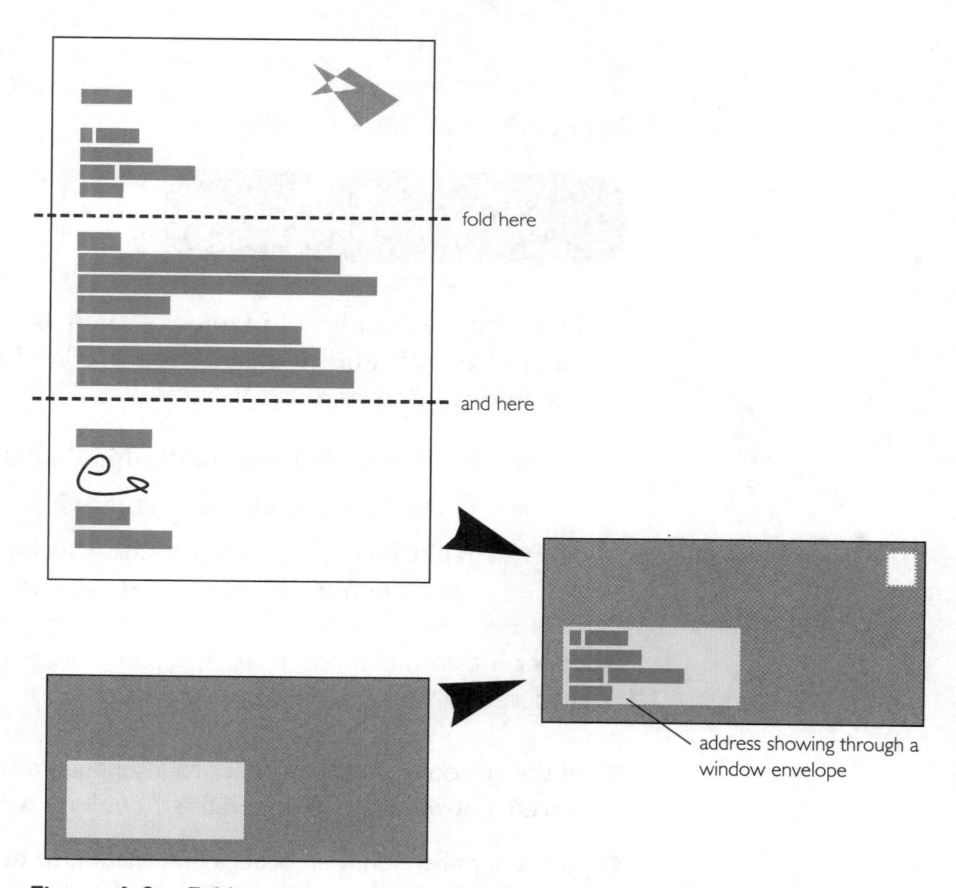

***Figure 1.8** Folding a sheet of A4 to show an address in a window envelope*

If the customer pays immediately the invoice may also form a **receipt**. Figure 1.9 shows a Post Office invoice/receipt for three stamps.

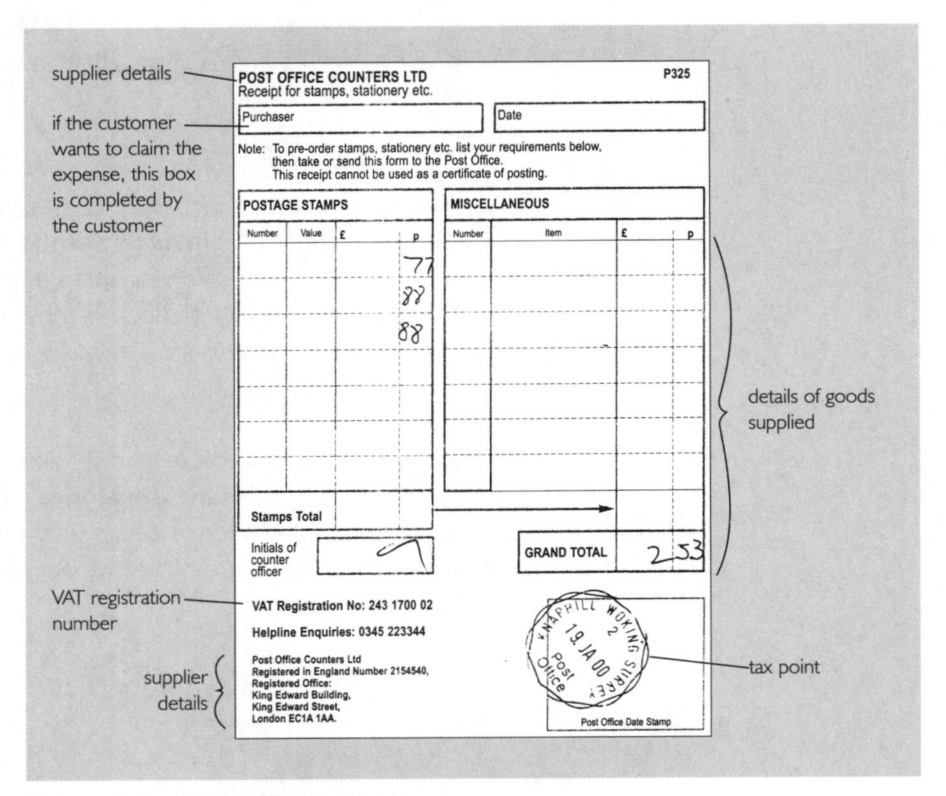

Figure 1.9 Post Office invoice/receipt

Exercise 1.6

Find some examples of invoices – such as telephone bills, electricity bills and itemised supermarket bills – and check the information on each.

- ★ **Is all essential information included?**
- ★ **Is the VAT calculated correctly?**
- ★ **What layout has been used? Has any of the text been enhanced so that it stands out especially?**

An **order** is a document to confirm that goods or services are required. It can be produced by the supplier or the customer.

- If the customer sends an order to a supplier, this document is called a **purchase order** because it confirms a purchase
- If the supplier sends an order confirmation to the customer, this document is called a **sales order** because it confirms a sale

Alternatively, the supplier may send the customer a form to complete to confirm an order. This is usually called a **booking form**.

Penhaven Country House Hotel

It is important that guests confirm their planned stay at Penhaven and they are asked to send a deposit with their booking (Figure 1.10).

The current tariff is sent with the booking form, so the 'terms' – the price of the room and other services – are clear to the guest before they sign the booking form.

BOOKING FORM

customer's details:

NAME ....

ADDRESS ....

....

....

TELEPHONE NO. ....

service ordered:

TOTAL NUMBER OF ROOMS REQUIRED ....

TWIN SUPER-DE-LUXE ....

DOUBLE SUPER-DE-LUXE ....

DOUBLE DE-LUXE ....

DOUBLE STANDARD ....

SINGLE DE-LUXE ....

COTTAGE SUITE ....

ARRIVAL DATE ....

DEPARTURE DATE ....

ARE YOU VEGETARIAN? ....

PETS? ....

MAY WE ASK WHERE YOU SAW ADVERTISEMENT? ....

DEPOSIT ....

ESTIMATED TIME OF ARRIVAL AT HOTEL ....

customer signs to confirm the booking:

SIGNED ....

DATE ....

seller's logo:

AA ★★★ RAC ★★★

PENHAVEN COUNTRY HOUSE

seller's details:

PARKHAM • Nr. BIDEFORD • N. DEVON • EX39 5PL
Tel. (01237) 451711/451388 Fax (01237) 451878

Figure 1.10 *Penhaven booking form*
Courtesy of Penhaven Country House Hotel

An order contains the same information as an invoice, setting out who is buying what, at what price and under what conditions. An order is usually given a unique number, which can then be quoted on the invoice. When an invoice is received this helps the accounts department to check that the invoice is for goods that have been ordered and that the price is correct. Payment may then be made more quickly.

Notice that the Post Office invoice/receipt in Figure 1.9 also serves as an order form. It saves the counter staff time if the customer fills in what stamps are needed and calculates the total due. Companies who regularly buy stamps like this are given blank forms to complete.

A **delivery note** may be prepared by the supplier for goods that are to be sent to the customer. This contains similar information to the invoice, but does not usually show price information because this is confidential. The delivery note is usually a multipart document – the customer is asked to sign it to confirm that the goods have been received in good condition, and is given a copy for filing. The delivery person returns the signed note to the accounts department. If there is any dispute about payment the supplier then has proof that the goods were delivered and accepted.

Exercise 1.7

Find examples of orders and delivery notes.

- ★ **Check what information is – and is not – shown on each document.**
- ★ **How many parts has each document? Who keeps which copies?**

Memos, e-mails and faxes

> **Internal communications**
> This means communication *within* an organisation, not involving anyone outside the organisation.

Memos are used for **internal communications**.

A memo is used in a number of situations:

- When you want to put some information into writing, e.g. to confirm a meeting date and time, evidence of action taken, or a record of a conversation
- When the person you need to tell something is not immediately available – you might send a memo which they will read the next time they are in the office

Did You Know?

Memo is short for **memorandum** – an informal written message.

- When you need to tell lots of people the same information – a single memo can be addressed to many different people

Memos are used for **informal** communications. More formal information would be put in a letter and addressed personally to the employee, e.g. a letter advising an employee of a pay increase, or a warning letter about his or her poor punctuality record.

A5 paper
is half the size of A4 paper.

Organisations often have a standard layout for memos. This will include the heading section (to say to whom it is going, who it is from, and the date) and then space for the message to be handwritten or typed. Memos can be quite short, so they are often printed on **A5 paper**.

Usually, a memo is printed in landscape orientation, i.e. the longer side at the top.

Activity 1.5

- ★ **Design a memo layout for Pam Turner, the caterer. Use A5-sized paper with landscape orientation.**
- ★ **Produce a sample memo, using your design. The memo is from Pam to her assistant, Jake. It is dated 5th July 2000 and is to confirm that a new client, Young Promotions, will require tea for 35 on Saturday 2nd August. Menu B2 is to be supplied at a cost of £4.75 per person.**
- ★ **Keep a copy of the memo in your portfolio.**

Look at the memo wizard layouts available to you with your wordprocessing software for some ideas. Don't copy the wizard layout exactly though, otherwise your design will not be original!

E-mail offers an alternative to sending memos, telephoning or writing to someone. So long as the other person also has e-mail facilities, you can send him (or her) an e-mail note.

- Some organisations have an internal e-mail system, and their staff can send e-mails rather than memos.

Chris Lane

Memos are used a lot at the Chris Lane club. Most staff work on shift systems, so they cannot rely on seeing each other to pass on information. Figure 1.11 shows an example of a memo sent by Janice when she was busy organising one of the many social events: a special banquet. The memo was produced using a Word wizard.

M E M O R A N D U M

DATE: March 12, 2000
TO: [*Names*]
FROM: [*Names*]
RE: [*Subject*]
CC: [*Names*]

[*Type your memo text here*]

a Word wizard is used to set up a standard memo

M E M O R A N D U M

DATE: March 12, 2000
TO: Reception / Carole
FROM: Janice
RE: Deliveries
CC: Jim, Ben

There will be a lot of deliveries for the Banquet next Friday.

- Tables from Browns - to go in the corridor behind the creche
- Benches from Wilsons - also to go in the corridor
- Table decorations from Daisy Chain - to go in the shed behind Jim's office

If I am not around when the deliveries are made, please make sure everything is put in the right place.

Thanks

Janice keys in the details

Figure 1.11 *Memo example*

Did You Know?

Some e-mail addresses end in **.com**, showing that the person is using a service provider, such as BT Internet, Compuserve or AOL, for the e-mail connection. Companies can arrange their own 'domain name' and then they put **.co.uk** at the end of the address. Universities usually have **.ac.uk** at the end of their addresses. Some government departments have **.gov.uk** endings, and others, like QCA, have **.org.uk** endings.

- **Many organisations are linked via the Internet and now have e-mail addresses. Within the organisation all members of staff have their own addresses. This means anyone with an e-mail facility can send messages to the organisation, or to individuals within the organisation.**

E-mail 'addresses' are made up of two main parts separated by the @ symbol:

- **Before the '@' symbol, the name of the person or company**
- **After the '@' symbol, the address of the company or the service provider**

Within both parts a 'dot' symbol is used to separate the information.

The author's e-mail address is ***firstclass@btinternet.com****. The author works for a company called First Class and the e-mail facility is provided by BT Internet.*

All staff at Pearson Education, the publishers of this book, have e-mail addresses formed from their name separated by a dot, and followed by @pearsoned-ema.com. So, to write to a Mr John Smith at Pearson Education, the e-mail address would be john.smith@pearsoned-ema.com

Did You Know?

E-mail addresses cannot include spaces or commas.

Exercise 1.8

Your school or college may have e-mail facilities. If so, find out what the e-mail address is. Does the e-mail address appear on any stationery?

Penhaven Country House Hotel

Maxine and Alan Wade decided to advertise their hotel facilities on the Internet. Part of the Internet package included an e-mail facility, so they can now be contacted by, and make contact with, their guests using e-mail as well as by letter or telephone.

For each of your local organisations, find out whether they have an e-mail facility.

★ Do they have only internal e-mail facilities, or do they also have a link via the Internet?

★ Is the e-mail address included on any stationery?

You might decide to contact the organisations through their website. Often these include an e-mail address.

E-mails can replace non-urgent telephone calls in a number of situations:

- When the person you are trying to contact seems to be always on the phone – you just get the engaged signal
- When the person you are trying to contact is not available – on holiday, off sick today, in a meeting, out to lunch, not in yet, or gone home already!

For the person you are trying to contact, it may also be helpful to receive an e-mail, rather than a telephone call:

- They may spend a lot of their day in meetings and do not want to be disturbed by telephone calls. However, they may deal with their e-mails whenever they have a few minutes between meetings.
- They may have an urgent deadline they are trying to meet, and need to concentrate on a particular task for the next hour or so.

E-mails are particularly useful when there are time differences between the people who need to communicate.

- Some office switchboards operate strict opening hours, say 9 a.m. till 5.30 p.m. If you work before or after those times you may not be able to telephone people working at these offices outside these hours. You may have the option to leave a message on an answering machine, but then someone is going to have to relay that message for you. However, you could send an e-mail message, which the person you want to contact should see when they next return to the office.

- Suppose you want to communicate with friends in America or Australia. The time difference between the UK and their countries means you may want to speak to them when they are asleep, and vice versa. It is easier to send e-mails during your normal working day; they can then reply during their own working day. When you first switch on your system, any e-mails sent during the night (UK time) will be waiting for you.

Also, as more and more people work on a freelance basis, and/or work from home, the times when you might want to send e-mails but not accept telephone calls are increasing. The e-mail facility allows people who work from home to switch their answering machine on when they do not want to be disturbed, but still send and receive messages via e-mail.

E-mails are also very useful for people who are always travelling. Sales representatives move from hotel to hotel carrying their laptops with them, and can easily maintain contact with their head office and clients through e-mail.

Finally, e-mails can be used to send documents as attached files:

- The attached file might be a business letter or invoice that is going to be posted, but you want the person to receive the information faster than the postal service can manage.

- The attached file could be some information that you want the other person to amend and send back to you. Sending electronic files in this way is the most efficient way for people to work together on a document, e.g. a report, without actually meeting.

This method of sending information is not as secure as some other methods (e.g. registered post, file transfer) but is fine for non-sensitive information.

More information about using the Internet, and sending and receiving e-mails, appears in another book in this series: *Intermediate GNVQ ICT Options*.

However, not everyone has e-mail and sometimes the information you want to send is not on the computer, so it cannot be sent as an attached file.

Fax
is short for facsimile.

Faxes can be very useful for sending hand-written notes or diagrams to someone when it would be difficult to explain something over the telephone. Hotels often send maps to their clients by fax.

Did You Know?

If you have an ISDN line no modem is needed to convert the messages before they are sent down the telephone line.

Fax machines can be used to send documentary information via the telephone network to someone who also has a fax machine (or a fax facility on an IT system). To send a fax, both sender and receiver must have a fax facility. There are several ways of having a fax facility:

- You may have a fax machine attached to a telephone line, and the document on paper
- You may have a fax facility on an IT system, linked via a modem to a telephone line, and the document as an electronic file
- You may have a fax facility on an IT system, linked via an **ISDN** telephone line, and the document as an electronic file

ISDN (integrated services digital network)
is an ITU definition for global digital data communications. Its purpose is to allow people, computers and other devices to communicate over standardised connection facilities.

If the sender is working from a fax facility on an IT system, a connection to the telephone network has to be made before the fax can be sent. If the sender is using a fax machine the document is simply fed into the machine (which is already connected to a telephone line) and the number dialled direct.

Whether the receiver has a fax machine or a fax facility on an IT system, the sender may get the engaged signal and would have to dial again until a telephone connection could be made. Fax facilities on an IT system can be customised to redial automatically, which saves the sender some effort.

Penhaven Country House Hotel

Most guests obtain information about how to reach Penhaven when they receive their brochure. (See page xix in the Case Studies section for more details about the procedures followed at Penhaven.)

However, if a guest makes a booking after 4.30 p.m. on the day before arrival, it is too late for directions to be sent in the mail, so Maxine faxes a map to them.

Figure 1.12 shows the fax cover-sheet, and the map attachment. Note that the cover-sheet is based on Penhaven's headed stationery, with the fax header information at the top.

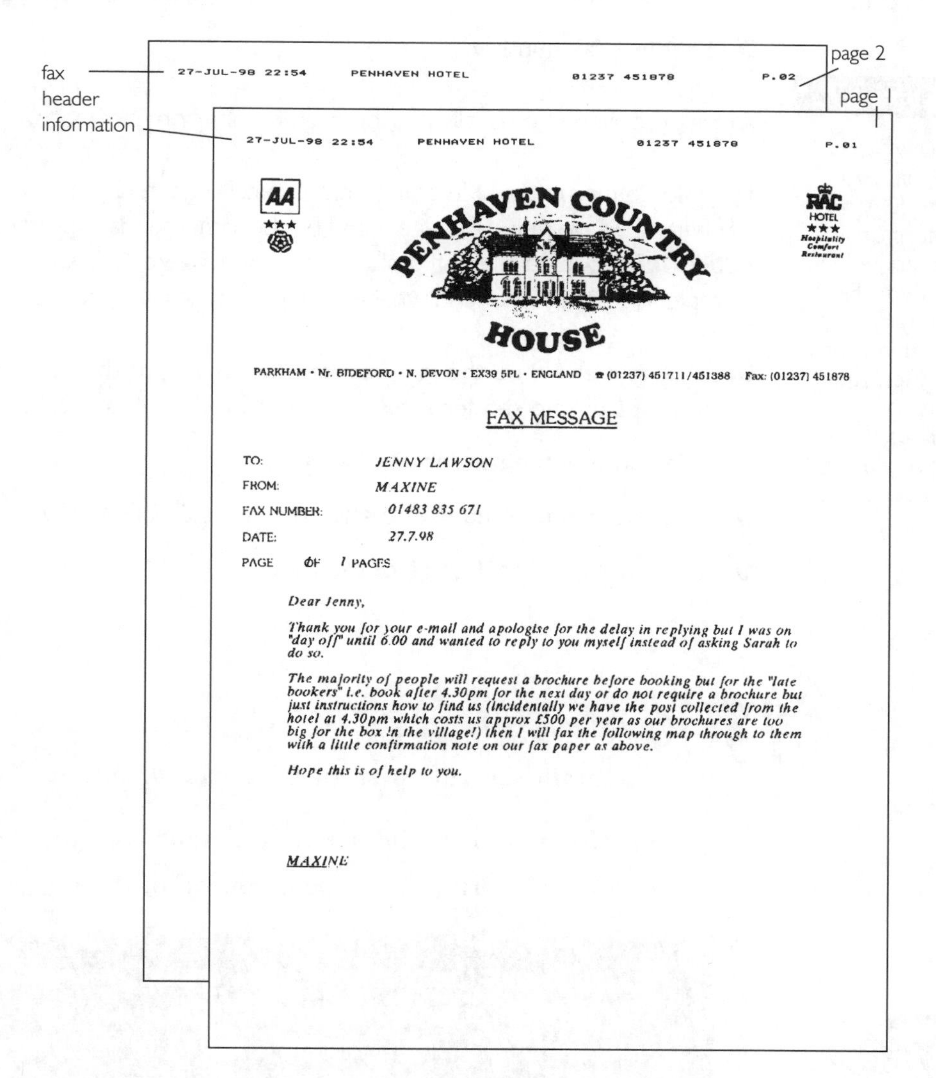

27-JUL-98 22:54 PENHAVEN HOTEL 01237 451878 P.01

PENHAVEN COUNTRY HOUSE

PARKHAM • Nr. BIDEFORD • N. DEVON • EX39 5PL • ENGLAND ☎ (01237) 451711/451388 Fax: (01237) 451878

FAX MESSAGE

TO: *JENNY LAWSON*
FROM: *MAXINE*
FAX NUMBER: *01483 835 671*
DATE: *27.7.98*
PAGE ΦF *1* PAGES

Dear Jenny,

Thank you for your e-mail and apologise for the delay in replying but I was on "day off" until 6.00 and wanted to reply to you myself instead of asking Sarah to do so.

The majority of people will request a brochure before booking but for the "late bookers" i.e. book after 4.30pm for the next day or do not require a brochure but just instructions how to find us (incidentally we have the post collected from the hotel at 4.30pm which costs us approx £500 per year as our brochures are too big for the box in the village!) then I will fax the following map through to them with a little confirmation note on our fax paper as above.

Hope this is of help to you.

MAXINE

Figure 1.12 *Penhaven's faxed directions*
Courtesy of Penhaven Country House Hotel

Did You Know?

ITU stands for International Telecommunications Union and is part of the United Nations Organisation. It coordinates worldwide telecommunications and tries to obtain agreement on international standards for data telecommunications

Did You Know?

Faxes received on an IT system arrive as bit-map files, so they cannot introduce viruses to your system. E-mails may have viruses within any attached files, and so virus software should be used to screen all incoming e-mails.

Exercise 1.9

- ★ **What are the advantages of using a fax rather than a telephone call?**
- ★ **What are the advantages of using a fax rather than an e-mail?**

The fax machine can be programmed to send some basic information along with the message being faxed, which then appears on each sheet of the fax received:

- Sender's name
- Sender's fax number

The fax received also usually has the page number on each page.

If you do nothing extra, at least the person receiving the fax knows where it has come from. However, it is polite – and has become standard practice – to include a cover-sheet as the first sheet of any fax. Figure 1.12 shows an example; note the layout and what information appears at the top of each sheet:

- The date and time the fax was sent (according to the date and time set on the sender's fax machine): 27-JUL-98 at 22:54
- The name of the sender: Penhaven Hotel
- The telephone number of the fax machine: 01237 451878
- The number of each page of the fax

Obtain several different fax cover-sheets.

- ★ **Compare what information is shown on these sheets.**
- ★ **What information appears on *all* of them?**

You could ask the person responsible for receiving faxes at your school or college to show you some examples. (You would not be allowed to read the rest of the faxes; these are probably confidential.)

Did You Know?

Organisations can send mailshots – also called junk faxes – direct to fax machines. Using a fax facility on an IT system, the automatic dialler is programmed to try each telephone number in turn. If a human answers, it rings off. If a fax signal is received the fax advert is sent.

The information in a fax may be confidential, so the sender may include a message warning the receiver of the fax. Then, if the fax arrives at the wrong person's machine they are asked not to read it, but to inform the sender that it has gone astray.

An interesting development in the uses of faxes is the **fax-back** facility. If your clients are likely to have a fax facility (and most do nowadays), by sending a form they can fax back, you save them writing a letter or making a telephone call.

Publicity flyers

Publicity flyers are adverts printed on single sheets of paper. Publicity flyers are like mini-posters: they can be used to advertise a service or an event. You will find plenty of examples in your nearest Tourist Information Office.

Activity 1.8

Look at the examples of publicity flyers shown on pages 30, 31 and 32.

- **Design a publicity flyer for Pam Turner's catering service.**
- **Make the flyer A5 size, and decide whether you want to use portrait or landscape orientation.**
- **Decide what information you will need to include on the flyer.**
- **Decide what fonts to use.**
- **Alternatively, redesign the flyer for St Breock Gallery (Figure 1.14 on page 31). Richard Haslam-Hopwood updates his flyer quite regularly, and if your design impresses him he may well decide to use it!**

Keep a copy of the flyer for your portfolio.

Include some clip-art or colour, if you think it improves the appearance of the flyer.

The Candle Shop

Figure 1.13 shows the publicity flyer produced for the Candle Shop. It is a single sheet of A5 (portrait orientation) with nothing printed on the reverse side. The design includes artwork of some candles (naturally!) and a map showing where to find the shop. Note the different sizes of fonts used for the text, and the white space on the right-hand side of the flyer.

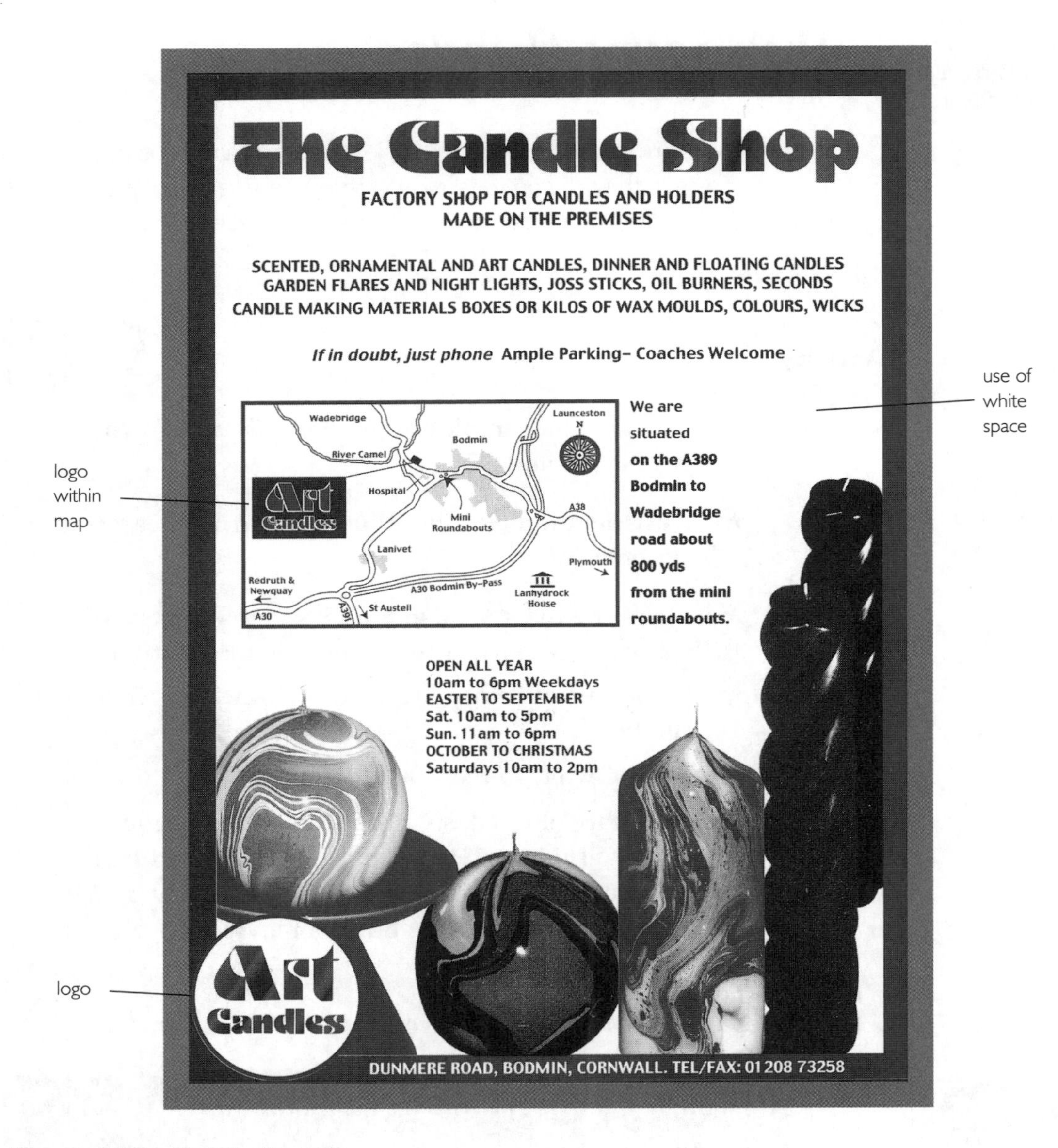

Figure 1.13 *Candle Shop flyer*
Courtesy of T. Bishop, Art Candles

St Breock Gallery

Richard Haslam-Hopwood's publicity flyer is double-sided A5 (portrait orientation) – see Figure 1.14. On one side, two colour photos of the inside of the gallery plus a map of how to find the gallery are arranged with essential information: the name of the gallery, opening times, the telephone and fax numbers. On the other side Richard has written a brief history of the St Breock Gallery.

two colour photos and a map

A BRIEF HISTORY

ST. BREOCK GALLERY was established over 25 years ago and is owned by Richard Haslam-Hopwood, an acknowledged expert on reproduction furniture. In the 1970's he had a Gallery just off London's Bond Street, called "Tomorrow's Antiques" and his traditionally made furniture received universal praise from many major household magazines.

…en on radio programmes and appeared on BBC Television Pebble … Office of Information made a film of his furniture which was shown …ll over the world.

… years the export of antique furniture has been increasing annually …te. Since 1988, this figure has reached a staggering £4 billion - an …400 million. Good antiques have now become a rarity and, as a …ensive.

…s of craftsmen, many of them ex-antique restorers, making good …tems he calls "Tomorrow's Antiques". Time is spent with each one … methods and materials are of the highest standard; Richard's maxim …hat you can see that matters, but more a question of what you …d reproduction will withstand the effects of modern day living - …nd air conditioning having ravaged many of our best antiques. They …iating asset, keeping pace with the ever increasing value of genuine …can also be made to customers own specification. You can even

…easing shortage of antique furniture is forcing antique dealers to … dwindling stocks by selling reproduction furniture - much of which … the Far East - so the public have to be more wary about the …ng copies as the real thing.

…te belief in British craftsmanship is reflected in the comment made … Thornton, the then Keeper of Furniture at the Victoria and Albert …id: "I know it is heresy to say this but top grade reproduction … be just as acceptable as the genuine article. It should be a question … commercial value." John Bly, on the BBC Antiques Roadshow, made …cently: "There are craftsmen out there making items that will, …ear in the salerooms of the future".

… beautiful furniture, the Gallery also stocks oils and watercolours …ntury to the current date. There is a special annual exhibition, in the … of selected artists, potters and craftsmen producing works of art …d's "Tomorrow's Antiques" criteria.

St. Breock Gallery

Cornwall's centre for fine Traditional Furniture
also
Antiques, 19th & 20th Century Oils & Watercolours,

Lower Gallery

Objets d'art
and
a selection
of
Local Crafts

Long Gallery

Open: Mon to Sat
10am - 5pm
Telephone:
(01208) 812543
Facsimile:
(01208) 814671

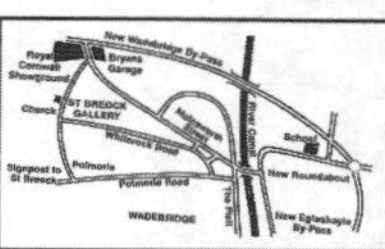

St. Breock Gallery,
St. Breock, Wadebridge,
Cornwall PL27 7JS.
(near the Royal
Cornwall Showground)

text on reverse

Figure 1.14 *St Breock Gallery flyer*
Courtesy of Richard Haslam-Hopwood, St Breock Gallery

Chris Lane

Marcus Pettifer is responsible for organising and promoting the social events for members of the Chris Lane club.

For each event, full-sized posters and smaller A5-sized publicity flyers are produced and placed in special holders on all tables in the club bar and restaurant area.

Figure 1.15 shows four examples of publicity flyers.

Figure 1.15 *Examples of Chris Lane publicity flyers*
Courtesy of Chris Lane Family Leisure Club

Exercise 1.10

- ★ Why do lots of publicity flyers appear on a single sheet of A5-sized paper?
- ★ What other sizes of paper might be used?
- ★ Look out for flyers that have a different size or style.
- ★ Look out for publicity flyers that involve folding a sheet of A4 paper into three.

Newsletters

Newsletters – sometimes called magazines – may be produced by an organisation to keep staff, clients or suppliers informed about what is happening within the organisation.

Chris Lane

Chris Lane produces a newsletter for members called *In Touch.* This gives details of social events, news about changes at the club and information about members, e.g. how well the tennis team are doing and who is 'Junior Member of the Month'. The current newsletter is displayed at Reception and other parts of the club, for members to help themselves to a copy.

Lush International

Lush produce a magazine called *Lush International Times* to send to all customers. It lists the latest products and gives news about special offers. This magazine is sent to all customers on Lush's mailing list.

Chris Lane

The Chris Lane newsletter has one-, two- and three-column styles. Some pages have a mix of numbers of columns: two columns at the top and three at the bottom. Figure 1.16 shows three sample pages.

TENNIS TALK

2000 brings loads of changes to the tennis programme. Director of Tennis David Gabb says he is really excited about how things are shaping up -

TENNIS LEAGUES

HECTOR & SANTIAGO

CLUB TEAMS

IN TOUCH WITH KIDSPORTS

AN EXCITING YEAR!

Chris Barton gives us an insight into how the Kidsports' Year is progressing..

KIDSPORTS SNACK BAR

IN TOUCH

NEWSLETTER APRIL - MAY 2000

The newsletter for the Members and Green Team of Chris Lane Family Leisure Club
Westfield Avenue, Old Woking, Surrey, GU22 9PF. Tel: 01483 722113 Fax: 01483 729848

Chris Lane FAMILY LEISURE CLUB WITH KIDSPORTS

CONTENTS

Social Snaps	2
Club Profile	3
Health & Fitness	4
In Touch with Kidsports	5 - 8
Tennis Talk	9
Social Whirlwind	10
Alpha Review	11

Someone You Know would love to join the Club!

Membership Referral Rewards!
See posters or ask Andy or Tamsin for full details on 01483 722113

Weekend Guest Passes
-see overleaf

JOIN THE CRUISERS
- See page 4 for details

ALPHA SUCCESS
See Page 11

Chris Lane Comments -
INVESTORS IN PEOPLE

Much is happening, as always, at the Club.

I am proud to announce that we have been awarded the coveted "Investors in People Award' My thanks to Simon Thorpe, our Training Director, for all his hard work in co-ordinating the Club's achievement of this award.

NEW MANAGEMENT TEAM MEMBERS

The new members of my management team, Andy Harris, Graeme Collins, Chris Barton, Paul Hoppe, and Marcus Pettifer are beginning to make a real impact organisationally around the Club.

The success of our business is about people whether it is happy members or excellent staff. We are conscious of "Walking our Talk" in our bar and restaurant area, which has been our Achilles' heel for the past 18 months.

After a few misfires we have finally made the long awaited appointment of Food and Beverage Director in Darren Nesbitt who starts April 1st. We appreciate that we need to get our act together quickly there for you all.

SOCIAL EVENTS

Some great social events such as the New Year's Part II - Myths and Legends, have come and gone and were very well supported and were also great value.

I know that I am not a terribly popular fellow at the moment with all my members. Some of the tennis and pool only members are disgruntled with me because of the changes in the membership structure, as they are not able to join at their previously discounted rates. Continued on page 3...

Turn to page 3 to hear what was said in the ladies' showers!..

IN THE SWING OF 2000...

...more about the Social scene on page 9

IN TOUCH with KIDSPORTS - Newsletter inside

Figure 1.16 Sample pages from Chris Lane newsletter
Courtesy of Chris Lane Family Leisure Club

Banner headline fills the width of the page.

The layout of a newsletter is usually in columns, to look like a newspaper. The front page may have a **banner headline** showing the title of the newsletter.

The rest of the newsletter is then divided into columns – the number of columns depends mainly on the width of the page. Columns need not be the same width throughout the newsletter, so each page can have a different layout.

The same type of heading may appear throughout the magazine – or, for more variety and to create interest, a number of different heading styles may be used.

Exercise 1.11

Look at a newspaper to see what heading styles are used.

- ★ **How many different styles are used on a single page?**
- ★ **What effect do these different styles have on readers?**

Newsletters may be produced on A4 paper (which may be easier for an organisation to produce in-house) or on 'broadsheets' like a newspaper.

Chris Lane

The Chris Lane newsletter is produced on A4 glossy paper. This gives readers the impression of a high-quality organisation.

Lush International

Lush's magazine is printed on recycled paper. The quality of the paper is similar to newspaper, giving the customers the (correct) impression that no money is being wasted on producing the magazine.

The magazine has 5 sheets, A2 size. Then, each A3 'page' is created by folding all the sheets once – just like in a newspaper – to make a magazine with 10 pages. To keep the pages secure, it is also stapled.

The general format for a newsletter is decided, together with which fonts and colours may be used to liven up the material.

Exercise 1.12

The material for a newsletter may be produced by many people. In a newspaper it will be a team of journalists.

- ★ **Does your school or college produce a newsletter? If so, who writes the articles?**
- ★ **Do any of your chosen organisations produce a newsletter? If so, who writes the articles?**

The job of the **newsletter editor** is to pull the articles together, following the general design, and lay out the pages in the most attractive way. Once this has been decided for one issue of the newsletter, the same layout may be used on the following issues.

Exercise 1.13

Look at one particular page in two different issues of a newspaper or magazine.

- ★ **Is there much difference between the layouts of these pages?**
- ★ **How is this helpful for the reader?**

Subeditor
controls what information is printed and the accuracy of that information. A subeditor must be very good at proofreading – and this has to be done quickly under the pressure of deadlines.

When an article is received from the writer, a **subeditor** reads it through and makes any changes he or she thinks are necessary.

These are the types of checks a subeditor will make:

- **Correct spelling, punctuation and grammar**
- **Correct spellings, particularly of people's names**
- **Correct facts – dates, places, who someone works for, their job title**
- **Correct tone – reflecting the 'image' of the newsletter**

Sometimes an article has to be cut down to fit the available space.

Did You Know?

When journalists prepare articles for newspapers they are paid to produce a certain number of words. Then the editor knows that the article will fit the available space.

The articles may be produced on word processors, but the editor is more likely to use desktop publishing (DTP) to produce the newsletter. This is because DTP offers more features for page layout. However, for your portfolio work the DTP features available on most word processors are fine.

Pictures are an important part of any newsletter design. A newsletter with no pictures would be quite dull, and the job of the editor includes making each page attractive enough to catch the readers' attention. The general design of a newsletter will include how much space is given to text, and how much to pictures. Colour may also be used to brighten up the page.

Did You Know?

Some word-processing software offer DTP facilities. However, in the publishing industry packages like Quark Xpress, PageMaker and Adobe Acrobat are used instead. If you have experience of using one of these packages you may be able to find work as a DTP operator.

Chris Lane

The Chris Lane newsletter includes photos of members. Colour is used for the written text and for many of the headings.

Lush International

Lush's magazine includes colour pictures of the products for sale. Figure 1.17 shows extracts from two pages in the *Lush Times* July 2000 issue. Notice the various heading styles used.

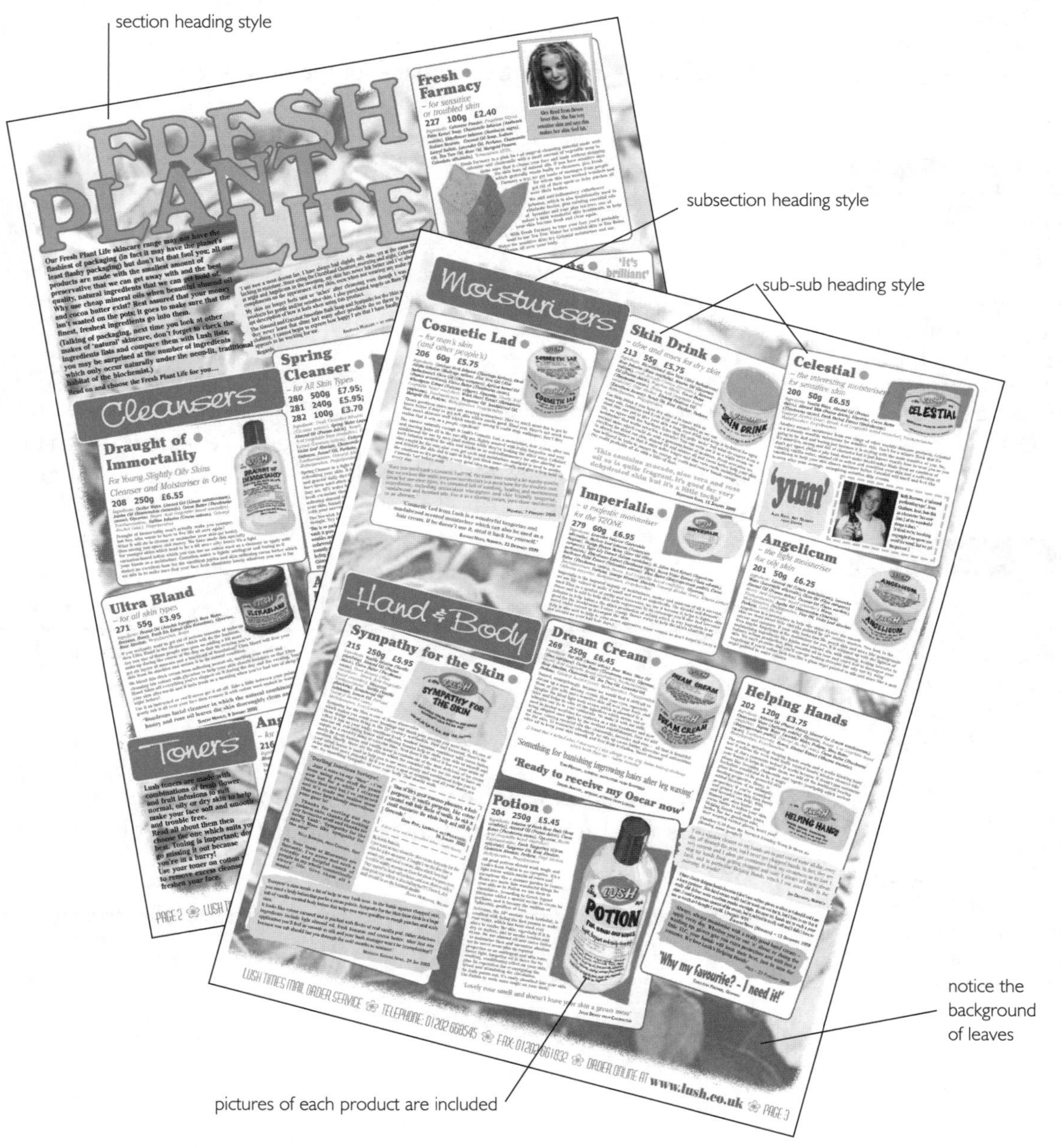

Figure 1.17 *Lush magazine extracts*
Courtesy of Lush

Working in a group of three or four, agree a general design for a one-page newsletter. This should include at least one graphic and at least one table.

- **Each person in the group first takes the role of 'journalist' and writes at least one article for the newsletter, using a word processor. Give one copy (on disk) to everyone else in the group.**
- **Each person is now to take the role of 'subeditor'.**

  Print out a draft of the articles (in double-line spacing).

  Check these articles carefully (including your own!).

  Mark up any changes you think are necessary.
- **Each person now takes the role of 'editor'.**

  Using the disk copy of each article, make the changes suggested by the subeditor and incorporate all the articles into a single page.
- **If you have too much material, make some cuts.**

  If you do not have enough, write some more to fill the space.

  Choose headings for the articles and a heading style for each one.

  Choose artwork to include in your page, and use colour if you wish.
- **Print out your finished page, and give copies to the others in your group.**
- **Compare each other's newsletters.**
- **Make notes on what was good about your newsletter, and what you could do to improve it. Keep a copy of these notes and your newsletter in your portfolio.**

It will help everyone if you use the standard proofreading symbols. *See page 226 in the Good Working Practice Guide for details.*

Drafts

When writing something new, it is sometimes difficult to think of exactly what you want to say. With a word-processing package, you can key in your first thoughts, knowing they will not be perfect. Then you can review it and improve it.

This is called **drafting** (and redrafting!). A word-processing package allows you to draft and redraft a letter until it says exactly what you want to say.

Each new version is called a **draft**. Figure 1.18 shows three drafts of the same document.

A document usually has lots of text, some tables and some artwork. When you are drafting it is the wording of the text that you are trying to finalise.

The standard style for a draft is for the text to appear in **double-line spacing**. This is useful because you may need space to write in corrections (see the first and second drafts shown in Figure 1.18).

Double-line spacing has one extra space line after each line of text.

Did You Know?

The term 'draft' is also used to describe a version, on-screen or printed, which does not include any formatting or graphics. If you have access to Word, see Tools/Options/View and select 'draft' to see what effect this has on-screen. Using draft view mode saves a lot of memory and allows the processor to concentrate on the editing you are doing, rather than having to update the screen all the time.

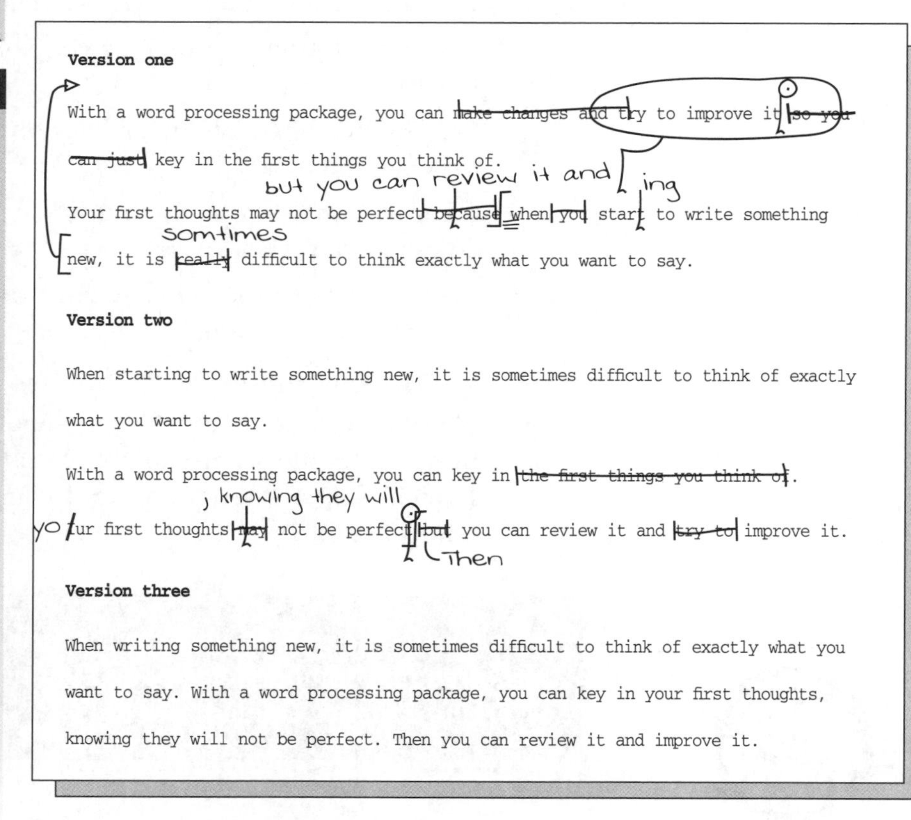

Version one

With a word processing package, you can ~~make changes and~~ try to improve it ~~so you can just~~ key in the first things you think of.

Your first thoughts may not be perfect ~~because~~ when ~~you~~ start to write something new, it is ~~really~~ difficult to think exactly what you want to say.

Version two

When starting to write something new, it is sometimes difficult to think of exactly what you want to say.

With a word processing package, you can key in ~~the first things you think of~~.

Your first thoughts ~~may~~ not be perfect ~~but~~ you can review it and ~~try to~~ improve it.

Version three

When writing something new, it is sometimes difficult to think of exactly what you want to say. With a word processing package, you can key in your first thoughts, knowing they will not be perfect. Then you can review it and improve it.

Figure 1.18 *Drafting and redrafting*

Flag
is text that says, for example: 'Figure 4 goes here'.

The artwork and tables can be replaced by '**flags**' showing where they will appear in the final version of the document. It is not necessary to print out the tables and artwork with every draft, because it is only the words you are thinking about changing.

Drafts can provide evidence that you have used a spellchecker, and so it may be useful to retain an early draft, annotated with the words that you corrected, while doing a spellcheck on your document.

It is important to label drafts, so that you will know which is the most recent, up-to-date version. This information can be included in a header or a footer:

- **Version number**
- **Date**
- **Who wrote the document**
- **The path name for the file**

Each version is checked by proofreading the draft. There are two types of proofreading:

- **Comparing the two drafts, the most recent version against the previous one, to make sure all corrections have been made as planned**
- **Reading through the most recent draft to make sure it still makes sense and to look for further improvements**

Both methods should be used.

It was thought that the introduction of word-processing packages would create the **paperless office**. Instead, users tend to print out many draft copies before they are satisfied with the finished document. The end result may be better, but often a lot more paper is used in the process.

To save paper you could keep one box for paper that has already been printed on one side and use this for printing out drafts. (Sometimes, what is already printed on the reverse side is more interesting to read!) However, take care that this does not jam your printer.

Reports

Reports are prepared in a number of situations:

- **As a one-off document, e.g. giving details of the findings of an investigation**
- **On a regular basis, e.g. giving details of the financial status of a company**

Reports are usually prepared to gather together relevant information to help people to make decisions.

- **When considering installing a new computer system, for example, a company may ask for a feasibility study to be carried out. From this study, a feasibility report will be produced. This report will help the management to decide how to proceed.**
- **When trying to correct a problem, e.g. too many staff absences, a senior manager or someone in the personnel department may investigate the situation and prepare a report explaining the findings. Using this report, the management may be able to decide how to reduce staff absences.**
- **When deciding whether to invest in a company, prospective shareholders can look at the information provided in the company's annual report. This gives a lot of information about the company's performance and financial status.**

Reports may also be provided just to give information.

Most borough councils produce a report showing where their income comes from and what council taxes are spent on.

Exercise 1.14

Make a list of six different reports.

Reports should show clearly all relevant information in as concise a way as possible:

- **Who wrote the report, i.e. the author**
- **For whom the report is written, i.e. the intended reader**

- What purpose the report has, e.g. to make recommendations regarding a particular issue
- What terms of reference the writer has used, e.g. any limitations on the investigation
- The findings
- The recommendations

Reports are **formal** documents.

- Reports may be for **internal** use, e.g. to explain health and safety procedures
- Alternatively, they may be used for **external** communications, e.g. design ideas to a prospective client

A report is a **structured** document which can have many different sections. It is important for the reader to be able to find information quickly and easily. For this reason, reports have the following features:

- Front cover, including title and author
- **Contents** page listing all sections and giving their starting page numbers
- **Headers** and/or **footers** on each page, including page number, the date the report was printed/published, and the title of the report
- **Bibliography** section showing what source material has been used
- **Appendices** for reference material that has been reproduced, or for material that supports the report but is not essential reading

It may also be relevant to have an index, especially if the report is to be published in book form.

Exercise 1.15

★ Look at the Contents page of this book. Note the layout used. The page numbers show where each section starts and are right-aligned.

★ Note that no information is provided in Appendices. Instead, there are several 'Guides'.

★ Note that an index is provided.

Standard documents and their purpose

Business letters and business cards

Invoices, orders and delivery notes

Memos, e-mails and faxes

Publicity flyers

Newsletters

Drafts

Reports

Agendas and minutes

Agendas

Minutes

Figure 1.19 *The outline of part of Chapter 1 of this book*

Reports can be as short as two pages but are more likely to be much longer. Within the report the many sections may each be divided into subsections. These subsections may also be divided into further subsections. Altogether, there may be as many as four **levels of heading** within one report.

To make these levels of heading clear to the reader, numbering can be used. Usually the headings are assigned different point sizes, and bold or italic may also be used.

Figure 1.19 shows the **outline** for part of this chapter. Note the differences in style between the different levels of heading.

Activity 1.10

Ask at least two of your chosen organisations for copies of their annual reports. Compare the overall structures of these documents.

- ★ **Is it easy to find the information you require?**
- ★ **Look at the heading styles used. How many different levels of heading are used?**
- ★ **Look at the general layout of the material. Is it easy to follow? Are diagrams used a lot?**

Company reports are supplied to shareholders. So, if you know someone who holds shares in a company they may lend you their copy of the company's annual report.

Did You Know?

With some word processors there is an option to view the 'outline' of a document. You can then reorganise the document: you can 'upgrade' or 'downgrade' a particular heading, move sections about and so on. The numbering of these sections can be allocated (and reallocated) automatically by the software.

Agendas and minutes

In some situations meetings take place and no record is taken: the discussion is 'off the record'. However, there are other situations where it is very important that notice is given that a meeting will take place (an **agenda**), that notes are taken during the meeting, and a written record produced (the **minutes**).

Exercise 1.16

Think of two situations where it is important that agendas and minutes are produced.

Agendas

An **agenda** is an internal document that lists details of a planned business meeting:

- The **title** of the meeting, explaining the purpose of the meeting
- The **time, date** and **venue** of the meeting, so those attending know when and where the meeting will be held
- A list of topics to be discussed, in order – a tick list or plan for the meeting to ensure that nothing is forgotten

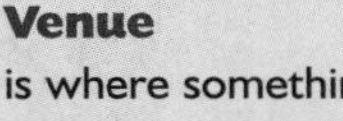

Venue
is where something takes place: the meeting place.

The list of topics usually starts with some 'standard' items:

- **Apologies** for absence – from people invited to the meeting who could not attend
- **Minutes of the last meeting** – a chance for those attending to refresh their memories as to what happened in the last meeting, before moving on to the discussions of the current meeting
- **Matters arising** – an update on items discussed at the previous meeting, which are not on the agenda for this meeting

The minutes of the last meeting should be agreed as being a fair record of the previous meeting, signed by the chairperson and then filed by the secretary. Then, at a later date, if there is any dispute there is a record of what was decided and proof that this was a true record according to those attending the next meeting.

The main discussion topics of the meeting are then listed. Finally, there are some standard closing items:

- **Any other business** – an opportunity for anyone at the meeting to introduce another topic for discussion, although the secretary ought to be warned about this before the meeting, and if time does not allow discussion, this topic may be postponed till the next meeting
- The **date** and **time** of the **next meeting** – no meeting should close without deciding when and where the next meeting will take

place: this allows those present to consult their diaries and agree a mutually convenient date

An agenda is sent to everyone who is invited to attend the meeting. The agenda is usually prepared by a secretary, and if someone cannot attend apologies should be sent to the secretary before the date of the meeting.

Word-processing packages provide wizards for agendas. Figure 1.20 shows three formats offered in Word 6, plus (bottom right) the first page of a notetaker's copy which has spaces for the notes to be made about discussions that take place, decisions that are made and action items. From this notetaker's version the minutes can be produced very easily.

Weekly Status Meeting

13/03/00
10:30 to 12:10
Building 1, Conference Room

Meeting called by: Note taker:
Type of meeting:

Attendees:
Please read:
Please bring:

Agenda

1. Meeting Overview	Phil	10:30-10:40
2. Topic A	Jane	10:40-10:55
3. Topic B	Peter	10:55-11:25
4. Topic C	Jim	11:25-12:10

Additional Information

Special notes:

Agenda **Weekly Status Meeting**

13/03/00
10:30 to 12:10
Building 1, Conference Room

Meeting called by:
Type of meeting:
Note taker:

Attendees:
Please read:
Please bring:

Agenda topics

10:30-10:40	Meeting Overview	Phil
10:40-10:55	Topic A	Jane
10:55-11:25	Topic B	Peter
11:25-12:10	Topic C	Jim

Special notes:

Weekly Status Meeting

13/03/00
10:30 to 12:10
Building 1, Conference Room

Meeting called by: **Note taker:**
Type of meeting:

Attendees:
Please read:
Please bring:

----- Agenda Topics -----

1. Meeting Overview	Phil	10:30-10:40
2. Topic A	Jane	10:40-10:55
3. Topic B	Peter	10:55-11:25
4. Topic C	Jim	11:25-12:10

Other information

Special notes:

Weekly Status Meeting

13/03/00
10:30 to 12:10
Building 1, Conference Room

Meeting called by: **Note taker:**
Type of meeting:

Attendees:
Please read:
Please bring:

----- Agenda Topics -----

Meeting Overview Phil 10:30-10:40

Discussion:

Conclusions:

Action items:	Person responsible:	Deadline:

Topic A Jane 10:40-10:55

Discussion:

Conclusions:

Action items:	Person responsible:	Deadline:

Figure 1.20 *Agenda templates*

Exercise 1.17

Find out which wizards are available on your word-processing software.

Minutes

So that those present can remember what was discussed at a meeting, what decisions were taken and what actions are planned, the secretary keeps a written record of the main points: the minutes.

Minutes contain the same headings as the agenda, but with the details filled in. On the right-hand side there is also an action column to show the initials of the person who has agreed to put that decision into action.

- **A list of who was present at the meeting and those who sent their apologies**
- **For each topic, a summary of the discussion that took place – not a word-for-word record, but the main points made, decisions taken and who is going to act as decided**

Minutes should be sent out as soon as possible after the meeting.

- **Those who attended can be reminded about what action (if any) they need to take.**
- **Those who could not attend the meeting can see what decisions were made and what actions are expected.**

At the next meeting, those present decide whether what was written was accurate, and can ask for amendments to be made to the minutes. These corrections are done by hand and initialled, before the minutes are signed as being a 'fair record' of the meeting.

You need to prepare an agenda for a meeting, hold the meeting and then prepare the minutes, for circulation to those who were invited to attend.

- ★ Working as a group, decide which topics should appear on the agenda. Individually prepare your agendas using word-processing facilities. (The agendas should have the same information, but you may present it differently.)
- ★ Hold the meeting to discuss the points on the agenda. Make notes during the meeting.
- ★ After the meeting, write up the minutes. Make sure you proofread your minutes carefully. It is important that there are no errors in the minutes. Print out a draft of your version of the minutes.

Again as a group compare your individual versions of the minutes. You should have a similar format, with headings to match the agenda.

- ★ Did you have the same content?
- ★ Did anyone miss anything important?
- ★ Were any mistakes made?

Make notes on your own version of the minutes to correct any mistakes you made, and to amend the content so that it truly reflects what happened at the meeting. Amend your minutes and print out a final copy. File both copies (your draft and your final copy) in your portfolio.

If you are a member of a group, e.g. a sports team committee, who regularly meet to discuss topics of interest to you, you may choose to write up the minutes for the meeting you attend. You will then need to compare your minutes against those prepared by the secretary of your committee.

Itineraries and programmes

An **itinerary** is a plan or record of a journey, including dates, times and places. It is often displayed in tabular form for ease of reading, and may be included within a letter.

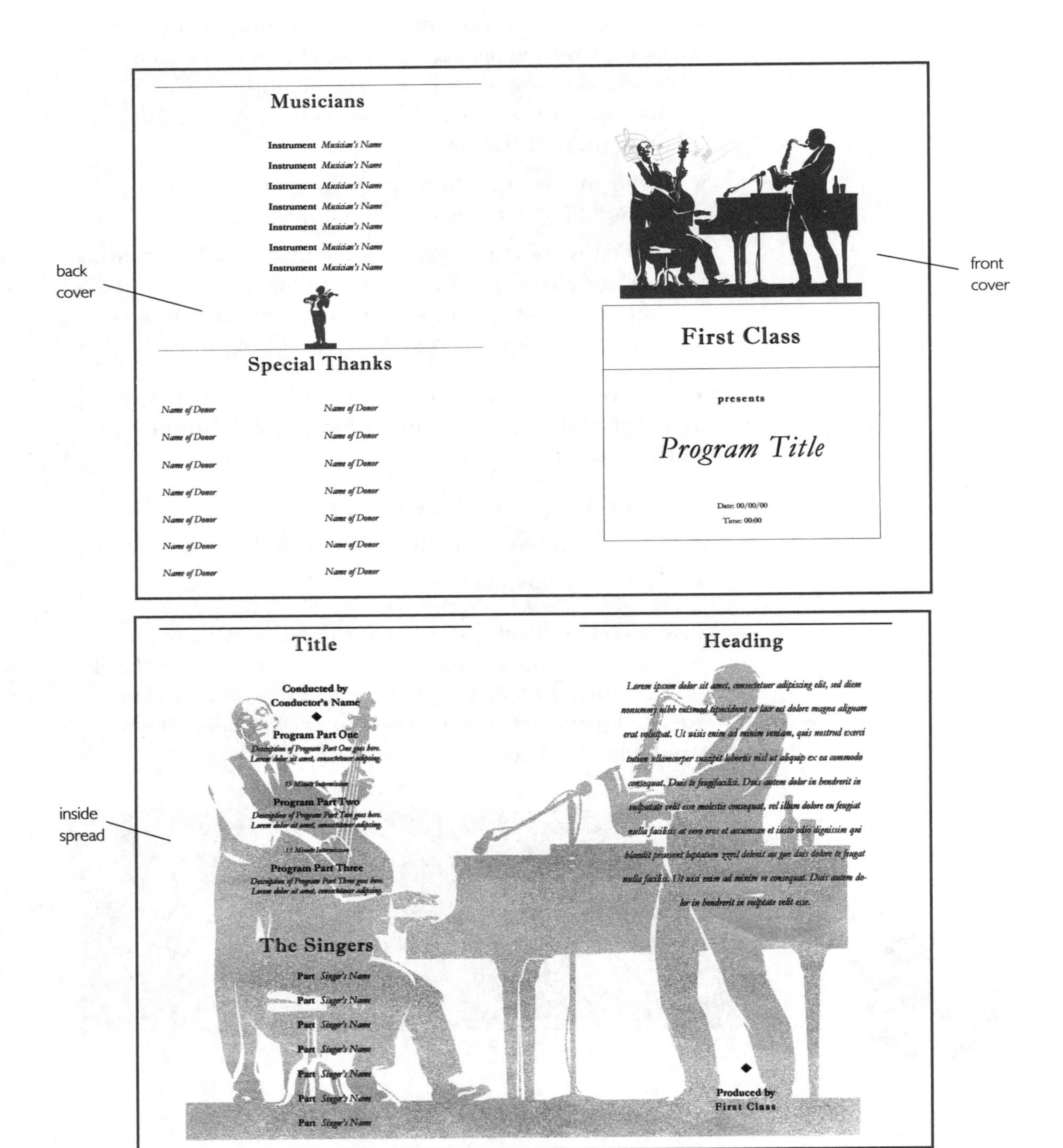

Figure 1.21 *Programme template*

A **programme** is a plan or record of an event, e.g. a theatre performance, an athletics event or an open day at a college. A programme may be a single sheet of paper, but is more likely to be a booklet.

Figure 1.21 shows a template for a program available on Publisher (American spelling). Notice that it is presented so that the front and back cover are side by side. Once the details of the performance have been entered, if this document is printed back-to-back on A4 paper it can be folded to form an A5 programme.

Activity 1.12

Information about itineraries and programmes is unlikely to be confidential, so ask your local organisations for examples of those they produce.

Your school or college may also produce an itinerary (e.g. for a field trip) or programmes (e.g. for school/college functions).

- ★ **Collect at least three examples in total.**
- ★ **Look for similarities and differences between the ones produced by local organisations and those your school or college produces.**
- ★ **Duplicate the information from one of the programmes, using a template on your wordprocessing or DTP software.**

Keep a copy of the original programme, and your version, in your portfolio.

Styles of writing

Before you start to prepare a document you must know what it is that you want to communicate. As you start to write (or type using the keyboard, more likely) you must decide how you will express your message. For this, there are two important things for you to remember:

- Your reader
- The occasion

Remembering your reader

The age and situation of your reader may be important:

- Your reader may be someone like you: the same age, doing the same course or in the same type of job.
- Your reader may be older than you. The people you write to in your chosen organisations are likely to be quite a few years older than you. They will have been in work for several years and may have higher qualifications than you.
- Your reader may be quite young, maybe as young as 6 or 8 years old. A child as young as this will be able to read, but may not understand many long words.
- Your reader may be old, e.g. a pensioner you are inviting to a Christmas party. Some old people have difficulty in reading, and a long letter may be too much for an elderly person to cope with. So, it is best to keep your message simple and short. Perhaps you could use a slightly larger point size too.

Did You Know?

For complete strangers it is polite to use formal language. With your friends and people you know quite well, you can be more informal.

Your reader may be someone you know very well, know slightly or have never met before.

The relationship you have with your reader is also important.

- Your reader may be someone who works for you, or someone you work for
- Your reader may be one of your clients, or one of your suppliers
- Your reader may be a prospective client – or a prospective employer – whom you want to impress

Did You Know?

There are software tools to help with style. Some of these assess the **reading age** that a passage requires. If the reading level seems too high, you can try shorter sentences and use simpler words.

Your reader will remember you by the way you express yourself: in words, sentences and paragraphs.

- Unusual words might impress the reader of a job application, but they might annoy someone needing directions to your house.
- Long sentences may be more difficult to follow, so try to make your sentences as short as possible.
- Paragraphs are used to divide your message into separate 'thoughts'. Grouping sentences into paragraphs can help the reader to follow what you have to say.
- Use correct punctuation and grammar. Failure to do this can mislead your reader.

These two sentences show how using punctuation can change the meaning:

The cakes, which were sliced, should have been served to the guests.

The cakes which were sliced should have been served to the guests.

In the first sentence, all the cakes were sliced and all these should have been served to the guests. In the second sentence only the cakes that were sliced should have been served to guests. It does make a difference!

Remembering the occasion

You remember the **occasion** by thinking about the style of your writing – not so much the font that you use (although that can be important), but how you put your message together.

- Formal occasions need a formal style
- Less formal occasions need an informal style

> **Did You Know?**
>
> With some software tools you can choose a writing style, such as Business Letter or Memo or Advertising or Report. The advice you get matches the style you choose.
> Other tools, such as a grammar checker, may offer a choice between Strict (all rules), Business and Casual. You may also be able to design your own set of rules to be used by the grammar checker.

Exercise 1.18

Suppose you were to write two letters: one is informal to a friend and the other is formal to a prospective employer.

- ★ **Apart from the body of the letters, what else would be different?**
- ★ **How would you start the letters?**
- ★ **How would you end them?**

One way of using the correct style is to use an appropriate standard document.

- For short informal notes within an organisation, send a memo or an internal e-mail
- For short informal notes to a contact outside your organisation, send an e-mail
- For formal messages, send a letter

There are also standard styles used within a number of other standard business documents, such as invoices, orders, delivery notes, agendas, minutes and itineraries.

Exercise 1.19

Apart from the many standard documents you have seen already in this chapter, can you think of any other types of standard formats or styles?

- ★ **Look at information about your school or college timetable. How is this presented?**
- ★ **Look at railway and bus timetables. How are these presented?**
- ★ **Look at some pages on teletext. Is a standard format or style in use?**
- ★ **Look at some pages on the Internet. Is a standard format or style in use?**

Look at the documents you have collected from your chosen organisations.

- ★ **Could any of them be better expressed?**
- ★ **Choose one section of one document, key it into your word processor and try to reword it in a simpler way.**

Tools such as a **thesaurus** may help you to replace particular words with more appropriate ones. This can help to improve the readability of a document.

Accuracy and readability of information

Data take many forms:

- Text
- Numbers
- Tables
- Charts and graphs
- Graphics

Figure 1.22 uses some of these types of data.

When creating a document, the data may come from various sources:

- **Your imagination – you invent the work while you are keying it in**

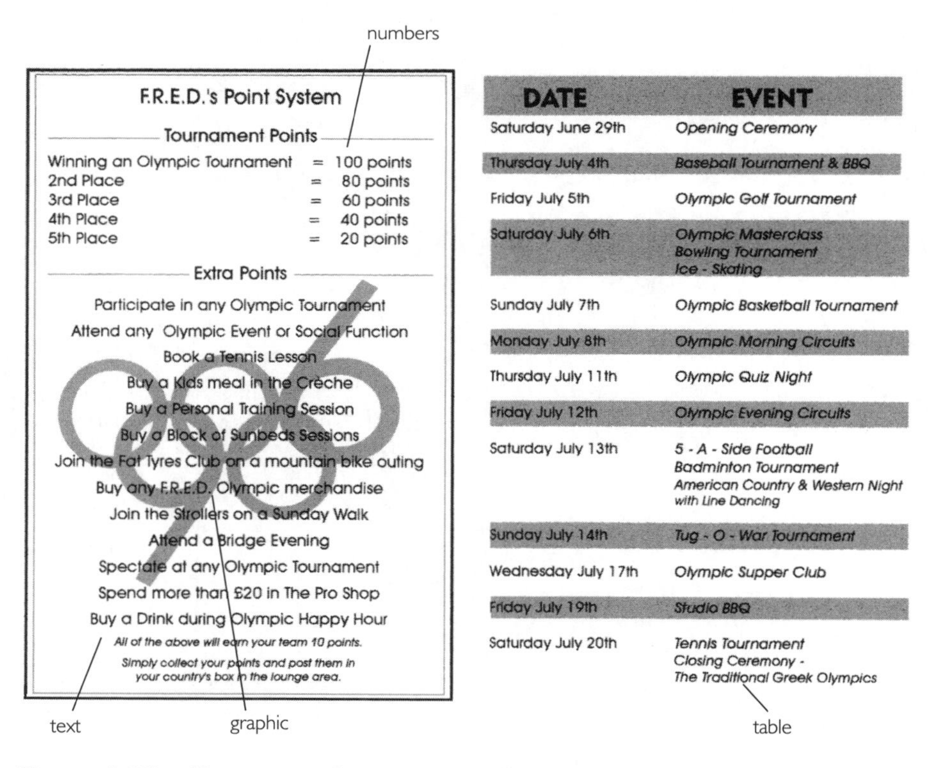

F.R.E.D.'s Point System

Tournament Points

Winning an Olympic Tournament = 100 points
2nd Place = 80 points
3rd Place = 60 points
4th Place = 40 points
5th Place = 20 points

Extra Points

Participate in any Olympic Tournament
Attend any Olympic Event or Social Function
Book a Tennis Lesson
Buy a Kids meal in the Crèche
Buy a Personal Training Session
Buy a Block of Sunbeds Sessions
Join the Fat Tyres Club on a mountain bike outing
Buy any F.R.E.D. Olympic merchandise
Join the Strollers on a Sunday Walk
Attend a Bridge Evening
Spectate at any Olympic Tournament
Spend more than £20 in The Pro Shop
Buy a Drink during Olympic Happy Hour

All of the above will earn your team 10 points.
Simply collect your points and post them in your country's box in the lounge area.

DATE	EVENT
Saturday June 29th	*Opening Ceremony*
Thursday July 4th	*Baseball Tournament & BBQ*
Friday July 5th	*Olympic Golf Tournament*
Saturday July 6th	*Olympic Masterclass* *Bowling Tournament* *Ice - Skating*
Sunday July 7th	*Olympic Basketball Tournament*
Monday July 8th	*Olympic Morning Circuits*
Thursday July 11th	*Olympic Quiz Night*
Friday July 12th	*Olympic Evening Circuits*
Saturday July 13th	*5 - A - Side Football* *Badminton Tournament* *American Country & Western Night with Line Dancing*
Sunday July 14th	*Tug - O - War Tournament*
Wednesday July 17th	*Olympic Supper Club*
Friday July 19th	*Studio BBQ*
Saturday July 20th	*Tennis Tournament* *Closing Ceremony - The Traditional Greek Olympics*

Figure 1.22 *Using more than one type of data*
Courtesy of Chris Lane Family Leisure Club

- Existing computer files – you may retrieve a file to make some changes
- Libraries – graphics in particular are available in this format

One of the most useful things about ICT systems is the facility for data storage. You can key in a letter, save it on a floppy disk and then, another day, retrieve the data file. No rekeying is necessary – unless you lose the file!

You can retrieve data from files of your own work, but you may also have access to other sources. If existing sources are available it makes sense to use them.

Did You Know?

*After a filename, the **file extension** shows what format the file is in. Word files are usually saved in .DOC format.*

If there are no existing sources you need to develop your own information. When starting to write something new, it is sometimes difficult to think of exactly what you want to say. With a word-processing package you can key in your first thoughts, knowing that they will not be perfect. Then you can review and improve them.

Rather than 'starting at the beginning', you can write your thoughts in the order they occur to you. It could be that the very last thing you think of ought to appear in your first paragraph.

Importing means taking data created on a different software application (and having a different file extension) and incorporating it into a document. It may involve converting the imported file into the same format as your document.

The original thoughts are your own, but by editing documents you can turn an early draft into a finished document that is good enough to appear in your portfolio folder.

You may decide to include a piece of clip-art to brighten up your text, or to catch your reader's eye. With a word processor your text will be stored as a document (probably in .DOC format). The clip-art may have been created using graphics software and will be stored in a different format (possibly .WMF format).

To incorporate the clip-art into your document, you need to **import** the clip-art file and insert it at the required position within your document.

It is a good idea to keep track of where your clip-art came from. This information can be put in your reference list or some other appendix. If you keep a record of the filenames of the clip-art used, you will easily be able to find them again.

You may want to produce a multimedia presentation, and for this you will be putting text, sound and drawings together. It is important that you fully document your presentation.

- **You should have a script (describing the events of your presentation) and/or a storyboard, showing these events pictorially**
- **You should have a list of all your source files, including the formats**

Documentation is important, because without full documentation those that come after you, and who may have to adapt what you have produced, will not have enough information to do their job properly.

Some of what you produce may be adapted, or copied directly, from other sources. You must observe copyright laws when using other people's material, and obtain their permission beforehand. In any report you produce that relies on information from other sources, it is also standard practice to acknowledge all those sources.

- **If a source has been particularly helpful you may include the details of your contact (name of person, company name etc.) on an Acknowledgements page in your report.**
- **All other sources should be included in a bibliography (perhaps as an appendix), or close by the material you have used. On page 62 of this book a poem is printed, and an acknowledgement is printed immediately after the poem.**

For this book, permission was obtained for the information used in the many case studies. Acknowledgements are listed on page xiv.

Did You Know?

The **Plain English Society** campaigns for legal and other government documents to be written as simply as possible. Check out their website. It offers useful advice on writing simply and clearly.

It is important that information presented in a document is accurate, up to date, relevant, timely and readable.

- **Inaccurate information can mislead and annoy readers**
- **In some situations inaccurate information can create legal complications, and may cause an organisation embarrassment or lead to financial penalties**
- **Information written in a complex way may fail to convey the meaning intended**

Exercise 1.20

Think of some situations where the accuracy of information in a document is so important that mistakes could result in a disaster of some sort.

When do mistakes creep in?

Mistakes can be introduced at several stages:

- **When you collect the information**
- **When you read the information to be keyed in**
- **When you key the information into the ICT system**

Your manager tells you to send a memo to remind staff about a meeting. He or she tells you the details and you make notes.

Here are some of the mistakes you could make while jotting down your manager's instructions:

- **The wrong date**
- **The wrong time**

- The wrong venue
- The wrong people to invite, e.g. missing someone off the mailing list

Verification involves comparing information. It checks the accuracy of **data transfer** from one form to another.

The only way to avoid this type of **data collection error** is to check your facts carefully. If you repeat the information to your manager, reading from your notes, your manager can **verify** that this information is correct, i.e. that you have successfully transferred his or her verbal instructions into your handwritten notes.

When you prepare the memo, using your notes, there are two different types of errors you could make:

- You could misread your own notes!
- You could miskey while you are entering the data

While keying in the memo for your manager, you misread the date of 5th July as 8th July.

It is difficult to prevent this type of error, apart from making your notes clear enough for you to read! However, when the memo has been prepared you could ask your manager to **proofread** it. This involves reading it through. He or she may then notice your error. Your manager will read the memo, comparing it with what he or she thought you had been asked to do. This is another verification check.

Validation checks are used to make sure the data is sensible or reasonable. It does *not* mean it is accurate. Data is checked against a rule or a list of acceptable values. If it matches, it is assumed to be correct. If it does not match, an error is flagged.

Punctuation includes commas, semicolons, colons, full stops, dashes, brackets, question marks and exclamation marks.

It is *not* possible for an ICT system to notice this type of error. However, ICT systems can be used to check some, but not all, common keying mistakes:

- Words spelt incorrectly
- Sentences ending with two full stops
- Repeated words
- Capital letters missing from the start of a sentence

Spellcheckers

Spellcheckers are a form of **validation check.**

The spellchecker helps you to correct your spelling and **punctuation**.

The spellchecker works by comparing each word against a list of words kept in a **dictionary**.

Did You Know?

Different dictionaries are available for different languages, e.g. English and American, so it is important that the correct dictionary is used. An American spellchecker will reject 'colour' and 'fulfil' – in America, these words are spelt 'color' and 'fulfill'.

The spellchecker scans the text in your document, looking for spaces and punctuation marks. A space or a punctuation mark tells the spellchecker that a 'word' has just finished. The group of characters between two spaces or punctuation marks – the 'word' – is then matched against 'words' in the dictionary.

If there is no match, it could mean one of two things:

- **You miskeyed the word and it needs to be edited**
- **The dictionary does not have that word in its list, and – if the word is correct – it could be added to the dictionary**

Sometimes a spellchecker will suggest that a word is incorrect when you know it is correct. This is often the case with proper names, for example 'GNVQ' and 'ICT'.

Exercise 1.21

Find out how to add words to your word-processor's dictionary to customise the dictionary.

A spellchecker is an excellent tool but, as the lager adverts say: 'It's good, but not that good.' What will spellcheckers miss? If there is a match it still does not guarantee that you did not make a keying error! For example, if you press 'm' instead of 'n' (they are close on the keyboard), you could key in:

- **worm instead of worn**
- **mane instead of name**

The spellchecker will not catch 'worm' and 'mane', because they are correctly spelt words.

This poem gives lots of examples of errors that will *not* be spotted by a spellchecker:

Eye have a spelling chequer
It came with my Pea Sea
It plainly marques for my revue
Mistakes eye cannot sea.
I've run this poem threw it,
Eye am sure your plea's too no,
It's letter perfect in it's weigh.
My chequer tolled me sew!

(Reproduced courtesy of the Midland Bank Pensioners' Association)

In groups, take a few lines each and try to rewrite this poem correctly!

The poem starts: I have a spelling checker, it came with my PC . . .

So, since spellcheckers are not foolproof you must use some other checking method to be sure your finished work is perfect: proofreading.

Proofreading

> **Proofreading** is used mainly to check the sense of your text. It can also be used to check that no tables have been split across two pages and that artwork does not 'overprint' text.

A **proofread** is a visual check of the content of your document.

- Print early drafts in double-line spacing, to allow plenty of room for you to correct by hand
- In later drafts include all tables and artwork, to allow you to check the layout, including the positioning on the page of any figures and tables

There are two types of proofreading:

- Comparing one draft against the next
- Reading through a draft

Both methods should be used.

Suppose you had a first draft and you had written corrections all over it. Then you (or a friend) edited the text to correct it. Figure 1.23 shows an example of both documents.

Your first job would be to proofread the second draft against the first to make sure that all the planned corrections had been implemented.

- **You should check each correction, one at a time, and tick them off on the first draft as you go**
- **You can then mark the second draft with any corrections that were missed and still need to be done**

Then – most importantly – file the old version away. You may need to keep it for your portfolio folder. Finally, you should read the second draft through at least once more.

- **Does it still make sense?**
- **Can you improve on it?**
- **Can you spot any mistakes that the spellchecker missed? (There is one deliberate mistake in the text of Figure 1.23. Can you find it?)**

First draft

The tag is punched with holes – to record the item type and other information –

Kimball tags are small pieces of card ~~punched with holes,~~ which can be attached to a garment, is and torn off when the item is sold. The part torn off is then put into a computer system

Some stores use tags with bar codes nowadays. This makes the process more automatic

More expensive items have a security tag which sets of an alarm if you try to leave the shop without paying/ for the goods ⊙

Second draft

Kimball tags are small pieces of card which can be attached to a garment. The tag is punched with holes – to record the item type and other information – and is torn off when the item is sold.

The part torn off is then input into a computer system.

Some stores use tags with bar codes nowadays. This makes the process more automatic.

More expensive items have a security tag which sets of an alarm if you try to leave the shop without paying for the goods.

***Figure 1.23** Drafts of a document*

You need a partner for this activity.

- **Each of you key in three paragraphs. Do not look at the screen while you touch the keys, and work as fast as you can. This way you are likely to make quite a few mistakes! Save your file and print out two copies of your document in double-line spacing.**
- **Swap documents with your partner and spend five minutes or so proofreading the work to find any errors.**
- **Load your partner's document file, make the corrections and resave the file.**
- **Print out the second draft and return both drafts to your partner.**
- **Check the editing work your partner has done to your own document, and mark up any corrections he or she has missed.**
- **Read through your own document once more, to see if you can spot any more errors.**

It may help you to see the errors more clearly if you mark corrections in red pen.

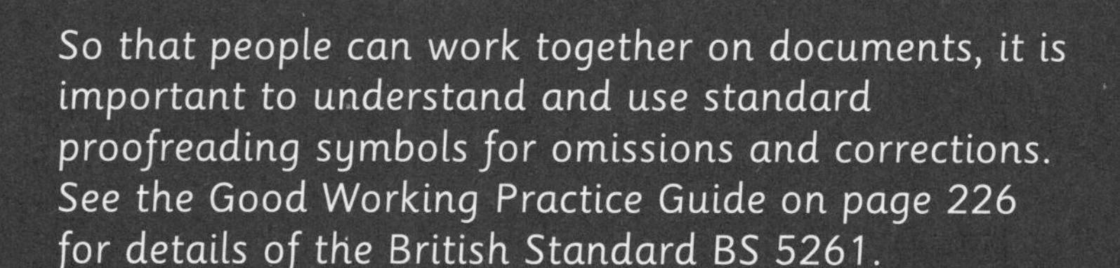
So that people can work together on documents, it is important to understand and use standard proofreading symbols for omissions and corrections. See the Good Working Practice Guide on page 226 for details of the British Standard BS 5261.

It is quite difficult to spot your own errors. Sometimes it is better to ask a friend to proofread your work. In return, you can proofread your friend's work.

Checking for accuracy

To make sure the end result is absolutely accurate, you will need to apply accuracy checks to your work.

There are two main types of accuracy check:

- **Validation checks: spellcheckers**
- **Verification checks: proofreading**

Transcription errors are the errors made when transferring data, from original course documents to the keyboard, or from one electronic form to another (e.g. reading a disk file).

These checks need to be made every time you 'transfer' data as **transcription errors** may have occurred.

Finally, how well you express yourself will depend on your communication skills. Spellcheckers cannot tell you when you use a word wrongly, so you may want to learn when and how to use grammar-checkers. Grammar-checkers rely on a number of rules:

- **Your sentences must have a subject and a verb that agree**
- **You should write mostly in an active voice rather than a passive voice**
- **When you are writing academic reports you should avoid writing 'I' (by using the passive voice)**

If you break any of these rules the grammar-checker will warn you.

Exercise 1.22

Find out how the grammar-checker works on your word processor.

Presentation

It is important to present information clearly as it may annoy or confuse your reader if your presentation is poor. A common mistake is to use inconsistent headings or layout. You should think of what you want to achieve with your document and what will appeal to your readers.

There are many techniques that can be used to help you to create effective documents.

Having decided **paper size**, you can plan the structure and layout of your document:

- Using titles and headings
- Setting up headers and footers
- Choosing page orientation: landscape or portrait
- Setting up templates and macros

Letters have a different layout from memos. Newspapers use several columns. Textbooks like this may only have a single column, but may use the margin for messages.

Exercise 1.23

Make sure you know how to set up headers and footers, including having different information on the first page, and on odd/even pages. Look at the pages of this book. Notice that there are only footers. Other books may have headers and footers.

- **Sometimes there are none on the front page.**
- **Sometimes there are different headers on odd and even pages.**
- **Sometimes the footer is the same on each page.**

A **template** is a special document used to set the style for all documents of a particular type, e.g. an invoice or a memo. Templates usually have the .DOT file extension. To make text styling as simple as possible a toolbar can be created, with each key on the toolbar representing one of the styles used. To assign a style, the keyboard operator simply places the cursor within a paragraph and clicks the required key on the toolbar. A **macro** is a sequence of instructions that can be 'called' by a single keystroke or by clicking a button on a toolbar. Most software applications allow you to set up your own macros.

Exercise 1.24

- ★ **Make sure you know how to set up and use a template.**
- ★ **Make sure you know how to set up a macro.**
- ★ **Make sure you know how to set up and customise toolbars on your word processor.**

Notice in Figure 1.24 that although the page orientation is portrait, it is possible to present some text in landscape orientation.

White space is the part of a page not covered in text. Each page will have margins at each edge. There may also be white space above and below headings, and around artwork and tables. Too little white space may give a 'cramped' impression. Too much white space may result in a document being longer than it needs to be.

Did You Know?

Most word processors offer demonstrations of how to use features of the software. These take a very short time to go through, and you can learn a lot from watching them.

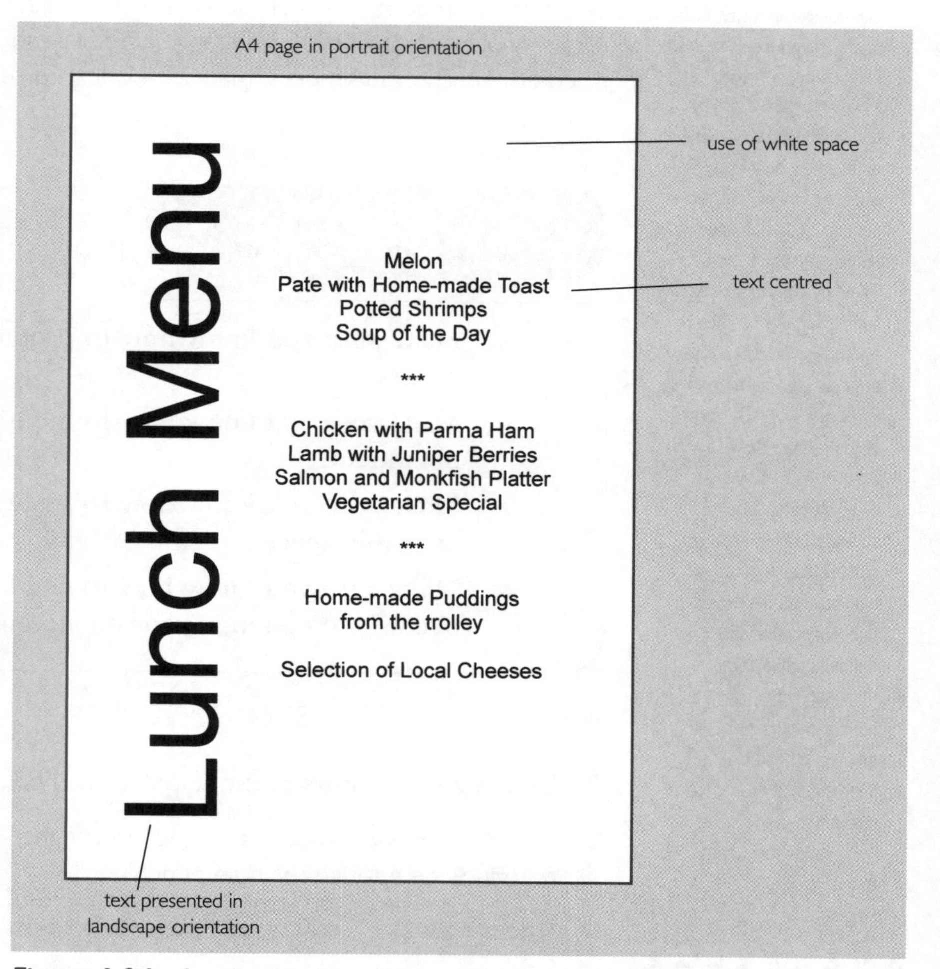

Figure 1.24 Landscape orientation within a portrait page

Left justification (or **justification off**) means the left-hand edge of the text will be straight but the right-hand edge will be ragged.
Right justification means that the right-hand edge will be straight but the left-hand edge of the text will be ragged. This would look strange on normal text, e.g. in a letter, but is used when text and graphics are incorporated in the same document. This style may also be used for special effects.
Full justification (or **justification on**) is used in newspaper columns, text books and for most business documents. It results in both edges of text being straight. The software adds extra spaces between pairs of words so that the words that do fit into one line fill the line completely. The spaces you key in are called **hard** spaces; the spaces inserted by the software are called **soft** spaces.
Centred text appears in the centre of each line. Centred text is often used on menus, programmes or the front pages of reports.

Exercise 1.25

Make sure you know how to control the orientation of pages, sections of text, and graphics.

You can then collect together relevant data and present it as information in the most appropriate way:

- Using graphs and charts
- Including pictures, drawings and clip-art
- Scaling images to fit the available space
- Using borders and shading

Suppose a document includes artwork, e.g. a graph, a pie chart and one piece of clip-art, then each one needs to be scaled to fit into the available space. A variety of borders would look strange, so a style should be adopted for all three diagrams, e.g. a simple single line. Shading could be used on the headings.

Exercise 1.26

- **Make sure you know how to produce graphs and charts.**
- **Make sure you know how to include clip-art into a document.**
- **Make sure you know how to scale images to fit the available space.**
- **Make sure you know how to add borders and shading to enhance your document.**

You should be able to design a good page layout:

- Deciding which **fonts** to use (typeface and point size)
- Including margins (top, bottom, left and right) – with the left margin wide enough for hole punching
- Choosing which justification to use (**left**, **right**, **full** or **centred**)
- Deciding on line spacing (single, double etc.)

- Planning white space to good effect
- Using **hanging indents** for lists
- Setting tabs (left, right, decimal etc.)
- Using tables to present data in columns
- Setting page breaks to control pagination and to avoid **widows** and **orphans**

Indent
is the amount of space between the margin and the start of the text. Text can be indented on either side, on both sides, or not at all.

Hanging indents
give the effect of a list. The list can be numbers/letters or bullet points.

Tabulation is used to create the effect of columns. Tab positions are set and then, when the tab key is pressed, the cursor jumps to the next tab position. The benefit of using tabs rather than hard spaces is that you can change them very easily. Depending on the software you are using, you will set up a **ruler** with tab positions marked. If you move the tab positions on the ruler, all text controlled by that ruler will move to the new positions.

A text file may be too long to fit on one sheet of paper. If so, the text has to be paginated, that is, divided into pages. **Pagination** is done automatically by the software, so no text is lost when printing. If you want to control pagination you must put a **page break** in to show where you want the new page to start.

Widow
is a single line of text at the bottom of a page, separated from the rest of the paragraph – its 'offspring' – which appears on the next page.

Orphan
is a single line of text at the top of a page, separated from its 'parent' – which appears on the previous page.

Exercise 1.27

Make sure you know how to use all of these features. If you are not sure about any of them ask your teacher for help, or use the online help facility to find some information.

Having produced the 'perfect' text, you need to think about **highlighting** important words or phrases. These will then catch the reader's eye.

You can **enhance** your text, tables and graphics by:

- Using bold highlighting for added emphasis. Words in **bold** stand out more and will be noticed. You should only use bold for headings or to highlight important words.
- Using **italics** or **underlining** to stress important words or phrases. If one word in a sentence is important for the sense of what you are saying – and if the reader might miss the importance otherwise – use italics. Here are two examples: In the event of fire, do *not* use the lifts. The cost is £25 *plus* VAT. Instead of italicising you can use underlining.

Did You Know?

The **page breaks** put in by the software are called **soft page breaks.** The ones put in by you are called **hard page breaks.**

- Using bullet points to make the text easier to follow. A list can be presented as a number of **bullet points**. You can choose what symbol to use for the bullet: •, ❑, ➩ or many others.

For simplicity it is best to stick to only one or two highlighting techniques, as using too many makes a document look cluttered.

Figure 1.25 shows two examples: one shows good highlighting; the other has too much.

<u>Using a word processing package</u>

When starting to **write something new**, it is sometimes difficult to think of exactly what you want to say. With a **word processing package**, you can key in your first thoughts, knowing they will not be perfect. Then you can review it and improve it.

The word processing package also offers a **spelling checker**, a **thesaurus** and a **grammar checker**.

The <u>spelling checker</u> highlights **words not found in the dictionary**. The <u>thesaurus</u> suggests **alternative words to use**. The <u>grammar checker</u> highlights sections of text where **you might have made an error**, e.g. using a *singular* noun with a *plural* verb as in 'The *<u>man are</u>* working' or a *plural* noun with a *singular* verb: 'The *<u>men is</u>* working'.

Too much highlighting

Using a word processing package

When starting to write something *new*, it is sometimes difficult to think of exactly what you want to say. With a **word processing package**, you can key in your first thoughts, knowing they will not be perfect. Then you can review it and improve it.

The word processing package also offers a spelling checker, a thesaurus and a grammar checker.

The **spelling checker** highlights words *not* found in the dictionary. The **thesaurus** suggests alternative words to use. The **grammar checker** highlights sections of text where you might have made an error, e.g. using a *singular noun* with a <u>plural verb</u> as in 'The *man* <u>are</u> working' or a *plural noun* with a <u>singular verb</u>: 'The *men* <u>is</u> working'.

Good use of highlighting

Figure 1.25 *Use of highlighting*

Exercise 1.28

- ★ Make sure you know how to enhance your text.
- ★ Check with your software what bullet point styles are available.
- ★ Make sure that you know the difference between left, right and full justification.

Subscripts are characters that appear below the normal print position, e.g. in H_2O, the '2' is subscripted.

Superscripts are characters that appear above the normal print position, e.g. in $y = x^2 + 4$, the '2' is superscripted.

You must present your information accurately:

- Using **upper** and **lower** case appropriately
- Using **subscripts** and **superscripts** where needed
- Editing your text using **cut and paste**

Notice that superscripts and subscripts are in a smaller point size than normal text.

Exercise 1.29

Make sure you know how to create superscripts and subscripts on your wordprocessor.

There may be several ways of doing this: choosing superscript/subscript effect for the font, or raising/lowering the text by changing the character spacing.

You should know how and when to use these techniques in a document. You may need lots of practice, creating many documents, before you can use them correctly.

Activity 1.16

Produce a four-page document demonstrating your skills in layout and design.

Make notes on your drawing to show what features you have used in presenting this information.

You might decide to produce this document using desktop publishing (DTP) software.

Organisations and their use of information

Organisations can range from corner shops to large international companies. In an organisation a group of people work together to make something or to provide a service. Examples are a supermarket, an airline, a hospital, the Royal Navy, a car manufacturer, a chemist, a bank, a farm and a newsagent.

In this chapter you have learnt about the different types of documents used by organisations:

- Why they are used

Activity 1.17

Prepare a report to explain the purpose of six standard documents. Decide who your reader is going to be, and make sure your report meets their needs.

- **Choose six types of standard document, e.g. business letter, memo etc.**
- **Write brief notes on each one to explain their purpose.**
- **Decide how you could categorise these standard documents, e.g. for internal versus external communication.**

Compare each of the six standard documents with the other five.

- **In what ways are they similar?**
- **In what ways are they different?**

Plan the content of your report to include at least one table and at least one graphic, to demonstrate your key skills in communication.

- How they are presented
- Their good and bad points
- Their differences and similarities

Using templates and macros

It is also important – and can save a lot of time – for organisations to develop and use standard layouts. You have already studied several standard documents. For each of these, a template could be set up by one person and then used by everyone in the organisation. This ensures that all business letters look the same, all memos have the same (important) information included, and so on.

Find out what templates are available on your word-processing system.

- **Print out two examples and annotate each of them to show how the template has been set up.**
- **For Activity 1.5 you prepared a memo for Pam Turner. If you did not set this up as a template, do so now.**
- **Print out the template and annotate to show what Pam has to do when using the template.**

If you are not sure how to set up a template file, search the online help for 'creating templates'.

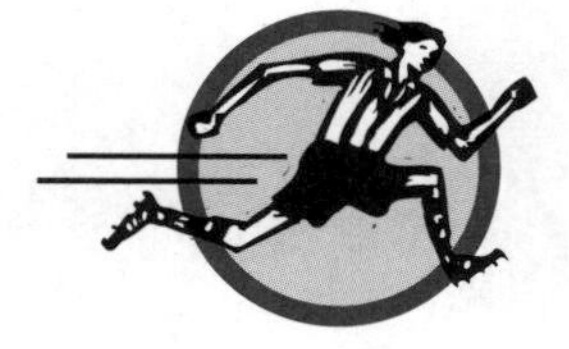

It is useful to include information such as the pathname of a document and today's date, in a header or footer of a document. In most word-processing applications this is provided as a special feature. You do not have to write a macro for it.

Exercise 1.30

What kinds of things are macros used for? Make a list of macros available to you, and make brief notes on what they do.

Activity 1.19

- ★ **In the template you prepared for Pam Turner's memo style, write a macro that automatically puts today's date on the memo.**
- ★ **Print out the memo to show that your macro works.**

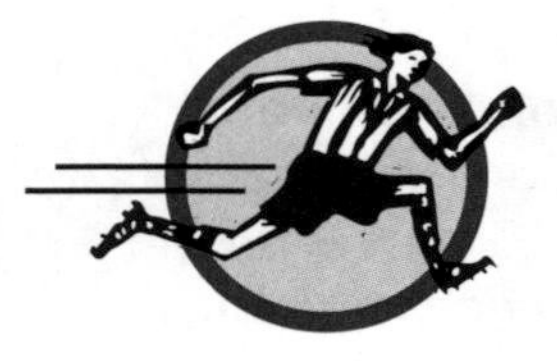

To insert the date (and time) anywhere in a document, select INSERT/DATE AND TIME.

Your portfolio should now contain many examples of your work in completing this chapter. You have collected sample documents from organisations, and produced similar documents using various presentation techniques. The next three activities complete your work for this chapter. (Remember that advice on how to present your portfolio material is given on page 241 in the Portfolio Guide.)

Activity 1.20

Review your portfolio of documents and identify six that you will present in your portfolio to show your ability to produce original documents.

In selecting the best six documents, use this checklist to decide which to include:

- ★ Do the six documents present a range of styles and occasions?
- ★ Has each document been written in a style that suits your reader and the occasion?
- ★ Is the purpose of each document clear?
- ★ Do your six documents show that you can vary the type of information you use: new information, existing information and information from different sources?
- ★ Have you included examples to show you can combine different types of information, such as text, sound, drawings, charts, images, colour and tables?
- ★ Do the six documents show that you have used appropriate presentation techniques to communicate your message?
- ★ Have you used presentation techniques consistently within each document?
- ★ Does your portfolio include early drafts of at least two of your documents, showing how you have changed your work to improve it, and that you have been using good working practices?
- ★ Are the final versions of your six documents accurate, without obvious errors?

Activity 1.21

Of the six documents in your portfolio, select two that are similar to documents you have collected from organisations, e.g. formal letters, publicity material (such as an annual report), and newspaper or magazine articles.

- ★ For each of these two documents, write notes comparing them with three examples you have collected from organisations.
- ★ Explain any differences between your documents and those produced by organisations.
- ★ Suggest improvements for each document.

Activity 1.22

Look back at your completed portfolio for this unit.

- ★ Review your work and suggest how you might improve it if you were to do it again.

Ask others for their opinions on your documents.

Revision questions

1. Give four examples of standard documents.
2. What is the difference between external and internal communications? Give two examples of standard documents used for external communication and two examples of documents used for internal communication.
3. What is meant by landscape orientation?
4. Explain the terms: typeface, point size and font.
5. Explain the difference between double line spacing and single line spacing. When might double line spacing be used?
6. Explain what agendas and minutes are used for. What information does each contain?
7. What is an itinerary? How might an itinerary be displayed?
8. When might a file be imported? How is this done?
9. Explain the difference between validation and verification.
10. Explain how to proofread a document.
11. What is a macro? How is a macro different from a template?
12. What are hanging indents? When are they used?
13. What is white space?
14. Explain the difference between a superscript and a subscript. Give examples of both.
15. Explain these terms: tabulation, pagination, widow and orphan.

2 Handling Information

- **Understand what information handling means and how it is used**
- **Create a database to store and process records**
- **Create a spreadsheet to store and process numerical information**
- **Search, sort, explore and predict information**
- **Discover trends and patterns from numerical information**

This chapter looks in detail at four topics:

- **Information handling and handling techniques**
- **Design of information handling systems**
- **Database methods**
- **Spreadsheet methods**

In your activities you will practise handling information, and produce a relational database and a spreadsheet to meet the needs of a user.

This chapter uses one case study – a sailing club called the Online Cruising Club (OCC). Background information about this case study, and others used in this book, appears in the Case Studies section starting on page xvi.

Information handling and handling techniques

This first section looks at data and information, sources of information and information handling techniques.

Data and information

At first sight the two words 'data' and 'information' seem to describe the same thing. In fact, there is a difference which, for this course in ICT, you need to understand.

The word information comes from the verb 'to inform' and this is the key to understanding the difference between data and information. Information has meaning – it informs the reader. Data has no meaning on its own.

The words in this sentence – taken one at a time – are good examples of data. Each word on its own has no meaning. It is only when they are strung together to make a sentence that the words mean something.

Similarly, numbers mean little until we know what the units are, what they are counting or measuring. So items of data are put together – in some structure – to make meaningful information.

DATA + STRUCTURE = INFORMATION

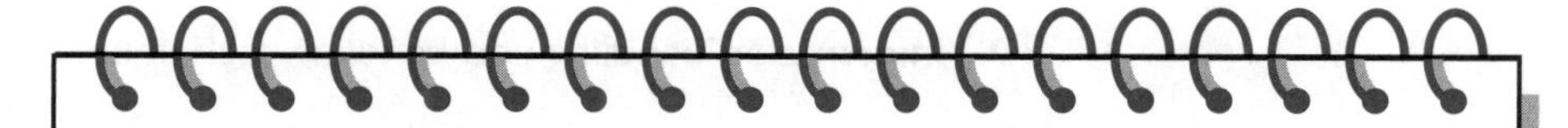

OCC

Here is some data:

The OCC committee has six officers (Commodore, Vice Commodore, Secretary, Treasurer, Sailing Secretary and Membership Secretary). The officers are (alphabetically) Angela, Gerry, Jenny, Linda, Mark and Tom.

continued

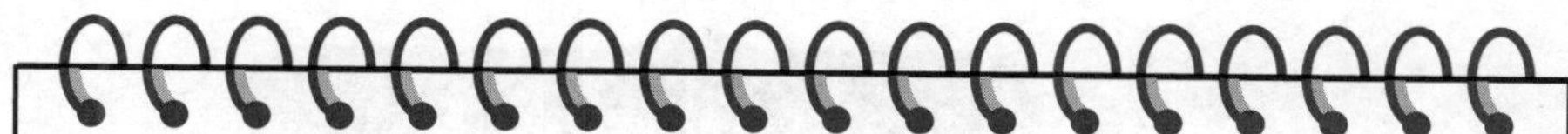

continued

Table 2.1 shows how this data can be structured into information, using a table.

OCC Committee 2000	
Commodore	Tom
Vice Commodore	Mark
Secretary	Angela
Treasurer	Gerry
Sailing Secretary	Jenny
Membership Secretary	Linda

Table 2.1 *Example of information*

There are many ways of structuring data: text in a letter, numbers in a table structure or spreadsheet, or names and addresses in database records.

Record-structured databases are rows of information in the form of one or more **tables**. Each row of a table is called a **record**. Records could be a person's name and address, information about a hotel in a travel database, or flights and destinations in an airport. In a **relational database** the tables of records are linked by **relationships** to form one larger database.

Exercise 2.1

Here are three examples of record-structured data:

- ★ **A directory entry – name, telephone number, address**
- ★ **A patient record – name, diagnosis, date**
- ★ **An order – item, quantity, price, total**

Think of three more examples of record-structured data.

Record-structured databases are discussed in detail starting on page 103.

Number-structured databases (spreadsheets) record numerical information in **cells**, in **rows** and in **columns**. You can use a spreadsheet to calculate results such as totals, or to produce graphs of the results, and to calculate or forecast results from given information. Spreadsheets are discussed in detail starting on page 125.

Exercise 2.2

Here are three examples of number-structured data:

- ★ **income and expenditure**
- ★ **sales forecasting**
- ★ **staff hours, rates of pay and tax**

Think of three more examples of number-structured data.

Internet pages, **CD-Rom** encyclopaedia pages and online help pages are examples of **hypertext databases.** These contain separate pages of information with items of text or graphics. The pages are linked so that pointing at a highlighted item – a **hot link** – results in a jump to a different page and reveals more information. Setting up this type of database is beyond the scope of this chapter, but you will access hypertext databases throughout your course – whenever you use the help facility on your computer, or explore the Internet.

Activity 2.1

When you are next online to the Internet, move the mouse around the screen and see how the cursor changes. Make a note of the different cursor symbols and the ways in which hot links like e-mail addresses are shown on screen.

Sources of information

There are many different sources of information – places where you can find out what you want to know. During your GNVQ course there will be many situations where you will need to do research. When looking for relevant information, you can choose to use sources like these:

CDs
Class notes and textbooks
Computer databases and the Internet
Directories and instruction manuals
Newspapers and magazines
People
Timetables
TV and radio

Exercise 2.3

Table 2.2 shows these sources of information and other details about them.

Copy the table, extending it to include 10 sources of information that you use regularly.

For each one, complete the other columns.

Source	Type	Order of information	Use
1. Telephone directory	Paper-based	Alphabetical on surname and initial	To find out people's telephone numbers
2. GNVQ textbook	Paper-based	In chapters; topics are listed alphabetically in index	To find out subject information
3. A daily newspaper	Paper-based	Grouped by section: front page for main news, back page for sports	Main news items, sports results and TV guide
4. Computer databases	Electronic		
5. The Internet	Electronic		
6. CDs			
7. Bus timetables			
8.			
9.			
10.			

Table 2.2 *Sources of information*

OCC

The address information about members is collected on a registration form, which they complete the first time they sail on *Overload*. Members who move house are expected to inform the membership secretary of their change in details. The full list of names and addresses is published each year in the OCC journal, so a special check is needed prior to publication.

Other items of information, such as subscription rates, are decided by the committee. The sailing secretary and membership secretary compile statistics, such as number of members booked to sail on a trip, or the number of members in a particular membership category.

Most sources of information are paper-based or available electronically, e.g. on the Internet. One extremely valuable source of information is people. People have knowledge, experience, beliefs and opinions, any of which might be important to your research. To obtain information from people, various methods can be used:

- Interviewing
- Questionnaires
- Observation

Interviewing is very time-consuming but may be the best way of collecting in-depth information, especially about people's opinions. The questions that are to be asked can be quite general, allowing the person to say exactly what they want. However, the interviewer should have a list of questions before the interview starts, and know exactly what information is wanted.

Questionnaires limit the responses that the person can give. Sometimes this a very useful way of collecting information, e.g. for application forms. The questionnaire needs to be carefully designed so that the questions are in a sensible order, there is no confusion as to what each question means, and there is enough space to write an answer to each question.

Sometimes interviewing is linked to a questionnaire, especially if the structure of the questions is very complex.

Observation is used when the activity has to continue, or needs to be seen to be understood.

- The simplest example is in conducting a survey of traffic passing a school. There is no need to stop the traffic. Information about the number of vehicles and the type of vehicle can be obtained just by watching them go by.
- Observation is also used during systems analysis. One way of finding out how a job is done is to sit alongside the person doing it and watch them carefully, taking notes and asking questions if anything is unclear.

When collecting information from people, the information needs to be transferred on to paper at some point. This then becomes the **source document**.

Activity 2.2

For each of these tasks you could work on your own or with a friend or two. Make notes on how you found the information and any problems that arose.

- ★ Look in the local telephone directory and find organisations of a particular type (e.g. doctors, hotels, stationery suppliers, tree surgeons, vets) whose name starts with the same letter as your surname.
- ★ Choose one instruction manual (e.g. for a mobile phone, a video recorder or replacing a toner cartridge) and make a copy of any diagram that is included to show the main parts of the equipment. In how many languages is the manual provided?
- ★ Using either an online database or your local library, find out what textbooks are available for students on your GNVQ course.
- ★ Make a search on a CD, e.g. an encyclopaedia like Encarta, and find all you can on a single topic, e.g. digital cameras, Charles Babbage, or the Human Genome Project.
- ★ Compare the way TV and radio listings are given in at least two newspapers.
- ★ Compare the way timetable information is supplied at a bus stop and at a railway station.
- ★ Collect examples of application forms and questionnaires. Notice how the form is laid out and what information is collected.

Information handling techniques

Information handling involves four main techniques:

- Setting up the information structure – the letter, the spreadsheet, the database or the web page

- **Inputting the data – called data entry**
- **Accessing the information and interrogation – trying to find the answers to questions**
- **Presenting results – as reports, tables or charts**

Setting up an information structure may seem straightforward, but the design of any information handling system is actually quite complex. So, before tackling this (on page 100), it makes sense to use information systems that have already been set up, and to learn from them what makes a good system – and what makes a poor one!

Presentation techniques are the subject of Chapter 1, in particular the presentation of reports using word-processing software.

In this chapter you will create tables and charts. This section concentrates on the remaining two topics: data entry and accessing information.

Data entry

For an information processing system the input originates from one of a number of possible sources:

- **A source document, e.g. the data-entry clerk keying direct to disk from an order form or an application form**
- **Online entry, e.g. a bank customer giving instructions to pay a bill by entering details directly on screen**
- **A telephone conversation, e.g. a booking clerk accepting a booking for theatre tickets by telephone**
- **A face-to-face conversation, e.g. a DIY store help-desk assistant interrogating the stock database on behalf of a customer**

Notice that when working from source documents (the first in the list), data entry can be batched. There is probably no urgency to enter the data, so long as it is done 'sometime today maybe'. The other three examples are all actioned immediately, although the DIY customer may have to queue for a while. In fact, all of the last three involve queuing, even if it is not apparent to the user:

- **When trying to make a telephone connection, the line may be busy**
- **When completing an online banking transaction, it takes time to download the web pages**

- When phoning to make a theatre booking, the telephone switchboard may have a queuing system, directing your call to the first available 'operative'

Some data entry may be automatic, e.g. using a barcode, but most is via the keyboard. The mouse is also used, but mostly to select choices offered on the screen.

Toggle key
is used to turn something on and off, like a light switch. You press it once to turn it on. To turn it off you press it again.

There are two main 'modes' of data input via the keyboard – **insert** and **overtype** – and to control which, you '**toggle**' the **Insert key** on the keyboard.

With word-processing software data is usually input in a free format. You just type what you want where you want it. Where you type is mostly controlled by moving the mouse around the screen and repositioning the cursor by a single click.

Exercise 2.4

Apart from using the mouse, how else can you move the position of the cursor around the screen?

With spreadsheet software data entry is often straight into the cell, so you need to be positioned on the correct cell before you start keying data.

Activity 2.3

Look for online help on data entry in your spreadsheet software. What tips are given to speed up moving from one cell to another?

Once you are positioned on the correct cell, you start to key in data. How this is understood by the software is covered in detail later in this chapter (page 129). With database software data can be entered straight into a table. However, it is more usual for a data-entry form to be designed.

Activity 2.4

- ★ **Find out if it is possible to create a data-entry form within your spreadsheet software.**
- ★ **Find out what online help is available should you want to create a data-entry form within your database software.**

So, to help the data-entry clerk, data-entry forms are displayed on the screen and are designed to make entry as easy and error-free as possible:

- **The data-entry screen is as close as possible to the original source document that the data-entry clerk will be working from**
- **The entries will be in the same order as the questions the booking clerk or the DIY help-desk assistant will be asking the customer**
- **The cursor will jump automatically to the next data-entry field as soon as the data-entry clerk presses return to signal the end of input for the previous field**

The design of data-entry forms is important. A poor design will frustrate the data-entry clerk and, for example, may slow down the process of taking orders. It may also result in mistakes being made.

Like the design of questionnaires, designing data-entry screens is a complex topic. Each screen has three separate 'areas':

- Header information, explaining what the screen is about
- Data entry fields, including the title of each field
- Closing information, including any final checks, and options to move to the next screen

There are many examples of data-entry screens on the Internet. Companies with websites are keen to obtain the names and addresses of those that visit the site. Such information is invaluable for marketing purposes. It is therefore becoming common practice to offer visitors the chance to take part in a free competition. All you have to do is complete the form – giving your private information free of charge to their marketing department.

Companies who use **e-commerce** to sell on the net genuinely need your name and address. Otherwise, how can they deliver the goods you have purchased?

Activity 2.5

Next time you are faced with an invitation to complete your name and address details on a web page, make special note of how you complete the form.

- ★ **How are the data-entry fields displayed? In what way are they different from the instructions explaining what you have to fill in?**
- ★ **In what order are the entries presented?**
- ★ **What do you press to jump from one field to the next?**
- ★ **What happens if you do not fill in all the fields?**
- ★ **What happens if you fill in a field with inappropriate data? For example, if a date is an invalid one are any checks carried out on this field?**

It is important that errors are not made during data entry. Methods of trapping errors – **validation** and **verification** – are explained in Chapter 1 (page 60).

Accessing information

To use an ICT system at all you must be able to find data already stored in that system. You must know where to look for the information, what instructions (or commands) to use, and how to say what it is that you want.

All data is stored in data files, and these are stored in **directories**. Directories are like filing cabinets. You might keep all correspondence files on customers with names starting with the letters A to D in one drawer, the ones for customers E to K in another drawer, and so on.

Each directory can also be split into subdirectories; and the subdirectories can be split still further, as shown in Figure 2.1.

There may be a limit to the number of files in any one directory; also, each name has to be unique within that directory.

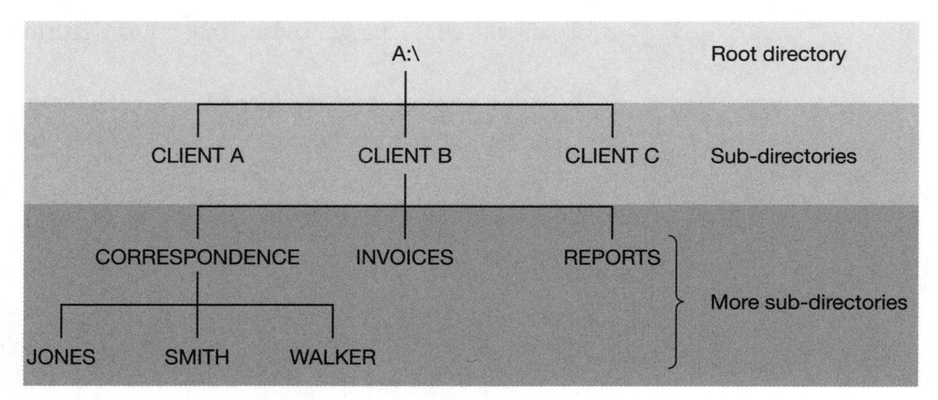

Figure 2.1 *Example directory structure*

> *It makes sense to decide where to store your data files before you have too many in one directory. This makes the process of backing up more manageable too. If your directory is well organised, arranging for just one subdirectory to be copied to a backup device is relatively simple. If all your files are in the one directory, backup could take a very long time, and you may be saving copies of files that do not need to be backed up.*

Produce a printout of the data files in one of your directories.

In ICT systems, data files created in one application have a special name ending (called a **file extension**) which allows the application software to recognise the file next time you want to access it. For example, this chapter has been written using word-processing software that uses the '.DOC' file extension.

Exercise 2.5

List the file extensions used by the software on your ICT system.

Importing files (rather than just retrieving them) involves a translation process. The same process (but in reverse) happens when you **export** data files for use in another software application.

File extensions are important. If you want to transfer data from one software application to another, the formats of the data files must be compatible. Knowing the file extension will allow you to check whether this type of file can be **imported**.

Each data file also has a name (called its **filename**) chosen by you.

It is important to choose names that are meaningful. Then, next time you see the name on the directory list you will remember what is in that file.

The **pathname** of a file is a combination of the following:

- The drive letter (the disk drive on which you have stored the data)
- The directory name
- Any subdirectory names
- The filename
- The file extension

You need to know all these – or at least recognise them from a list offered by your software – before you can locate a data file! This chapter is stored on a floppy disk. Its pathname is A:\GNVQ\BOOK\CH2.DOC. The backward slashes (\) separate the different parts of the pathname.

Exercise 2.6

Write down the pathnames of three different data files to which you have access.

Sometimes the information you need is not available just how you want it.

- **There may be more information than you need, and you may need to search for what you really need, from all that is available to you**
- **The information may not be in the order you want it, so you may need to sort the data into an order that suits you**

Search and sort facilities are available on most software applications: word processing, spreadsheets and databases. These two terms are easily confused, but it is important that you know which to use.

The word 'sort' is used in many ways. If you look it up in the thesaurus of your word processor you will find it is either a noun or a verb. As a noun, 'sort' could mean 'kind' or 'person'. Figure 2.2 shows the alternatives for the meaning 'kind'.

In ICT, sorting means rearranging records in a file into some order, typically numerical or alphabetical.

The telephone directory is sorted into alphabetical order by surname. It is also sorted by a second field – first name – so that 'Jones John' comes before 'Jones Peter'.

Activity 2.7

Key in the word 'sort' and position your cursor on the word while you select the thesaurus facility. Find out the alternative for the verb 'to sort' meaning 'to arrange'.

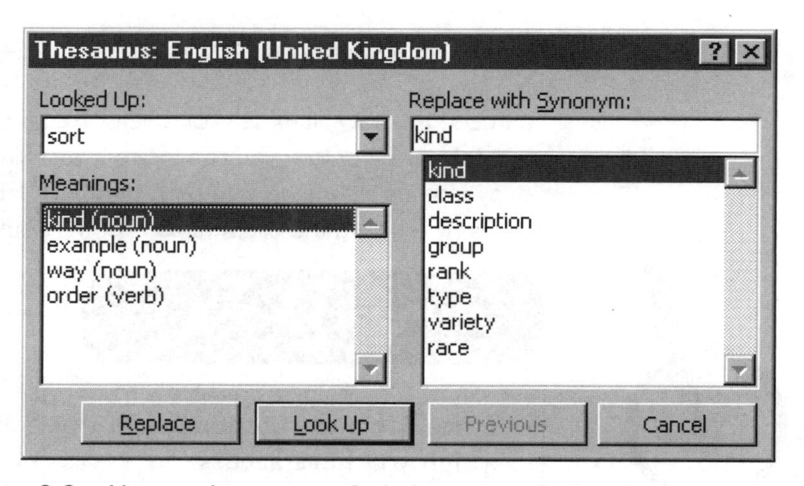

Figure 2.2 *Using a thesaurus to find alternatives for 'sort'*

So, in theory, sorting involves rearranging data into an order. In practice, the data stays exactly where it is, but is displayed or printed in the order that you ask for.

With most modern software the records may be stored in any order, usually the order in which they were entered. The order in which they are printed is controlled by **key fields** and **index files**, which the software creates to keep track of the location of each record.

In ICT, then, to sort a database means to present a listing of items – on screen or on paper – in a given order.

Activity 2.8

Find out how to use the sort facility on your word-processing software.

- ★ **In what situations is it available?**
- ★ **When might you want to use this facility?**

How data is sorted depends on the type of data.

- Text is sorted alphabetically
- Numbers are sorted numerically

Data can be sorted in two different ways: **ascending** or **descending**.

- Text sorted in ascending order (going up) will put Andrew before Zach. Descending order (going down) will put Peter before Paul.
- Numbers sorted in ascending order (going up) has the smallest numbers first. Descending order (going down) has the largest numbers first.

Activity 2.9

Collect examples of indexes and contents lists in books or magazines, and at least one timetable, e.g. a bus or train timetable. For each example, use a highlighter pen to show which data has been sorted, and decide what order has been used.

Exercise 2.7

Think of an example where data might be sorted in descending order.

Look at the example in Figure 2.3. Into what order has the data been sorted? The names and addresses shown in Figure 2.3 are fictitious. Why is it not possible to publish actual data from the OCC database in this book?

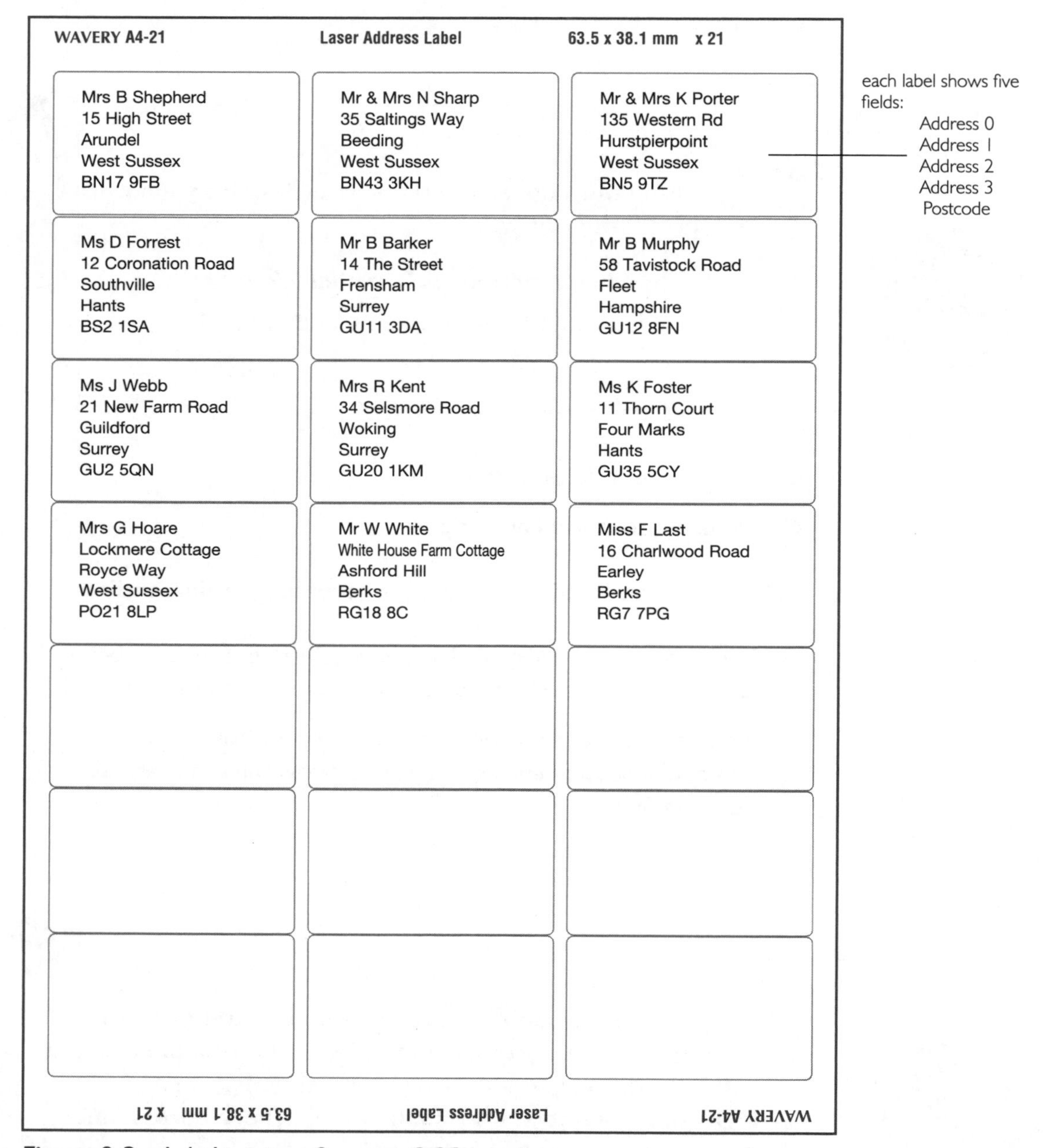

Figure 2.3 Label printout for some OCC members

Searching is different from sorting. On word-processing software you can use the **Find function** to search the text for a particular word or phrase that you have included in the text. This facility only allows a simple search, but you can choose to look for whole words only, or words that sound like the one you key in.

Activity 2.10

Explore the Find function on your word-processing software. Write notes on how it works. Find is often used with the Replace function. How does this work? How can it help you to edit your data efficiently and accurately?

You could use online help to find out more about this facility.

Sometimes, to access the information you want you have to search a large source of information for a small amount of information that is going to be useful for you.

Contents list
is arranged in the same order as the pages of the book and tells you on what page each chapter starts.

Index
the entries are arranged alphabetically, and each entry points to the pages within the book that might give you what you need on that topic.

This book has over 260 pages. To find out about one particular topic you could look at every single page until you spotted what you want. This could take ages! If you are already familiar with the book, it might be that referring to the **contents list** *will speed up your search. If this is not helpful enough, you might decide to refer to the* **index**.

Exercise 2.8

While doing this exercise, time yourself and think about what 'data' you are using to complete the exercise.

- ★ **In this book, on what page does the Good Working Practice Guide start?**
- ★ **Where is 'justification' explained in this book?**

If you are accessing information using a computer, you have to give the computer instructions as to what you want to find.

To complete the first part of Exercise 2.8, a computer (or someone who does not know how to find out this type of information) would have to be given these instructions:

- *Go to the contents page.*
- *Start at top line of text and check each line until you find 'Good Working Practice Guide'.*
- *Tell me what page number it starts on.*

Exercise 2.9

Write similar 'instructions' for accessing the index.

If you are searching for information on an ICT system, rather than a paper-based file, having found the correct data file you will probably want to look at a particular record or group of records. If a data file relates to all the people employed by a company, then this data file is separated into many records, each one related to one particular employee. Each record may have details of the employee such as these:

- Name
- Address
- Job title

These details are stored in separate fields within the record, one field for name, one field for address, and so on. Each record is the same 'shape', that is, it has the same fields. It is easier to imagine this if you draw a table as shown in Figure 2.4.

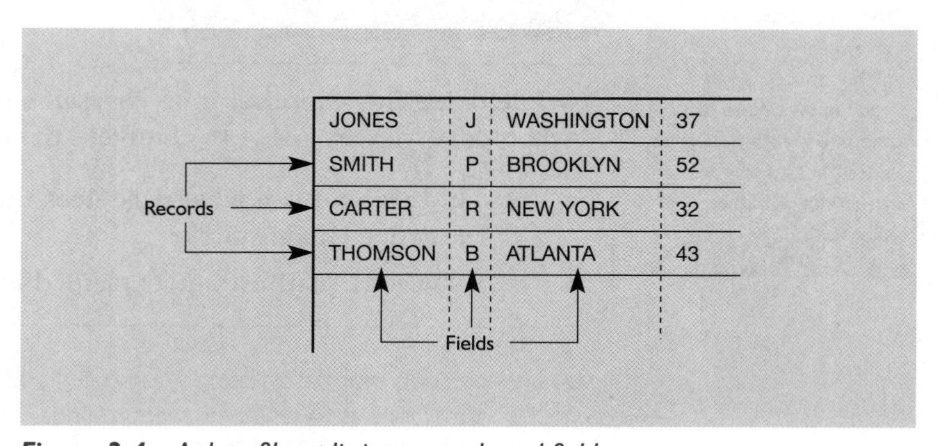

Figure 2.4 *A data file, split into records and fields*

To find information about a particular employee, you must know something about him or her which will uniquely identify the record. This is called the **key**. Usually, one data item is used as a **key field**. In the case of the employee file, it will probably be an employee number.

Exercise 2.10

What would you expect the key field to be in a data file held by a bank about each of its customers? Think of three more data files and suggest what information might be kept in each record, and what field might be the key field. For example, think about data held by libraries, electricity companies and schools or colleges.

> **Relational operators**
> = (equals), < (less than), > (greater than), ≦ (less than or equal than), ≧ (greater than or equal to)

A search instruction always includes a **condition**, and the condition always includes a **relational operator**.

These are all examples of simple conditions:

- *surname = "Lawson"*
- *crewtotal < 10*
- *age > 18*
- *credit ≦ 100*
- *balance ≧ 0*

Sometimes accessing information is not so simple, because to present it in a meaningful way the information requires a more complex structure. Suppose you want to know the telephone number of Joe Brown. First you look for the Browns. There are lots of them! So then you look for those with a first name of Joe. Surname is the **primary sort field**; the first name is the **secondary sort field**.

> **Logical operators**
> AND, OR and NOT

More complex conditions can be created by joining together two or more simple conditions using **logical operators**.

> **Did You Know?**
> You can use logical operators to reduce (or increase) the amount of information available to you. AND narrows down a search. OR opens up a search.

These are all examples of complex conditions:

- *surname = "Brown" AND firstname = "Joe"*
- *surname = "Lawson" OR surname = "Lawrence"*
- *credit ≦ 100 AND balance ≧ 0*

Once you know which record (or group of records) you want to access, you need to enter a command which will make the software search for that data. Exactly how you do this will depend on the software you are using. Some use a Find command; others use Select. There may be an icon with a pair of binoculars. Some offer you a blank record and ask you to fill in the data items you want to match.

Activity 2.11

Check how searching (or finding) works on your spreadsheet software.

Most database software will allow you to **search on a match**. This means you can find a record which has a data item that exactly matches a data value that you key in. For example, you may match on CUST_NAME = "SMITH" and get a printout of all customers whose surname is Smith. CUST_NAME is the **field title**. The computer will look at every record and, in particular, at the data in the field called CUST_NAME. If the data in the field matches, then that record is **selected** for printing.

Activity 2.12

Investigate how to find particular data within your spreadsheet software. Write down an explanation that would help someone who has never used this software before.

You may also want to **search on a range**. For this, you might use a search command including the test: PRICE > 100. This might find all records of products which have a sales price greater than £100. You might need to write more complicated instructions that ask for records **within a range**.

Activity 2.13

Find out what commands you should use to find particular records on your database software.

- **Write down the command you would use to find a matching record.**
- **Write down the command you would use to find a range of records.**
- **Use these commands to produce printouts of data extracted from the database file.**

If you are not quite sure about how to spell a person's surname, for instance, you can use a **wildcard search**.

If you search on CUST_NAME = "SM", you will be given records for people with surnames Smith, Smithson, Smythe – anyone whose surname starts with 'Sm'.*

Activity 2.14

Find out what wildcard features are available on your word-processing, spreadsheet and database software.

- **Write down how you would use these features and explain what effect they would have.**
- **Produce a printout of data to support your notes.**

Design of information handling systems

All organisations collect data – about their employees, their customers and their suppliers. Some also collect information about their competitors.

- All organisations are required to obey Health and Safety regulations. They have to display information to all staff about special measures in place, for example if a fire is discovered. These instructions are likely to be stored as a word processed file.
- Some organisations have reason to collect data because of the nature of their business. For example, estate agents would keep details about the houses they have to sell, as well as the people who have registered with them as looking for a new home. These would be stored in a database.
- Numerical information is usually processed on a spreadsheet. We look at the practical problems of this in greater detail on page 125. Some organisations use a spreadsheet for planning and costing purposes.

You need to plan the design of a system and specify what processing is needed. This will help you to decide the type of data structure to use and hence which type of software to use to store the data – word processing, spreadsheet or database.

The design process involves many stages:

- Defining the purpose of the system
- Defining the needs of the users
- Identifying what processing is needed
- Using ICT to create a storage structure
- Identifying the required information
- Collecting information for storage
- Entering and editing the information
- Processing the information

The starting point for any information processing system is to answer these two questions:

- What is its purpose?
- What does the user need?

OCC

- **The main purpose of keeping a database of members' names and addresses is for mailing out newsletters. The user needs a speedy and accurate method of producing labels every month.**
- **The purpose of the spreadsheet used by the membership secretary (Figure 2.13 on page 125) is to keep a record of members analysed by type, from which the subscription income can be forecast. Accurate calculations are required.**
- **The purpose of the spreadsheet used by the sailing secretary (Figure 2.20 on page 141) is to keep track of bookings and to forecast charter income.**

Finding out what the user needs, and defining the purpose of the ICT system, involves detailed discussions with the user. There may be a slight problem at this stage:

- **You may understand nothing about your user's business. For example, you may know nothing about how a sailing club is run. You may need to learn some new terminology!**
- **The user may know nothing about ICT systems. Your contact at the sailing club may find it difficult to explain what is currently done, and even more difficult to guess how an ICT system may improve things.**

Somehow, you must bridge this gap. You need to discuss the needs of a user to the point where you think you understand what is needed and can plan a way to deliver the information using an ICT system. Writing down what you understand to be the purpose, and listing the needs of the user is a good idea. If both you and the user agree to this statement at the beginning, then later efforts need not be wasted because of misunderstandings. From this information, you might then go on to produce a suitable design.

Exercise 2.11

You need to identify at least one third-party user for whom you will design an ICT system. In total, you need to design two systems, one relational database and one spreadsheet, but these could both be for the same third party. Start thinking now about who you know, and who might be willing to act as your third-party user for your portfolio material.

Having established the purpose of the system, you need to define its requirements:

- What data you need to store
- The order in which data is needed – for access and for printing reports
- The output needed – printed or on screen
- Details of special outputs such as graphs and charts
- The calculations and formulae and functions that are to be used
- Details of complex searches and 'What if?' queries that will be needed

Most of this information might be gleaned by looking at the information that is currently kept. This stage includes collecting information for storage, entering and editing the information and processing the information. Data handling is the processing of records in a database. We call this structured data, and consider the practical problems of processing it in greater detail next. Sometimes, data is recorded in a spreadsheet, and this is discussed on page 125.

Database methods

We often use the term 'database' instead of 'record-structured database'.

Simple databases (called **flatfile databases**) comprise a single table. More complex databases, called **relational databases**, comprise several tables linked by relationship.

Within a table there are two main database components: **records** and **fields**, as shown in Figure 2.4 on page 96.

In this section you will learn to identify the database components in a given data handling problem, and set up records to store these.

Records and fields

A database table is divided into many **records**, all the same 'shape'; each record holds the same kind of information but about a different person, thing or event:

- **If a database file keeps information about the employees in a company, for each employee there will be one record. The same information will be kept about each employee.**
- **If a database file keeps information about the products available for sale in a supermarket, one record will contain the details for a particular stock item. The same information will be kept about each stock item.**

Exercise 2.12

Think of three different database files – related to people, things and events – and for each one, write down what information may be kept in one record within that file.

One of your database files could be for your third-party user.

- If a database file keeps information about holiday bookings, one record will hold the information about one holiday booked. The same information will be kept about each booking.

In each record of the database file there are a number of **fields**; these contain the data items:

- In the employee database file the records will have fields for the employee's name, address, telephone number, job title etc. (Figure 2.5(a)).

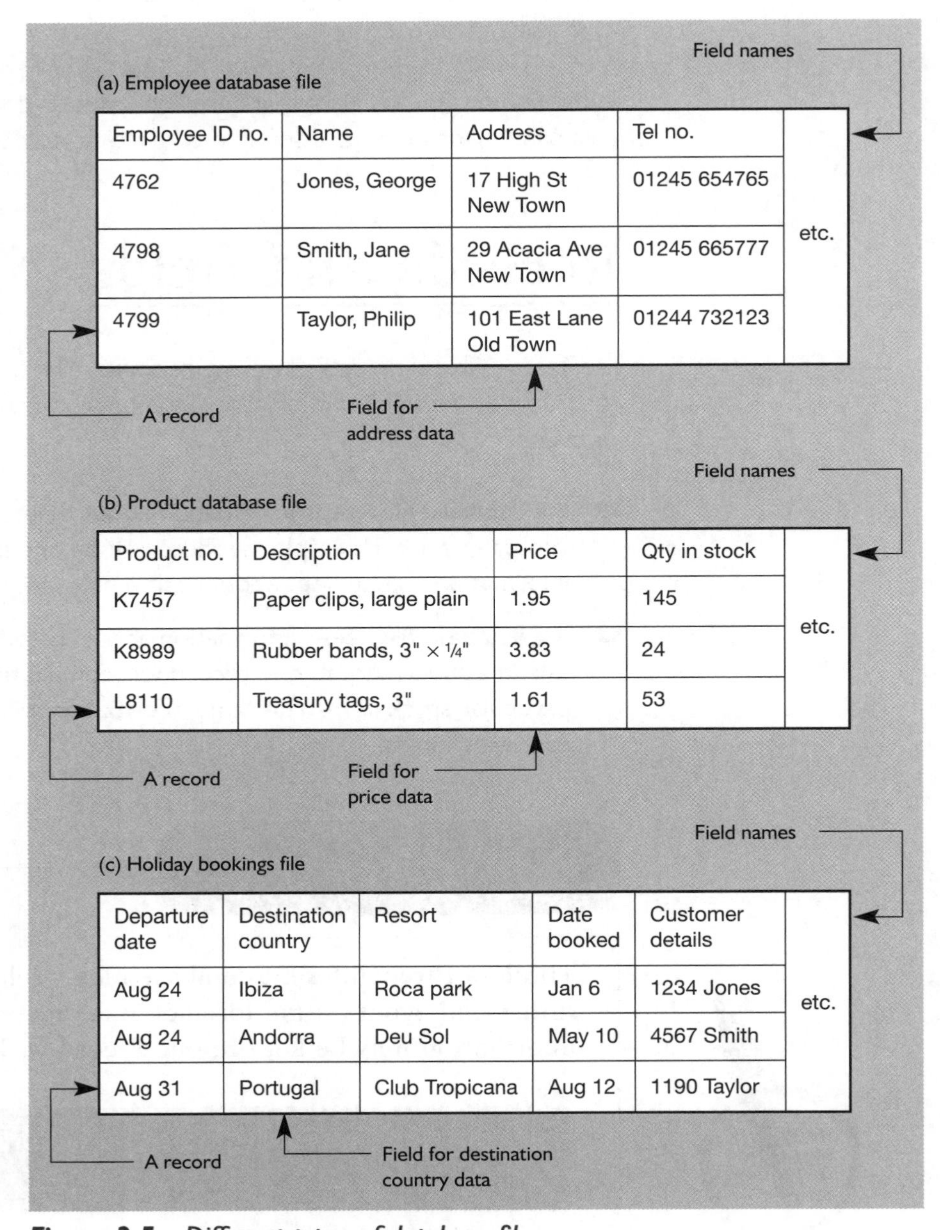

(a) Employee database file

Employee ID no.	Name	Address	Tel no.
4762	Jones, George	17 High St New Town	01245 654765
4798	Smith, Jane	29 Acacia Ave New Town	01245 665777
4799	Taylor, Philip	101 East Lane Old Town	01244 732123

(b) Product database file

Product no.	Description	Price	Qty in stock
K7457	Paper clips, large plain	1.95	145
K8989	Rubber bands, 3" × ¼"	3.83	24
L8110	Treasury tags, 3"	1.61	53

(c) Holiday bookings file

Departure date	Destination country	Resort	Date booked	Customer details
Aug 24	Ibiza	Roca park	Jan 6	1234 Jones
Aug 24	Andorra	Deu Sol	May 10	4567 Smith
Aug 31	Portugal	Club Tropicana	Aug 12	1190 Taylor

Figure 2.5 *Different types of database files*

- In the product database file the records will have fields for product number, product description, price, quantity in stock etc. (Figure 2.5(b)).
- In the holiday bookings database file the records will have fields for departure date, destination country, resort, date booked, customer details etc. (Figure 2.5(c)).

OCC

In the OCC members' address database (Figure 2.6, on page 108), each record holds the address details for one household. If two people in the same family belong to the OCC they only appear once in the database, so they only receive one mailing of each newsletter.

Within each record the fields kept for each household are: the people to send the mailing to (Addressee), their address (3 lines) and a postcode.

In the Sailtrips database each record holds the information for one sailing. The fields are: departure date, the number of days sailing, and a title (or description of the sailing) (see Figure 2.11, on page 120).

When designing a database file you need to list all the fields that will appear in each record. For each field you need a unique **field name**. This will be used when you interrogate the database file.

For the employee database file the field names might be: EMP_NAME, EMP_ADDR, EMP_TELNO, EMP_JOBTITLE.

It makes sense to choose field titles which are as meaningful as possible.

Exercise 2.13

For each of the database files from Exercise 2.12, list the fields, using a unique name for each.

Data types and key fields

Each field has a data type: character, numeric, date etc., which determines how the data will be stored. There are three main types of data that you need to know about:

> **Did You Know?**
>
> Dates are actually stored as the number of days since some date a long time ago. Exactly when that starting date was, will have been set up by someone when your software was first installed.

- Character (sometimes called text)
- Number (integer and decimal)
- Date

In the records of a product database file there are fields for product number, product description, price, quantity in stock etc. In deciding what data types to use to store or display this data, you need to think about the values it might have. Table 2.3 shows an example.

Field	***Possible values***
Product number	Character string – only letters of the alphabet or numbers, no decimal point or other characters
Product description	Text/character string – may include numbers, e.g. ½ to describe thickness of string etc.
Price	Currency – two decimal places for pence
Quantity in stock	Number – integer, cannot be less than zero

Table 2.3 *Deciding data types for a database*

Activity 2.15

These are the fields in the database for holiday bookings: departure date, destination country, resort, date booked, customer details. For each field, suggest what values the data might take and create a table (similar to Table 2.3) to record this information.

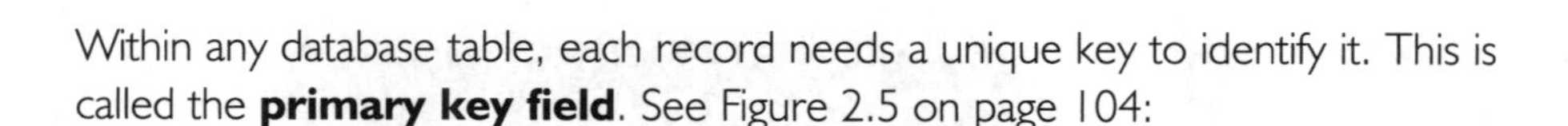

Within any database table, each record needs a unique key to identify it. This is called the **primary key field**. See Figure 2.5 on page 104:

- In the employee database file the key field is Employee ID no.
- In the product database file the key field is Product no.
- In the holiday bookings file there appears to be no key field.

It would be sensible to add an extra field – booking number – and use that as a key field.

In a relational database two or more tables are linked by relationships.

You will need to decide how much data needs to fit into each field, and therefore how long each field needs to be. This is called the **field length.**

Exercise 2.14

For your three databases (Exercise 2.12), decide on a type and length for each field.

When deciding on the length of text fields, look at some sample data and see what the longest possible entry could be. Choose a field length at least as long, perhaps a few characters more.

Foreign key
is a field in one table that 'points to' the key field in another table.

OCC

A relational database has been created of members' names and addresses for mailing out newsletters. To save postage, one copy of the newsletter is mailed to each household, even if several members live at the same address.

For example, there are more than 125 members, but they live at only 80 addresses.

Figure 2.6 shows how the data tables for Addresses and Members are linked. In the Members table, the field Address no. is a foreign key. It points to the address of that member in the Addresses table.

- **If a list of all members and their addresses is needed, the report is produced mainly from the Members table, but pulling address data from the Addresses table.**
- **When only labels are required, data is simply taken from the Addresses file.**

continued

continued

MEMBERS table

surname	first name	member ID	address code	mem type	date joined
Forrest	Diane	57	298	C	05/05/99
Hoare	Grace	85	61	F	16/09/93
Murphy	Barry	134	95	F	01/01/93
Porter	Keith	148	106	F	20/06/80
Porter	Joy	149	106	A	20/06/80
Shepherd	Brenda	169	118	F	07/12/84
White	William	267	197	LM	18/09/99
Kent	Rosemary	288	216	F	30/09/84
Barker	Brian	318	241	F	13/04/85
Last	Fiona	351	264	F	22/01/00
Sharp	Annie	399	306	F	23/06/87
Sharp	Nick	400	306	A	05/11/89
Foster	Katie	413	315	C	21/11/94
Webb	Joan	417	319	F	20/12/95

Keith and Joy Porter live at the same address

member ID is the key field for the Members table

address code is a foreign key in the Members table, and points to records in the Addresses table

ADDRESSES table

Ref	Addressee	Address 1	Address 2	Address 3	Postcode
61	Mrs G Hoare	Lockmere Cottage	Royce Way	West Sussex	PO21 8LP
95	Mr B Murphy	58 Tavistock Road	Fleet	Hampshire	GU12 8FN
106	Mr & Mrs K Porter	135 Western Rd	Hurstpierpoint	West Sussex	BN5 9TZ
118	Mrs B Shepherd	15 High Street	Arundel	West Sussex	BN17 9FB
197	Mr W White	White House Farm Cottage	Ashford Hill	Berks	RG18 8CN
216	Mrs R Kent	34 Selsmore Road	Woking	Surrey	GU20 1KM
241	Mr B Barker	14 The Street	Frensham	Surrey	GU11 3DA
264	Miss F Last	16 Charlwood Road	Earley	Berks	RG7 7PG
298	Ms D Forrest	12 Coronation Road	Southville	Hants	BS2 1SA
306	Mr & Mrs N Sharp	35 Saltings Way	Beeding	West Sussex	BN43 3KH
315	Ms K Foster	11 Thorn Court	Four Marks	Hants	GU35 5CY
319	Ms J Webb	21 New Farm Road	Guildford	Surrey	GU2 5QN

address record 106 shared by Keith and Joy Porter

address code is the primary key field for the Addresses table

Figure 2.6 *Relational database for Members and Addresses*

When deciding on numeric fields, you are choosing not how the data is stored (which is controlled by the software), but how it is displayed.

- **How many decimal places will you need to produce the required level of accuracy? For money amounts, you usually use two decimal places (for the pence), but on a telephone bill you will notice more decimal places on the itemised list of call charges.**
- **Do you want the pound sign to appear?**
- **Do you want a comma to separate the figures in large amounts? For example, would you prefer to see 123,456 or 123456?**

For dates, you also control how they are displayed rather than how the data is stored.

Activity 2.16

Find out what date formats are available on your database software. Write notes about this.

Database facilities

Relational databases are a recent development, but are now widespread.

Did You Know?

Before relational databases were invented other structures were used, such as **hierarchical databases**. The earliest databases were called ***flatfiles***.

Relational databases allow you to manage all the data for a particular situation within a single database.

- The data is stored in tables
- Queries are used to extract data from one or more tables, to create a new table
- Information in tables can be viewed on screen, edited directly or through data-entry forms, and printed out
- Reports can summarise data, giving grouped totals and presenting the information in whatever order you want
- If you want to, you can write macros to automate your database – this does not involve actual programming and there are wizards to help you

- You can also write modules, using a language like Basic, to customise your database.

Cue card
is a reminder note that helps you to operate the software more successfully.

How your database software works will affect how you approach this section. Unlike spreadsheet software, where most packages do things in very similar ways, database software can be very different. Even upgrading from an older version to a newer version of the same software package can be a bit tricky at first. So, it is important that you read the online help carefully before tackling this section. Most packages offer online help, e.g. in the form of **cue cards**, and/or they offer demonstrations.

Find out the name of the database software that you will be using. Find out what online help it offers.

In this section you will create a relational database comprising at least two tables with at least one relationship linking them.

Entity
is a thing about which you decide to store data, e.g. a person, or an object like a car. Sometimes an entity is an event, e.g. the booking of a ticket, or the payment of a bill.

These are the steps you will need to follow:

- Set up a table for each '**entity**' and enter data into your tables
- Set up a query to extract data from your tables
- Set up relationships between your tables
- Design a report to present the results of your query

Tables

Tables are the basic building blocks of a database. They hold the data for a single entity and have rows (for records) and columns (for fields).

Activity
2.18

For your database software, find out how to set up a table, how to enter data into it, how to sort the data on one field and how to print out a table.

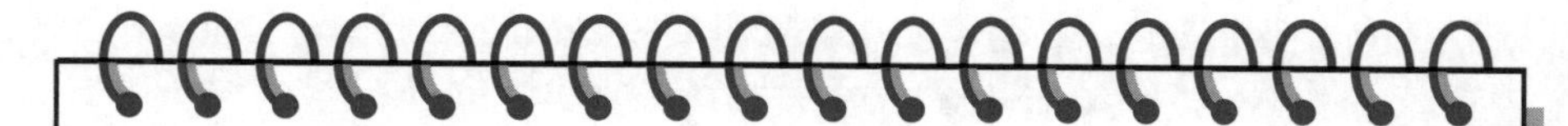

OCC

The OCC database has one table of all members and another for all addresses. Figure 2.6 on page 108 shows part of these tables.

For reasons of confidentiality you cannot be shown actual data from the OCC database, so dummy names and addresses are given in this book instead.

Exercise 2.15

Why is it not possible to publish actual data from the OCC database in this book?

Activity 2.19

Set up a database for something of interest to you.

- ★ **Create one table, making sure your data includes at least one text field and one numeric field.**
- ★ **Enter the data for ten records. Use real or imaginary data to test your database design.**
- ★ **Sort your records on one numeric field and print out the data.**
- ★ **Sort the data by one text field and print it out.**

You could choose something from this list: a CD or other collection, a Christmas card list or friends' telephone numbers. Or you could set up a database to meet the needs of a third-party user.

At this stage you need not explore how to create a form for data entry. However, when you have completely set up your database and tested it fully, you may decide that entering data through a data-entry form is a more sensible option.

Activity 2.20

Think again about the database you set up in Activity 2.19. Can you extend or improve the database by adding another table?

CD COLLECTION DATABASE

Suppose your table had information like: title of CD, artist, CD number. This is fine for CDs that involve only one artist. You can print out your list in Artist order and easily see what you have by one particular singer or band.

Suppose now that you work as a DJ, and that you have hundreds of CDs, including compilations.

How can you amend and/or extend your database design to allow you to locate tracks by any particular artist?

CHRISTMAS CARD LIST

If you want to send separate cards to several people all living at the same address, you might decide to save postage by putting them all in the one envelope. This is similar to the OCC problem of mailing out newsletters, so you can solve it by having a separate address table.

FRIENDS' TELEPHONE LIST

Suppose your table had information like: friend's first name, friend's surname, telephone number. How would you hold details of friends who have more than one telephone number, e.g. a telephone number at home, plus one at work, or a mobile telephone? There seems to be two options, as shown in Figure 2.7: duplicate the name data for each telephone number, or allow space for every type of phone for everyone. Both options are wasteful of space! Instead, it is better to have a second table.

What about keeping track of e-mail addresses as well? They may have one at school or work, and one at home.

Whatever your choice of database, review the data you have stored. Think of extra data that would be useful, and create at least one more table to hold this data.

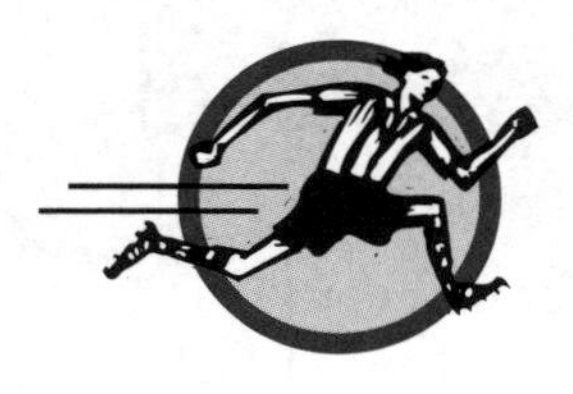

While you are 'prototyping' your database it makes sense to input only a few records for each table. This should be enough for you to test that the database works, but not so much that too much of your time is spent keying in data.

First name	Surname	Telephone
Jim	Brown	01482 927927 (H)
Jim*	Brown*	0207 940 1127 (W)
Mary	Gordon	01203 911437 (H)
Mary*	Gordon*	07771 673401 (M)

1st	Surname	Home tel	Work tel	Mobile
Jim	Brown	01482 927927	0207 940 1127	**
Mary	Gordon	01203 911437	**	07771 673402

* shows duplicated data
** shows wasted space

Figure 2.7 *Two options for a telephone database*

Relationships

It would be unusual for a relational database to have only the one table. Most have many tables, all linked by relationships.

So, having created tables you then need to link them by relationships. This may be done in some database software separately from raising queries, and/or at the same time.

Find out how to set up a relationship between two tables using your own database software. Discuss this with others in your class. Are you all using the same database software? If not, check how alternative database software works. What is the same? What is different? The net result should be the same!

There are four types of relationship: one-to-one, one-to-many, many-to-one and many-to-many.

One-to-one relationships link one record in a table with exactly one record in another table, and this relationship works both ways. The records in the second table link to only one record in the first table.

OCC

Members' contact details are kept in separate tables (Figure 2.8), one for each method of contact: home telephone, work telephone, mobile telephone, e-mail address. This is an example of a one-to-one relationship. It is useful when not everyone has data for all possible fields – it avoids 'blanks' within a single table.

Note that, in the Mobile table, for example, the membership number is the primary key field. It is also a foreign key, pointing at the Members table.

One-to-many and many-to-one relationships are actually the same, just looking at the link between the tables, from one table or from the other.

- A **one-to-many relationship** links one record in one table to many records in another table.
- A **many-to-one relationship** links many records in one table to exactly one record in the other table.

One example of where this may happen is with coded fields. Coded fields are used to save space within a table, but maybe a fuller form is needed to appear on reports. One table holds the complete list of codes together with their full forms just once – this is sometimes called a **lookup table**. The coded table then holds the short codes many times. Overall this should save space. Figure 2.9 on page 117 gives an example of a lookup table.

Original table design:
5 × 12 = 60 fields

mem no	tel no (home)	tel no (work)	e-mail	mobile
85	01243 614310			
148	01373 932782	01373 565307		
169	01903 983871			
267	01635 199873	01252 990075		07710 351559
288	02392 561103	02492 561101		
318	01252 893752	0170 9733905		
351	01189 968609	01189 857752	fiona.last@hgv.co.uk	07970 675571
399	01903 115515		anniesharp@freeserve.co.uk	
400	01903 615512			
413	01420 463994			
416	01202 376625			
417	01483 477875	01482 259605		

HOME TEL table

mem no	tel no (home)
85	01243 614310
148	01373 932782
169	01903 983871
267	01635 199873
288	02392 561103
318	01252 893752
351	01189 968609
399	01903 115515
400	01903 615512
413	01420 463994
416	01202 376625
417	01483 477875

2 × 12 = 24

WORK table

mem no	tel no (work)
148	01373 565307
267	01252 990075
288	02492 561101
318	0170 9733905
351	01189 857752
417	01482 259605

2 × 6 = 12

MOBILE table

mem no	mobile
267	07710 351559
351	07970 675571

2 × 2 = 4

EMAIL table

mem no	e-mail
351	fiona.last@hgv.co.uk
399	anniesharp@freeserve.co.uk

2 × 2 = 4

Total fields in split tables
= 24 + 12 + 4 + 4
= 44

Figure 2.8 *Contact details tables*

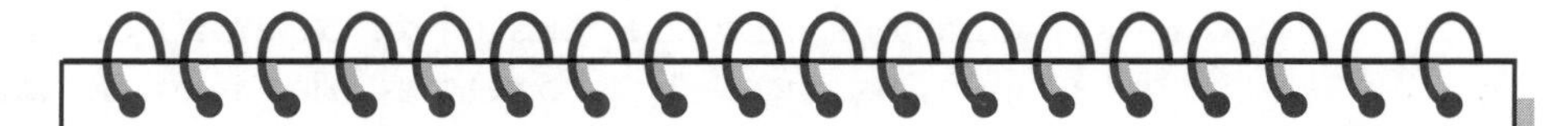

OCC

Within the Members file, one field has the membership type. This is an important field because the amount of subscription depends on the membership type.

Figure 2.9 shows the Members table and its many-to-one relationship with the Subscription table.

On internal reports the Membership code from the Members table is printed. On letters to members the full form (from the Subscription table) can be used.

Many-to-many relationships do exist in real life but cannot be processed on relational databases without a rethink of the relationship. (You may be pleased to know that you do not have to cope with many-to-many relationships at this level.)

OCC

During a season many sailing trips are organised. The yacht *Overload* has 10 berths, so on any one trip up to 10 members can sail. Members are allowed to sail as often as they like (or can afford!) during the sailing season.

This is an example of a many-to-many relationship.

Many members sail on each sailing trip. Members sail on many sailing trips. However, to record this on a database an extra entity – or table – is invented, called Booking.

Each booking represents one member's decision to sail on a particular trip.

One sailing should have 10 bookings. A member may make as many bookings as he or she wishes.

Figure 2.10 shows how these three tables are linked.

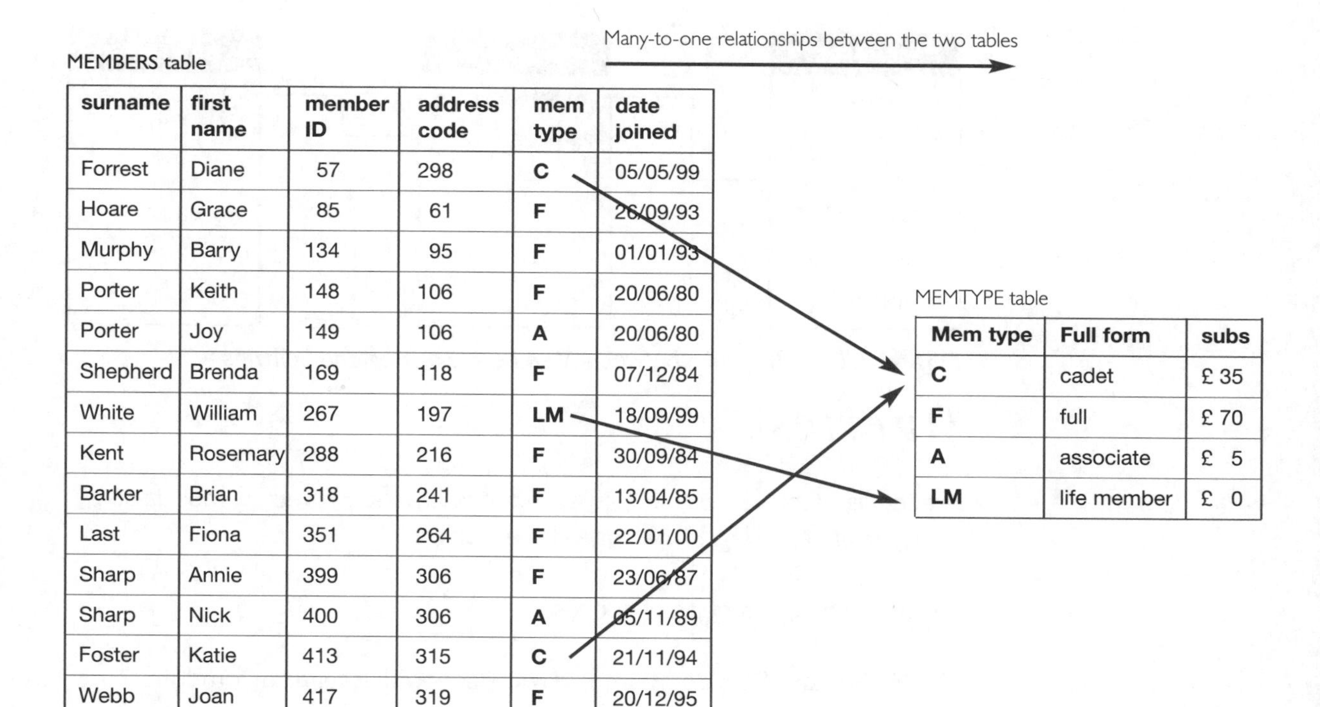

MEMBERS table

surname	first name	member ID	address code	mem type	date joined
Forrest	Diane	57	298	C	05/05/99
Hoare	Grace	85	61	F	26/09/93
Murphy	Barry	134	95	F	01/01/93
Porter	Keith	148	106	F	20/06/80
Porter	Joy	149	106	A	20/06/80
Shepherd	Brenda	169	118	F	07/12/84
White	William	267	197	LM	18/09/99
Kent	Rosemary	288	216	F	30/09/84
Barker	Brian	318	241	F	13/04/85
Last	Fiona	351	264	F	22/01/00
Sharp	Annie	399	306	F	23/06/87
Sharp	Nick	400	306	A	05/11/89
Foster	Katie	413	315	C	21/11/94
Webb	Joan	417	319	F	20/12/95

MEMTYPE table

Mem type	Full form	subs
C	cadet	£ 35
F	full	£ 70
A	associate	£ 5
LM	life member	£ 0

Report produced from MEMBERS table *and* MEMTYPE table

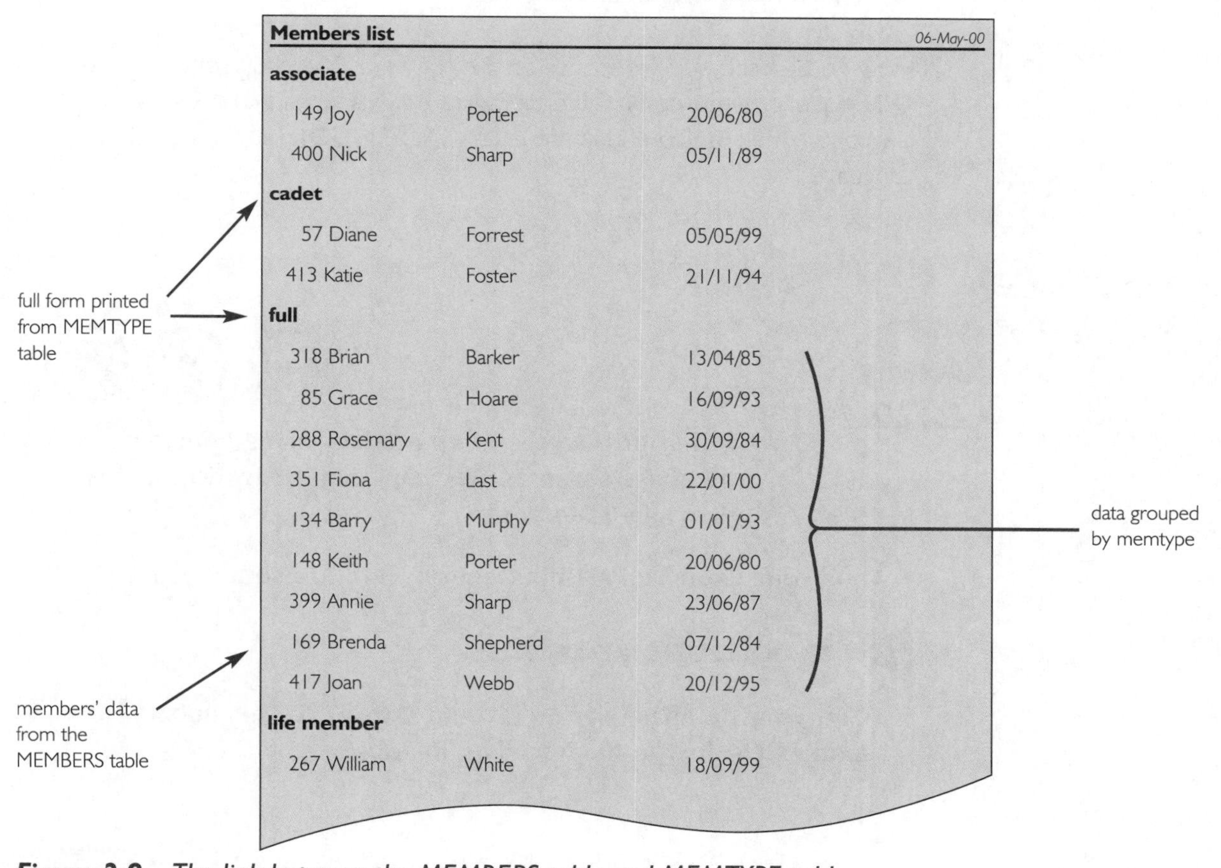
Members list *06-May-00*

associate

149 Joy	Porter	20/06/80
400 Nick	Sharp	05/11/89

cadet

57 Diane	Forrest	05/05/99
413 Katie	Foster	21/11/94

full

318 Brian	Barker	13/04/85
85 Grace	Hoare	16/09/93
288 Rosemary	Kent	30/09/84
351 Fiona	Last	22/01/00
134 Barry	Murphy	01/01/93
148 Keith	Porter	20/06/80
399 Annie	Sharp	23/06/87
169 Brenda	Shepherd	07/12/84
417 Joan	Webb	20/12/95

life member

267 William	White	18/09/99

Figure 2.9 *The link between the MEMBERS table and MEMTYPE table*

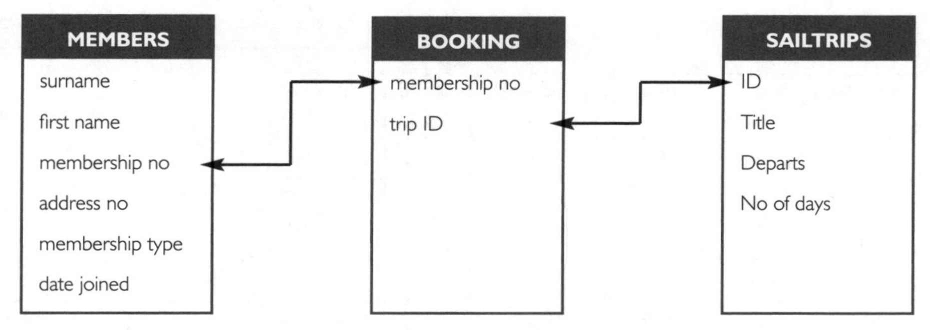

Figure 2.10 *The links between Members, Booking and Sailtrips*

Queries

A query is simply a question that you want to have answered by your database. It may relate to a single table, or to linked tables.

Here are some examples of queries:

- **How many CDs do I have in my collection that feature Tom Jones?**
- **How many Christmas cards do I need to buy?**
- **Which of my friends are on e-mail?**

How you ask the query depends on the software. Microsoft software uses **QBE** (query by example). Other software may use a particular query language – they usually end in the letters QL, e.g. **SQL** (Structured Query Language).

★ **Find out how to set up a query using your own database software. Watch a demonstration if this is available to you.**

For your database, set up a query. Here are some examples.

CD COLLECTION DATABASE

Can your database design give an answer to this query: How many CDs do you have by The Beatles?

continued

continued

CHRISTMAS CARD LIST

You are planning to send your Christmas cards before the second-class postage deadline. Can your database estimate the cost of your postage bill? Could your database take into account cards that you may hand deliver? If not, could you add a field to record this extra information?

FRIENDS' TELEPHONE LIST

In April 2000 some telephone numbers changed. If a similar change happened again, could your database provide a list of all numbers that would have to be changed?

Share this information with others in your class. Check how other database software works. It may be important in your first job that you can work on a different database from the one you usually use. So, take this opportunity to learn as much as you can about the many different databases on the market.

Reports

Reports are used to view your data, either on screen or on paper. A report is based on data within one table. This could be a single table, or a single data table created as a result of a query involving more than one table.

OCC

Many reports are produced from the OCC database:

- **A list of all members' names in alphabetical order – taken from the Members table, sorted into alphabetical order on Surname (see Figure 2.11)**
- **A list of sailing trips in departure date order – taken from the Sailtrip table, sorted on Departure field (see Figure 2.11)**

continued

continued

- A list of who is sailing on a particular trip – taken from a query table which selects all members who have a booking on a particular trip (see Figure 2.12 on page 123)

This last list is based on the Booking table, but pulls in data from the Members table (name of member) and Sailtrip table (description of trip and departure date).

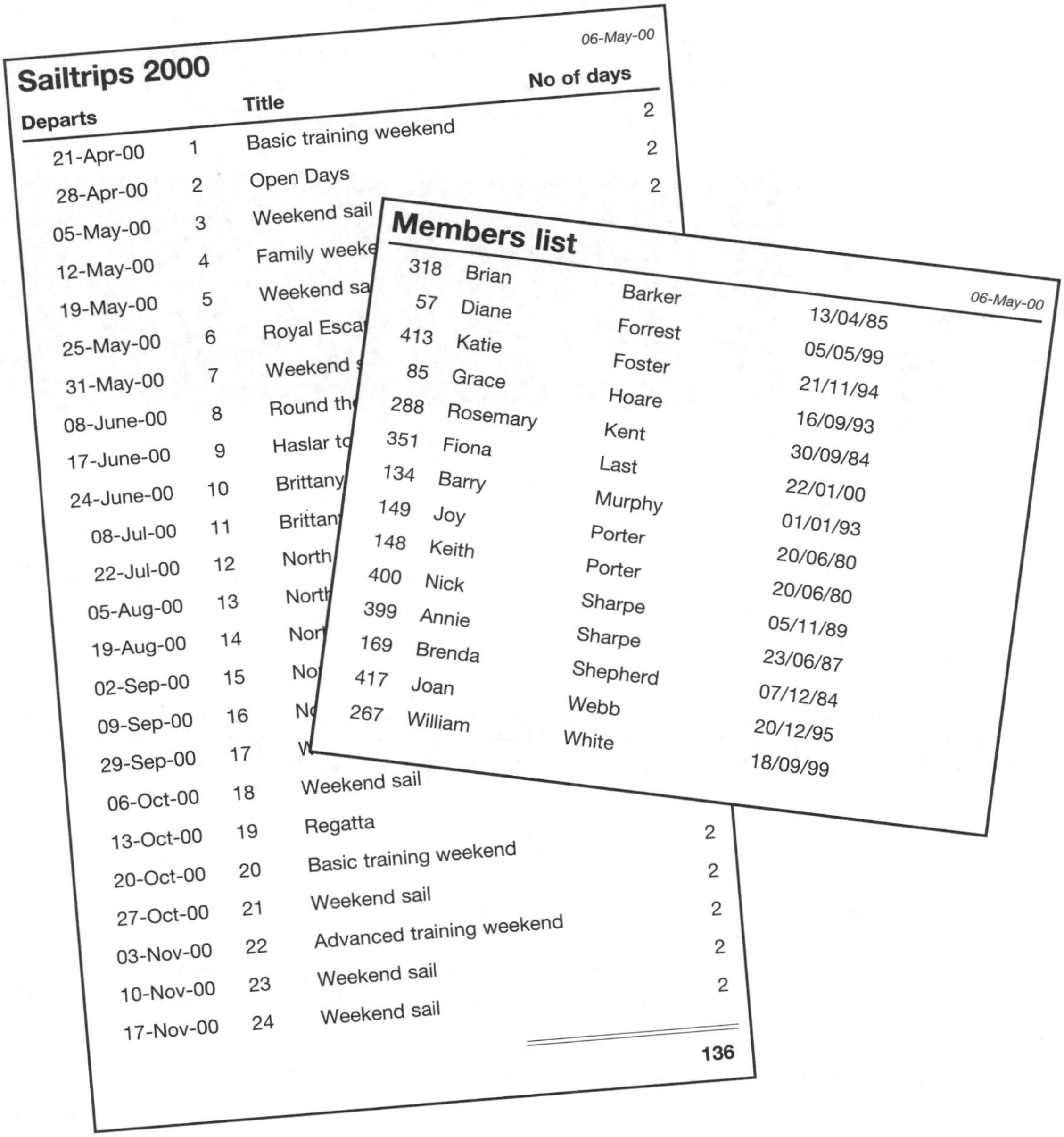

Sailtrips 2000 *06-May-00*

Departs		Title	No of days
21-Apr-00	1	Basic training weekend	2
28-Apr-00	2	Open Days	2
05-May-00	3	Weekend sail	2
12-May-00	4	Family weeke	
19-May-00	5	Weekend sa	
25-May-00	6	Royal Esca	
31-May-00	7	Weekend s	
08-June-00	8	Round th	
17-June-00	9	Haslar to	
24-June-00	10	Brittany	
08-Jul-00	11	Brittan	
22-Jul-00	12	North	
05-Aug-00	13	North	
19-Aug-00	14	Nor	
02-Sep-00	15	No	
09-Sep-00	16	N	
29-Sep-00	17	W	
06-Oct-00	18	Weekend sail	
13-Oct-00	19	Regatta	
20-Oct-00	20	Basic training weekend	2
27-Oct-00	21	Weekend sail	2
03-Nov-00	22	Advanced training weekend	2
10-Nov-00	23	Weekend sail	2
17-Nov-00	24	Weekend sail	2
			136

Members list *06-May-00*

318	Brian	Barker	13/04/85
57	Diane	Forrest	05/05/99
413	Katie	Foster	21/11/94
85	Grace	Hoare	16/09/93
288	Rosemary	Kent	30/09/84
351	Fiona	Last	22/01/00
134	Barry	Murphy	01/01/93
149	Joy	Porter	20/06/80
148	Keith	Porter	20/06/80
400	Nick	Sharpe	05/11/89
399	Annie	Sharpe	23/06/87
169	Brenda	Shepherd	07/12/84
417	Joan	Webb	20/12/95
267	William	White	18/09/99

Figure 2.11 *Reports produced from the OCC database*

Each report has a general structure:

- **Report header – appears on first page only**
- **Page header – appears at the top of every page**
- **Report detail – appears within a page, and is repeated for each record in the table on which the report is based**
- **Page footer – appears at the bottom of every page**
- **Report footer – appears at the very end of the report, only once**

When designing your report you need to decide what information you would like to appear on each page, or only at the start, or only at the end. These fields should then be positioned within the report structure to make the output match what you want. Note that you may choose to have an empty section – you do not need to have something printed at the foot of every page. If this is the case, this section is left blank in your design.

In Microsoft Access everything that appears on a report – whether it is a label/heading, a total or other calculation, or a field from a table – is called a **control**. *In a single report you may have as many as 20 controls and each one needs to be placed within the design of the report, in the appropriate section. This can take a while to do, so the software also provides a wizard to speed up the process.*

Activity 2.23

Find out how reports are produced using your database software. If your software offers wizards, see how they work.

One of the strengths of databases is the facility to sort the data into an order that is helpful to the user. When designing a report, the order in which the report detail section appears is very important and, usually, easily controlled.

Activity 2.24

Find out what sorting options are available within your database software.

Grouping of report details should also be possible, but this changes the structure of a report. The new structure includes a group header and a group footer:

- Report header
- Page header
- **Group header** – appears *ahead* of those report details belonging to this group
- Report detail
- **Group footer** – appears *after* those report details belonging to this group
- Page footer
- Report footer

The group header appears as many times as there are groups, and this depends on what you decide is a group.

OCC

One particularly useful report is a list of who is sailing on *each* trip. This is printed out in two different ways:

- **Grouped by member – shows what each member has booked for this season**
- **Grouped by sail trip – shows which members have booked for each trip**

Figure 2.12 shows these two report designs.

When designing grouped reports it is usual to place data that applies to the whole group within the group header (or group footer). The group footer usually contains any totals.

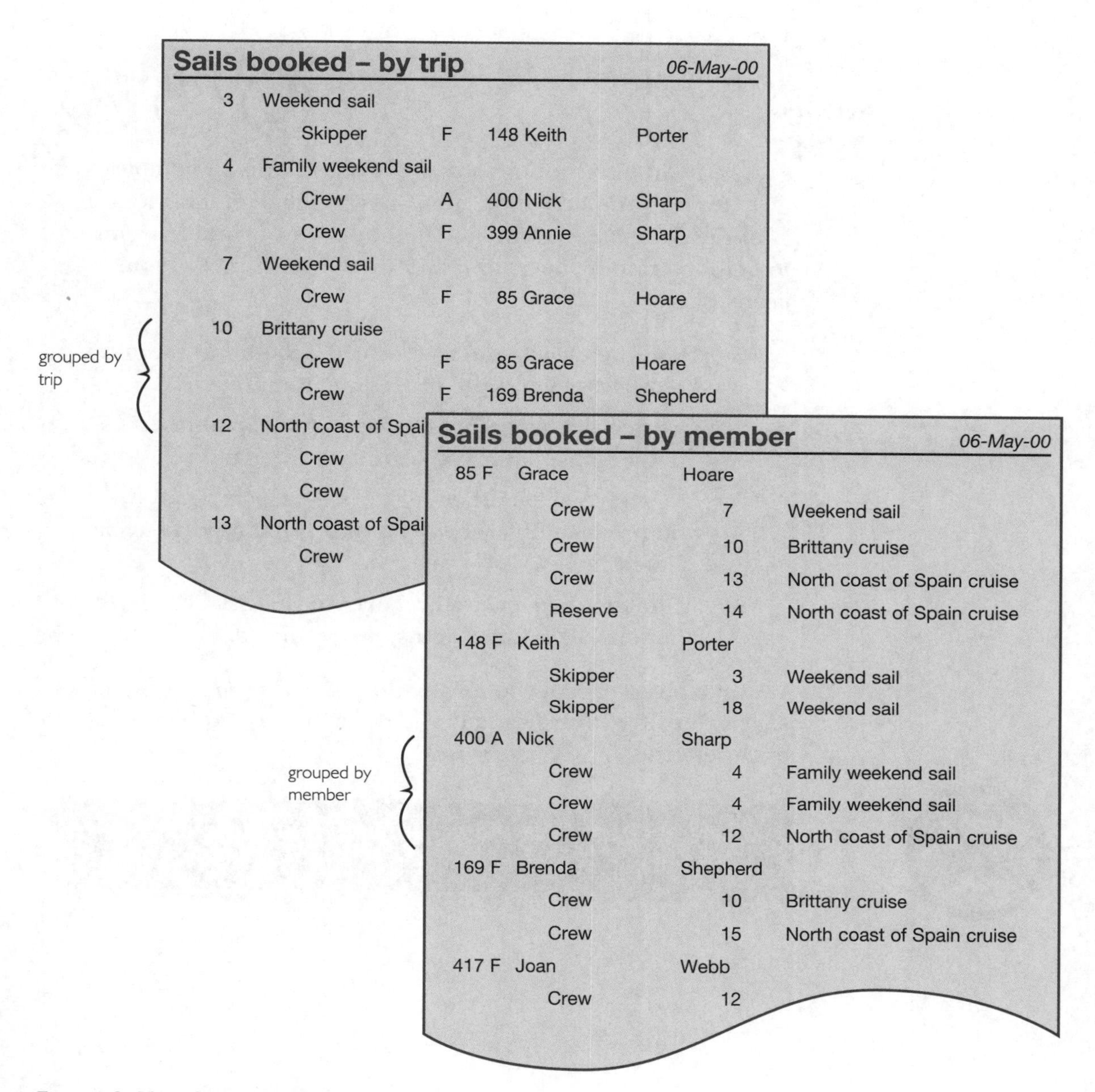

Figure 2.12 *Grouped reports*

Activity 2.25

If you have not already created a relational database for a third-party user, do so now. Include a description of the database system and annotate your printed output to demonstrate its operation and show how it meets your user's needs.

- ★ Describe clearly the user's needs, the information to be processed and the processing required.
- ★ Create table structures using suitable field names, field lengths, data types, primary keys and relations.
- ★ Use database facilities to enter data, sort, search, and produce different types of printed reports using related tables.
- ★ Annotate your printed reports so that it is clear why and how all printed items are produced.

You must also produce an evaluation of your work, so make suggestions for improvement and describe any problems experienced.

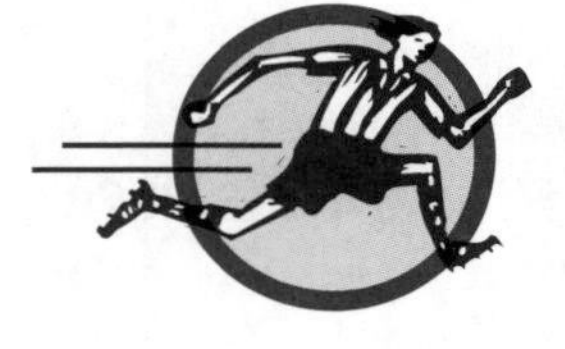

Remember to check the accuracy of your data and keep backup copies of all files.

Spreadsheet methods

Spreadsheets are used to store and analyse numerical information so that you can solve numerical processing problems.

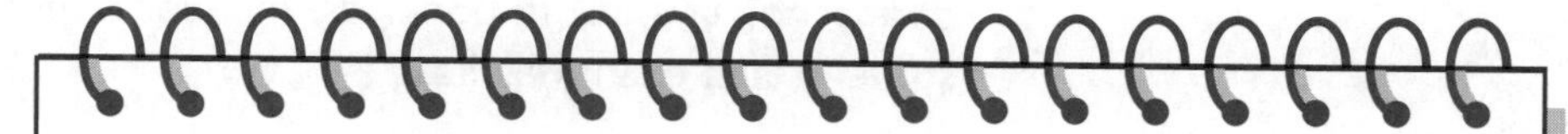

OCC

Linda, the Membership Secretary, keeps track of how many members belong to the OCC. According to their membership type (full, associate, cadet etc.), members pay a different annual subscription. To be able to budget properly, Gerry (the Treasurer) needs to know how much he can expect to receive in subscriptions in total.

Figure 2.13 shows this information.

	A	B	C	D	E
1	Subscription income – forecast				30-Apr-00
2					
3	**Membership**	**Code**	**Number**	**Subs**	**Income from subs**
4	full members	F	126	£70	£8,820
5	life members	LM	3	£0	£0
6	associate members	A	44	£5	£220
7	cadets under 25	C	17	£35	£595
8	outport members	O	14	£35	£490
9	non-sailing members	N	3	£35	£105
10	Total membership		207		£10,230
11	Average per member:				£49

Figure 2.13 *OCC's expected subscription income*

In this section you will explore spreadsheet methods used to solve numerical processing problems:

- **Presentation techniques**, e.g. using borders and shading
- Using **formulae** and **functions**, and calculating results (such as totals)
- Creating **charts** and **graphs** from numeric data, and identifying patterns in graphs or charts

- Changing values in a cell to predict results – '**what if?**' queries using trial and improvement techniques

The components of a numerical processing problem include items, dates, totals and calculations.

- **Items** are the things about which calculations are necessary, e.g. goods, holidays, room bookings, number of people, quantity, costs, students and exam results
- **Dates** are important in most numerical processing problems. It is necessary to keep a record of when things are sold, when a holiday is booked and when the holiday is to start, when exams take place and when results will be available.
- **Totals** are often needed: the total sales for a week, the total number of people booked for a holiday flight, the total number of items ordered, the total number of students entered for an examination, and so on
- **Calculations** are often needed. In invoicing, VAT (value added tax) at 17½% has to be calculated. In payroll, PAYE (pay as you earn) tax and National Insurance (NI) contributions have to be calculated. In sales, a discount may be allowed and a salesperson may earn a commission based on the number of sales made.

DOS-based system
will use the keyboard only, using arrow keys to move about the spreadsheet and to highlight particular areas.

Windows-based system
will use a mouse.

Numerical processing problems are often solved using spreadsheet software. These components of the problem have to be placed within the spreadsheet structure to model the problem and find a solution.

Exactly how you use the spreadsheet software depends on whether you are using a **DOS-based system** or a **Windows-based system**.

Activity 2.26

★ Find out how to load your spreadsheet software.
★ Find out how to retrieve a spreadsheet file, and how to print it out.
★ Write notes on how to do this.

Layout of a spreadsheet

The spreadsheet is laid out in **rows** and **columns** as shown in Figure 2.14. Note that the columns are labelled A, B, C, ... and that the rows are numbered 1, 2, 3, ...

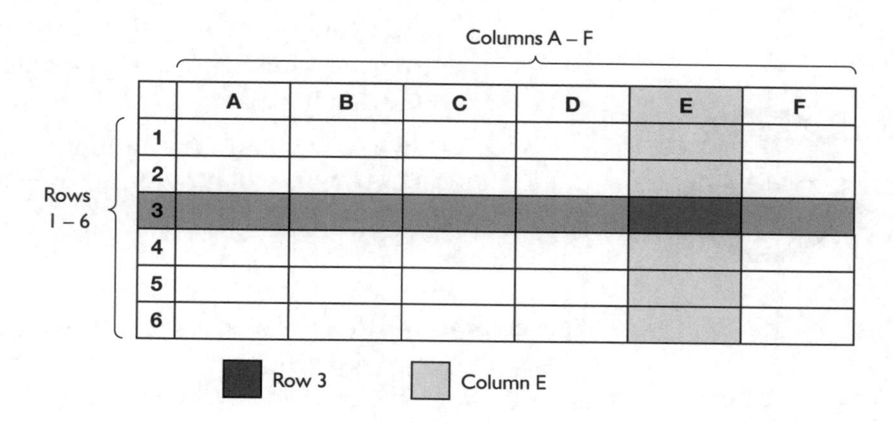

Figure 2.14 *Spreadsheet layout*

Cells are labelled by their column and row numbers. In Figure 2.14 column E is shaded, and so is row 3. The cell at the intersection of row 3 and column E is called E3 – the letter first and then the number. E3 is an example of a **cell reference**.

Exercise 2.16

Look at Figure 2.13 on page 125 and identify what is displayed in these cells: A1, B5, C10, D9, E1, E9, E10 and E11.

When designing a spreadsheet you decide how many rows and columns you will need. To begin with, all columns will have the same width – called the **default width** – which will be set by your spreadsheet software.

Activity 2.27

- Find out what the default width of columns is on your spreadsheet software.
- What happens if you enter data that is wider than the column width?
- Try keying in the alphabet into cell A1. How is this displayed? Key 'HELLO' into cell A2. What effect does this have?
- Now try keying in the number 12345678901234567890 into cell B1. What effect does this have?

If the **column width** is not wide enough to display your data, you will have to increase the width. You may also want to reduce the width of some columns, either to save paper or to improve the overall look of the spreadsheet.

Activity 2.28

- Find out how to change the width of columns using your spreadsheet software.
- Can you also control the row height?
- Write notes that would help someone who has never used your spreadsheet software before.

Sometimes, what you see on the screen does not match what is printed out. With some spreadsheet software you think all your data can be seen, i.e. your column width is wide enough on the screen, but when you take a printout some data is lost or **truncated**. This is a design fault within the software, but it is up to you, the user, to check this carefully.

Activity 2.29

Experiment with different column widths – say 6, 7, 8, 9 and 10 characters – and fill these columns with data of varying lengths. See if the data displayed is always printed in full.

Each cell of a spreadsheet can hold only one of four different types of data:

- **Numeric** – for numbers, including **currency** and **dates**
- **Character** – for messages, text, labels and so on
- **Formula** – calculations based on other data within the spreadsheet
- **Blank** – contains nothing!

OCC

In Figure 2.13 on page 125 there are examples of all four:

- **Numeric data is entered into cells C4–C9 and D4–D9.**
- **Text is entered into cells in row 3 and column A.**
- **Formulae are entered in column E and rows 10 and 11.**
- **Row 2 is blank. Cells B1, C1 and D1 are also blank.**

The first character you key helps the software to 'know' what type of data you are entering and to decide how to display it.

- If you start with a digit, the software assumes you are entering a number
- If you start with a letter of the alphabet, the software assumes you are entering some text

Activity 2.30

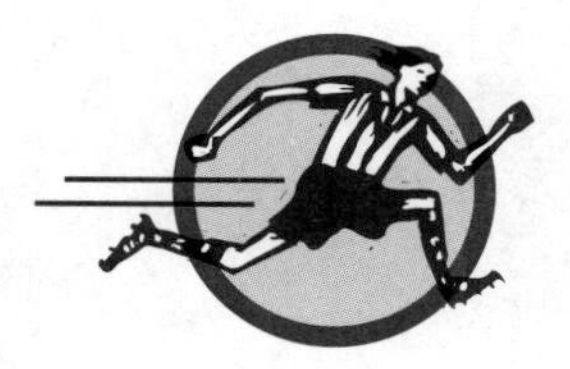

Starting with a blank spreadsheet, key your name in cell A1 and press return. How does the software display this text? In cell B1, key a number (e.g. your age) and press enter. How does the software display this number?

All text cells left aligned and all numeric cells right aligned

	A	B	C	D	E	F
1		Jan	Feb	Mar	April	TOTAL
2	Black	42	56	71	30	199
3	Blue	45	60	80	28	213
4	Green	12	15	20	9	56
5	Yellow	24	32	38	21	115
6		123	163	209	88	583

Figure 2.15 *Different alignments within a spreadsheet*

Figure 2.15 shows that the software automatically displays numbers right-aligned and text left-aligned. If the automatic (default) display does not suit you, you can control how the data in a spreadsheet is displayed; see page 133.

Activity 2.31

Enter this in a blank cell: =4+5 and then press return. What happens?

The third option for the contents of a cell – a formula – is what makes spreadsheet software so useful.

> ***Did You Know?***
>
> **Formulae** is the plural of formula. Sometimes 'formulas' is used instead.

- Formulae can be used to calculate sums, adding numbers in one row or column.
- Formulae can be used for more complicated calculations, using the usual maths symbols.
- The value displayed in each cell is automatically updated. So, if you change any of the numbers that form part of a calculation, the spreadsheet recalculates all formulae for you.

Explore how your spreadsheet software reacts to what you enter in a cell.

- ★ What happens if you enter something starting with a plus (+) sign or an equals (=) sign?
- ★ What happens if you enter something starting with a quote mark (')?
- ★ What happens if your data includes a slash mark (/) or a dash (-)?
- ★ What happens if you type a zero, a space and then some digits, including one slash mark, e.g. '0 1/5'?

Check that the entries in Table 2.4 'work' the same on your spreadsheet software. Then copy and complete Table 2.4 to show how your spreadsheet software reacts to what you enter.

What was entered	***How it was displayed***	***How the software interprets the data***
+27/3	9 (right aligned)	Worked out 27 divided by 3; treated it as a formula
27/3	27-Mar	Thought it was a date
27-3		
+27-3		
=27/3		
.75		
0 3/4		
'27/3		

Table 2.4 *Data entry to a spreadsheet*

Exercise 2.17

Some cells in a spreadsheet are left blank. Why is this? What is the difference between an empty (blank) cell and one that contains a space?

It is important to include **titles** on your spreadsheet. Otherwise, it may not be clear what the spreadsheet does, or when it was produced. There are several types of title within a spreadsheet.

- The **main title** appears at the very top and should include a description of the spreadsheet
- At the top of each column you should have a **column title**, to label the data in that column
- At the start of every row you should have a **row title**, to label the data in that row

You may also include a message on the final row of the spreadsheet, e.g. explaining any codes that you have used. Some rows may be left blank for spacing purposes: these do not need row titles. Some rows may have lines of dashes, to create the effect of ruling off before a total: these do not need titles either. Any row (or column) that has a **total** calculated from other rows (or columns) should be carefully labelled (Figure 2.16).

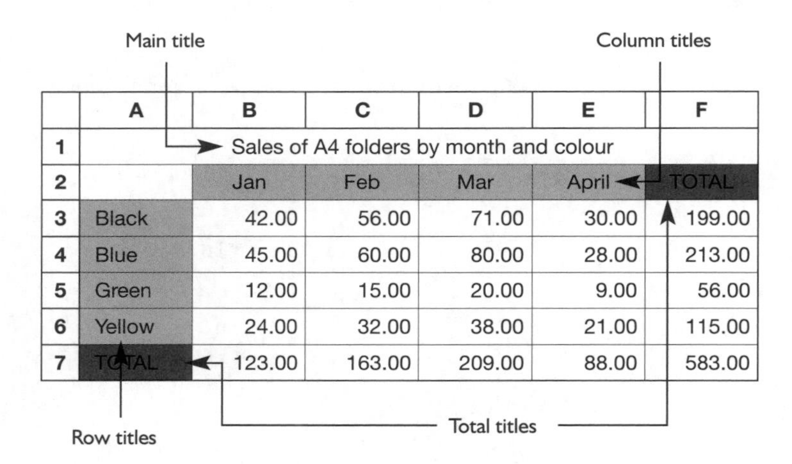

	A	B	C	D	E	F
1		Sales of A4 folders by month and colour				
2		Jan	Feb	Mar	April	TOTAL
3	Black	42.00	56.00	71.00	30.00	199.00
4	Blue	45.00	60.00	80.00	28.00	213.00
5	Green	12.00	15.00	20.00	9.00	56.00
6	Yellow	24.00	32.00	38.00	21.00	115.00
7	TOTAL	123.00	163.00	209.00	88.00	583.00

Figure 2.16 *Titles on a spreadsheet*

Exercise 2.18

Looking at Figure 2.13 on page 125, identify which cells contain the main title, the row titles and the column titles.

If the data in each cell was presented just as you keyed it in, the end result could be quite unattractive and, possibly, difficult to read. **Cell formats** control the presentation of information in a cell. Cell formatting is used to improve the overall look of the spreadsheet, and your aim should be to make it easier for a reader to understand. Here are some examples of what can be done to improve the presentation of data within a spreadsheet.

- Controlling the position of text or labels, e.g. right-align text to match numeric data in a column, centre headings
- Displaying numbers in currency format, e.g. with a pound sign preceding them
- Deciding on the numbers of decimal places to be shown, e.g. most currency is shown with two decimal places
- Choosing between different date formats, e.g. 'dd-mm-yy' (12-06-99) or 'dd mmm yyyy' (12 Jun 1999) – or showing time in the 24-hour format

OCC

In Figure 2.13 on page 125 the money amounts are shown with a £ sign. The subscriptions are in whole pounds, so no decimal places are used. The average per member is not actually £49 – this result has been rounded to the nearest pound, by formatting the cell as 'currency with no decimal places'.

It is especially important that information 'lines up' within the columns of a spreadsheet. This is called **justification** or **alignment**.

- For text data left-alignment is normal for row titles and for most data items. You might choose to centre the text (and its column heading) if you prefer.
- For numeric data, which involves only whole numbers (integers), it is usual to right-align the data. Then the units are all in a line, and the tens are all in a line and so on. If the numbers have a decimal point (e.g. with a column of currency data) it would be normal to align on the decimal point.

Figure 2.17 shows three examples of layout choices: all data cells centred, numeric data aligned on a decimal tab, and numeric data with two decimal places.

All data cells centred

	A	B	C	D	E	F
1	Sales of A4 folders by month and colour					
2		Jan	Feb	Mar	April	TOTAL
3	Black	42	56	71	30	199
4	Blue	45	60	80	28	213
5	Green	12	15	20	9	56
6	Yellow	24	32	38	21	115
7	TOTAL	123	163	209	88	583

Numeric data right aligned on a decimal tab

	A	B	C	D	E	F
1	Sales of A4 folders by month and colour					
2		Jan	Feb	Mar	April	TOTAL
3	Black	42	56	71	30	199
4	Blue	45	60	80	28	213
5	Green	12	15	20	9	56
6	Yellow	24	32	38	21	115
7	TOTAL	123	163	209	88	583

Showing decimal places

	A	B	C	D	E	F
1	Sales of A4 folders by month and colour					
2		Jan	Feb	Mar	April	TOTAL
3	Black	42.00	56.00	71.00	30.00	199.00
4	Blue	45.00	60.00	80.00	28.00	213.00
5	Green	12.00	15.00	20.00	9.00	56.00
6	Yellow	24.00	32.00	38.00	21.00	115.00
7	TOTAL	123.00	163.00	209.00	88.00	583.00

Figure 2.17 *Examples of data alignment within a spreadsheet*

OCC

In Figure 2.13 on page 125 the entries in the left-hand column are left-aligned. The column headings (Number, Subs and Income from subs) are right-aligned. The numeric data is automatically right-aligned.

Activity 2.33

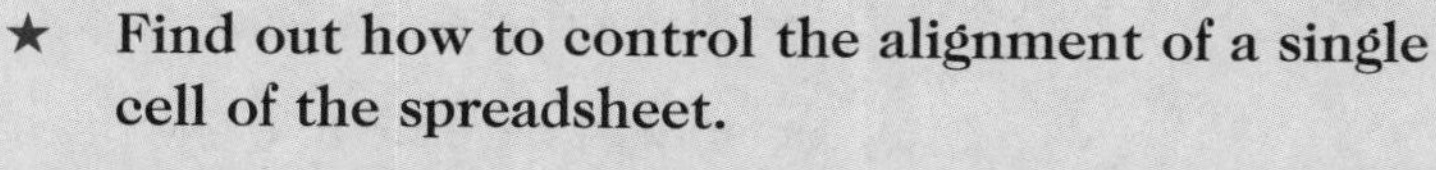

★ Find out how to control the alignment of a single cell of the spreadsheet.

★ Find out how to control the alignment of a block of cells.

★ Write notes on how to do this.

You might also decide to incorporate colour and/or shading into your spreadsheet. Figure 2.16 on page 132 includes shading for the row and column titles with darker shading for the TOTAL titles.

Activity 2.34

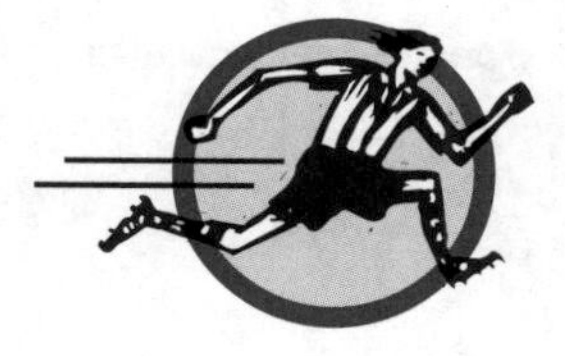

★ Find out what display formats are offered with your spreadsheet software.

★ Enter some data into a spreadsheet and choose a variety of display options to show what you can do.

★ Print out your spreadsheet, and make notes on how you achieved the effects shown.

When setting up a spreadsheet to hold information, it helps to identify the different components of a numerical processing problem and to try to match their data types to those available on a spreadsheet.

- The **item**, i.e. the thing you are interested in, will have a name or a description which can be stored as a string of characters. Examples could be holiday destinations, such as SPAIN, PORTUGAL or FRANCE. It could be examinations, such as GNVQ ICT, GNVQ LEISURE AND TOURISM and GNVQ SCIENCE. These items will usually be placed as **row titles** or **column titles** in a text field.
- **Numeric data** relating to the items will be stored as a numeric data type. This will be all the numbers involved in the problem, e.g. the number of students entered for GNVQ ICT, the number entered for GNVQ LEISURE AND TOURISM, and so on. It is important that this data is entered with 100% accuracy. All calculations will be based on this data and so, if anything is incorrect, the results will be incorrect too.
- **Dates** may be used to label rows or columns, or be part of the data used in a calculation. This may happen, for example, if the fine

on a library book depends on the numbers of days it is overdue. Dates that are simply row or column labels can be entered as text. Dates used for calculations are actually stored as numbers within the spreadsheet.

- **Formulae** are used to make the calculations required to solve a problem. This could be a simple **total**, e.g. the cost of a list of items (calculated using a column sum), or a more complicated **calculation**, e.g. the cost of a quantity of goods (calculated as quantity times price), or the VAT due on an item (calculated as 0.175 times the price).

Calculations are the most important part of a spreadsheet, so we will now look at them in some detail.

Calculations

Calculations can be done automatically by the spreadsheet software, so writing the formulae to perform the calculations is an important part of solving the numerical processing problem. All calculations that can be done on a calculator can also be done using spreadsheet software. This includes the usual four operations:

- Addition
- Subtraction
- Multiplication
- Division

Activity 2.35

- ★ Find out how to add two data items in a spreadsheet.
- ★ Find out how to subtract one data item from another.
- ★ What symbols do you use for multiplication and division?
- ★ How do you make sure the result appears in a particular cell?

Look in the online help for 'addition'.

To help you to write formulae, the spreadsheet software offers lots of built-in **functions**.

Find out what functions are available with your spreadsheet software.

SUM
this function displays the result of adding the contents of cells. Two dots are used to identify a **range of cells**. B1..B3 means B1, B2 and B3.

One special function allows you to **sum** a row or column of numeric data items. You must tell the software where to start adding, where to stop, and where to put the result. Exactly how this is done will depend on your software.

Activity
2.37

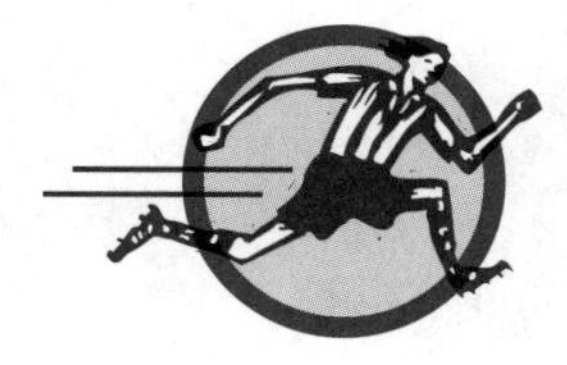

- ★ **Copy the data shown in Figure 2.18 on page 138.**
- ★ **In cell B4 enter this formula: +SUM(B1..B3)**
- ★ **What happens?**
- ★ **In cell B4 enter this formula instead: +SUM(B1,B3)**
- ★ **What happens?**

Activity
2.38

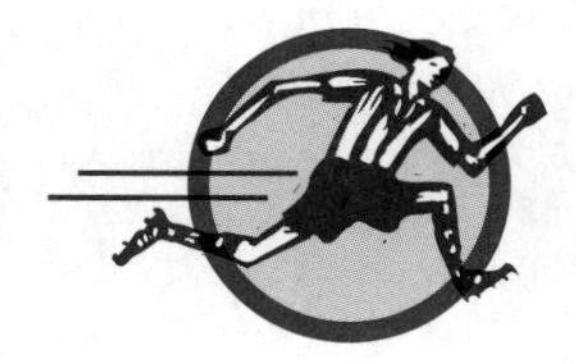

- ★ **Find out how to add up all the numeric data items in a single row of a spreadsheet.**
- ★ **Write notes to explain this process to someone who does not know how to use your spreadsheet software.**
- ★ **What happens if you try to add up data that is not numeric?**

	A	B	
1	First	4	
2	Second	9	
3	Third	13	
4			

Figure 2.18 *Using a formula to add the contents of cells*

Activity 2.39

Access some spreadsheets and look at the formulae they use. Look in particular at the IF and AVERAGE functions. Work out which cells are linked to other cells by formulae.

Your software may have an AUDIT option which allows you to trace the links between cells. This is particularly useful if a cell displays an error value and you cannot work out what is causing the problem.

IF
this function allows you to control what appears in a particular cell, depending on a condition.

AVERAGE
this function adds the contents of a range of cells and then divides by the number of cells, producing the average for those cells.

When you write a formula you will refer to other cells using the **cell reference**. If you want to copy a formula, you have two options:

- **Relative cell referencing** results in the copy of the formula being correct 'relative' to its new position
- **Absolute cell referencing** results in an exact copy of the formula, with no change being made to take into account its new position

Did You Know?

Placing a dollar ($) symbol before the column letter and/or row number makes a cell reference **absolute**.

In Figure 2.16 on page 132 the formula in cell B7 is +SUM(B3..B6). It adds up the other numbers in column B. This formula was ***replicated*** *across row 7. Table 2.5 shows the contents of the other cells in row 7. Notice that, when copying across a row, the column numbers are changed automatically.*

Cell reference	*Contents*	*Displayed value*
A7	TOTAL	TOTAL
B7	+SUM(B3..B6)	123.00
C7	+SUM(C3..C6)	163.00
D7	+SUM(D3..D6)	209.00
E7	+SUM(E3..E6)	88.00
F7	+SUM(F3..F6)	583.00

Table 2.5 *Formulae in row 7 of the spreadsheet shown in Figure 2.16*

Replication copying the contents of one cell to a range of other cells.

Use **replication** to copy formulae wherever possible. If you only enter the formula once, you have only one chance of making a mistake. If you enter it many times you are quite likely to introduce an error.

If you do not want the formula to be replicated 'relatively', you need to insert \$ symbols before the column letter and/or row number, to fix that cell 'absolutely'. This is useful if the spreadsheet includes a **constant value**, e.g. the VAT rate.

Activity 2.40

- ★ Copy the spreadsheet shown in Figure 2.19, which calculates net pay after deduction of tax at 23%.
- ★ Enter the formula in cell B3 and copy this cell to cells B4 and B5.
- ★ Check that the values are correct.
- ★ As shown in the figure, experiment with removing just one of the \$ symbols, e.g. the ones before the column letter. Do you still get correct values?
- ★ What if you remove the other \$ symbols, i.e. the ones before the row numbers?

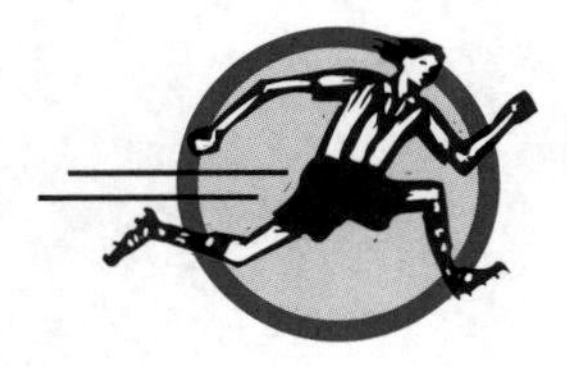

	A	B	C
1	Tax rate	23%	
2	Gross pay	Tax	Net pay
3	£100.00	£23.00	£77.00
4	£150.00	£34.00	£115.50
5	£200.00	£46.00	£154.00
6			
7	Gross pay	Tax	Net pay
8	£100.00	£23.00	£77.00
9	£150.00	#VALUE!	#VALUE!
10	£200.00	£4,600.00	−£4,400.00
11			
12	Gross pay	Tax	Net pay
13	£100.00	£23.00	£77.00
14	£150.00	£34.50	£115.50
15	£200.00	£46.00	£154.00

Formulae used

B3	+A3*B1	C3	+A3−B3
B4	+A4*B1	C4	+A4−B4
B5	+A5*B1	C5	+A5−B5
B8	+A8*$B1	C8	+A8−B8
B9	+A9*$B2	C9	+A9−B9
B10	+A10*$B3	C10	+A10−B10
B13	+A13*B$1	C13	+A13−B13
B14	+A14*B$1	C14	+A14−B14
B15	+A15*B$1	C15	+A15−B15

Using both $ signs works but is not actually necessary

The formula is replicated down column B so $B1 becomes $B2. B2 holds text so the calculation is impossible.

The cell B3 holds a number (23.00) so the calculation is possible, but incorrect.

A single dollar sign before the new number works because it is the new number that would change in this replication.

Figure 2.19 Absolute addressing

OCC

The Sailing Secretary wants to design a spreadsheet to keep track of the number of bookings made to date, and to calculate the expected income from charter fees.

In total there are 24 sailing trips planned for the 2000 season, as shown in Figure 2.20. Note that each trip lasts for 2, 3, 4, 7, 14 or 15 days. The charter fee is £26 per day. A maximum of 10 people can sail together, but if there are fewer than five the trip may have to be cancelled.

Trip	Trip details	Departs	Days	Booked	Berth days	£ Due	Cancel?
1	Basic training weekend	21–Apr–00	2	8	16	£416	
2	Open Days	28–Apr–00	2	8	16	£416	
3	Weekend Sail	05–May–00	2	5	10	£260	
4	Family weekend sail	12–May–00	2	10	20	£520	
5	Weekend sail	19–May–00	2	10	20	£520	
6	Royal Escape Race	25–May–00	4	10	40	£1,040	
7	Weekend sail	31–May–00	4	9	36	£936	
8	Round the Island Race	08–Jun–00	3	7	21	£546	
9	Haslar to Brittany passage	17–Jun–00	7	5	35	£910	
10	Brittany cruise	24–Jun–00	14	9	126	£3,276	
11	Brittany & Golfe de Gascogne cruise	08–Jul–00	14	7	98	£2,548	
12	North coast of Spain cruise	22–Jul–00	14	10	140	£3,640	
13	North coast of Spain cruise	05–Aug–00	14	10	140	£3,640	
14	North coast of Spain cruise	19–Aug–00	14	7	98	£2,548	
15	North coast of Spain cruise	02–Sep–00	7	10	70	£1,820	
16	Northern Spain to Haslar passage	09–Sep–00	15	6	90	£2,340	
17	Weekend sail	29–Sep–00	2	7	14	£364	
18	Weekend sail	06–Oct–00	2	2	4	£104	cancel?
19	Regatta	13–Oct–00	2	7	14	£364	
20	Basic training weekend	20–Oct–00	2	1	2	£52	cancel?
21	Weekend sail	27–Oct–00	2	3	6	£156	cancel?
22	Advanced training weekend	03–Nov–00	2	5	10	£260	
23	Weekend sail	10–Nov–00	2	3	6	£156	cancel?
24	Weekend sail	17–Nov–00	2	1	2	£52	cancel?
	Number of sailing days		136			£26,884	
	Number of berth days:				1034		
	Maximum income from sailing berths:					£35,360	

Figure 2.20 *OCC's sailing programme and bookings*

Activity 2.41

- ★ Create a spreadsheet to solve the OCC's numerical processing problem.
- ★ Adjust column widths to suit the data, and choose appropriate display options. Include a main title, column headings and row headings.
- ★ Calculate the total expected charter based on the number of bookings to date, and the maximum charter income if all 10 berths are taken on every trip.
- ★ Use the IF function to display a warning message for trips that may have to be cancelled.
- ★ Use the AVERAGE function to calculate the average number of bookings per trip.
- ★ Print out your spreadsheet, both before and after editing it.
- ★ Write notes on how you solved this numerical processing problem, and the calculations used in the spreadsheet.

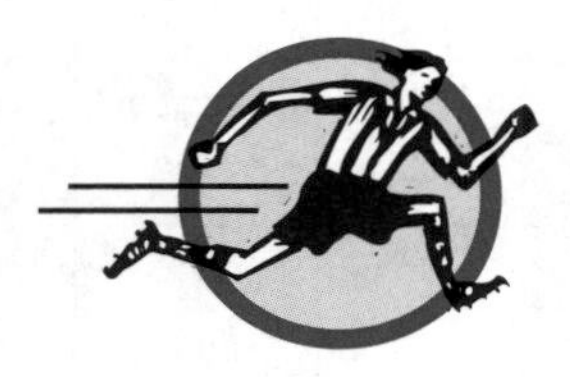

You might decide to use a spreadsheet to store database information. This works well until you decide to sort the data. Because the rows and columns of a spreadsheet do not necessarily mean records and fields as in a database, some software allows you to sort the items in one column (say), leaving all the other data items where they are. If you do this the data belonging to one record will appear in the row of another record!

Activity 2.42

Create a spreadsheet to hold data for five records of information. Investigate how sorting is done. See if you can sort one column at a time.

Spreadsheet facilities

Once a spreadsheet has been set up, there are many facilities on offer:

- You can **interrogate** the spreadsheet to find information, print selected parts of the spreadsheet or the whole worksheet.
- You can automatically create **charts** and **graphs** to present the data in a more user-friendly way.
- You can use **trial-and-improvement** techniques to carry out a **'what if?'** query and hence to solve a particular prediction problem.

Interrogating a spreadsheet

In Activity 2.10, you explored the **find function** on word-processing software. The Find function works differently on a spreadsheet: you can search by rows or columns, and look in cells, notes or within formulae.

Activity 2.43

- ★ **Explore the Find function on your spreadsheet software. Write notes on how it is different from the Find function on your word-processing software.**
- ★ **Explore the Filter function on your spreadsheet software.**

A **printout** of a spreadsheet usually shows the values for each cell, rather than the formulae that were used to calculate those values.

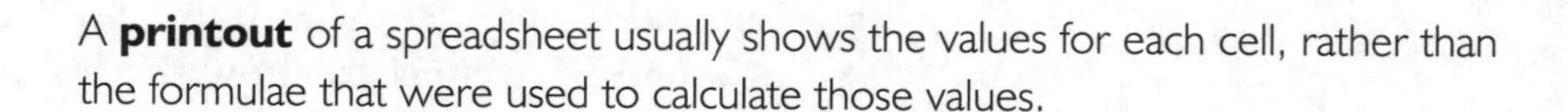

Activity 2.44

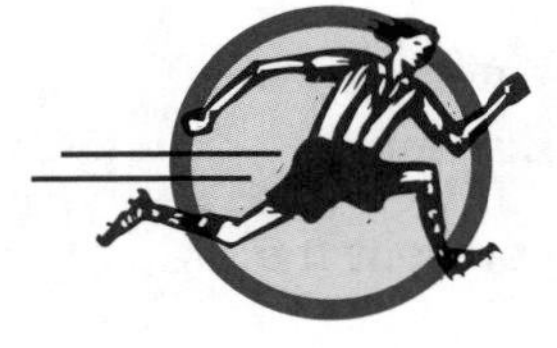

★ Find out how to control how much of a spreadsheet is printed, and how to control pagination.

★ Find out if your spreadsheet software allows you to print out the formulae used in each cell.

Charts and graphs

When you present numerical information in the form of line graphs or charts they should be made easy to understand. Spreadsheet software provides many facilities to title and label graphical information appropriately and clearly:

- Main titles on charts
- Axis titles, and axis scale labels
- Legend titles
- Data or series labels
- Colours and patterns

Activity 2.45

Using your online help facility, watch a demonstration of how to create a barchart. Make notes if you think you will not be able to remember what to do.

★ Using the spreadsheet you created in Activity 2.41, produce a barchart to show the number of berths booked on each trip to date.

★ Why would it *not* be appropriate to produce a barchart for the expected charter income for each trip? If you are not sure, produce this chart and see how informative it is.

★ What other charts might be useful for this particular spreadsheet?

Make sure you include a main title and titles for both axes.

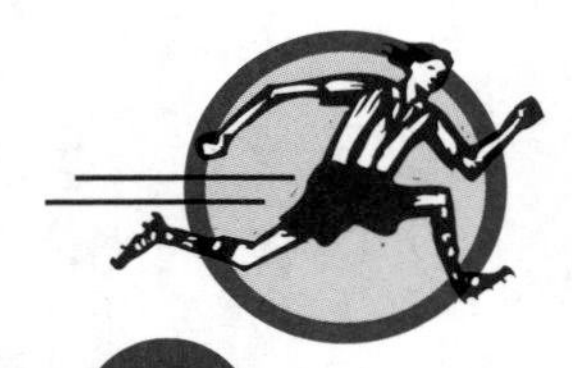

OCC

Figure 2.21 shows the breakdown of members by type as a pie chart.

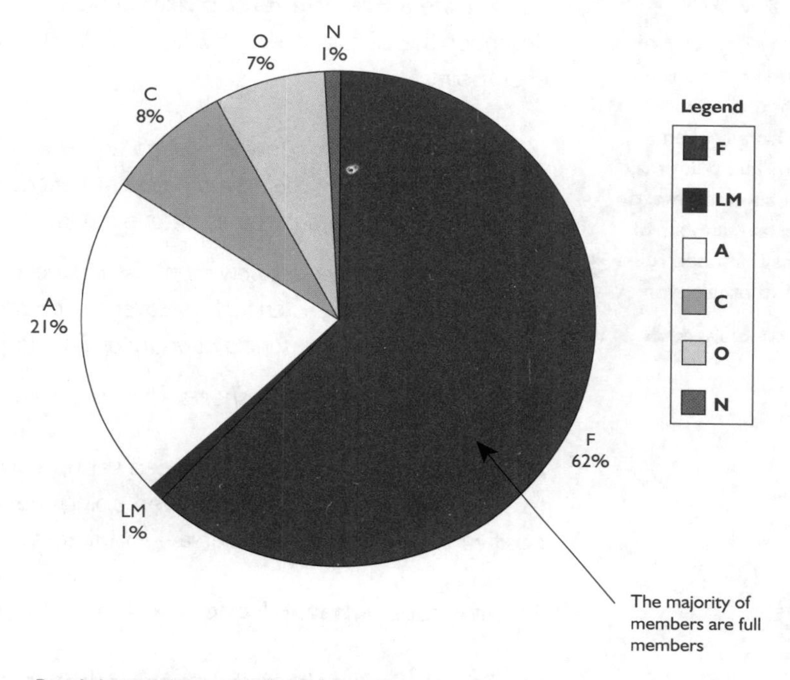

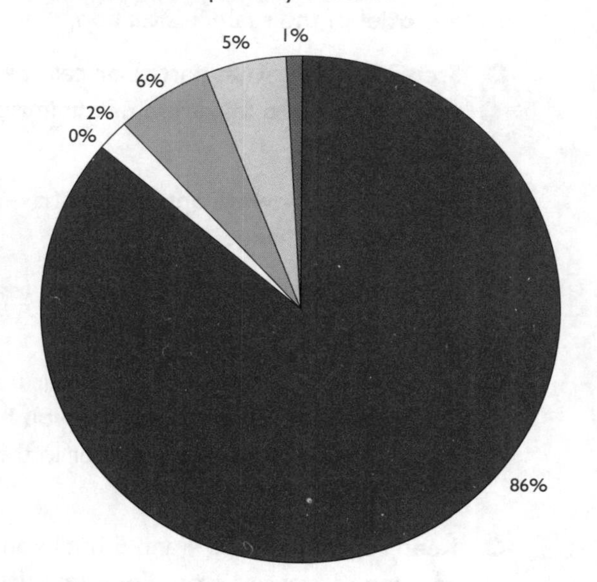

Figure 2.21 *OCC membership by type: pie chart*

Exploring trends and predicting results

One purpose of a spreadsheet is to explore trends and to predict results. You can calculate break-even points and carry out 'what if?' queries using spreadsheet software.

Break-even point is where there is no profit and no loss – you have broken even. The point may be a point in time, or a certain number of items that need to be sold to break even.

To calculate a **break-even point** you need to set up a spreadsheet that describes the calculation, with one row (or column) for each possible break-even point.

If you want to work out when a loan will be repaid (i.e. when you owe nothing), each row could be a payment period. So if you pay back the loan monthly each row can represent one month.

If you want to work out how many T-shirts need to be sold before the profit made on each one is enough to cover the overheads (rent, lighting etc.) then each row could represent a quantity of T-shirts.

Figure 2.22 shows spreadsheets which show how quickly a loan can be repaid.

As soon as the spreadsheet has been set up you need only look in one column to see at what point (the break-even point) the value has changed from positive to negative or vice versa – or hit zero.

To carry out a **'what if?' query**, you must loop through a number of steps:

- Step 1: Set up the data in a spreadsheet. Your spreadsheet is then a **model** of the real-life situation.
- Step 2: Identify what particular cell (or cells) hold the data that you are trying to maximise or minimise, or that meet some criteria
- Step 3: Identify what options you have, i.e. what cells hold data that you can change
- Step 4: Try a new value. It does not really matter what value you try!
- Step 5: See what happens. Did your new value make the situation better? Or worse? Are you heading in the right direction even? Do you need to go further in the same direction, or did you overstep?
- Keep repeating steps 4 and 5 until you are close enough to your solution to want to stop. For some problems you have to find the exact solution; for others you just need to be 'close'.

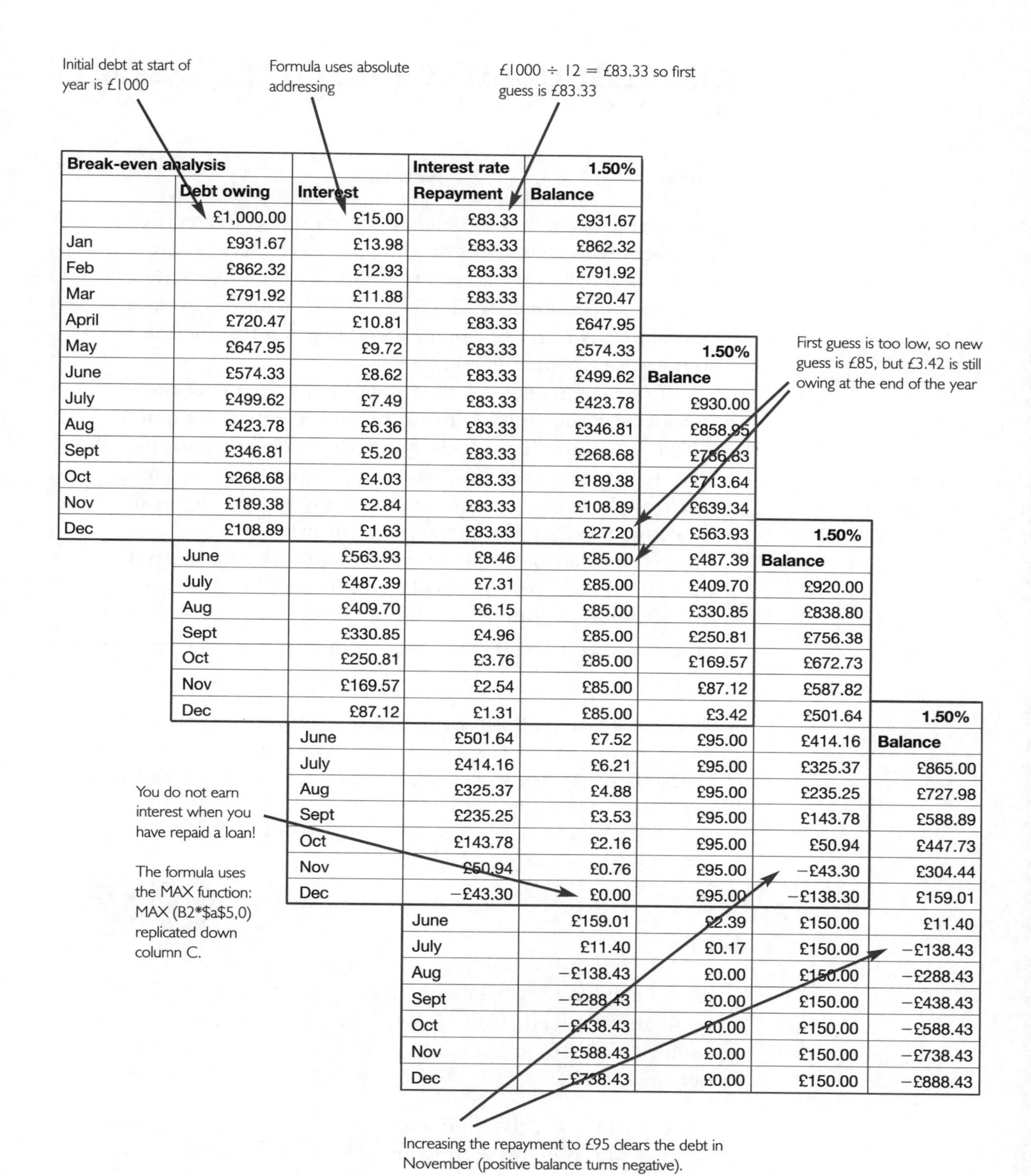

Break-even analysis			Interest rate	1.50%
	Debt owing	Interest	Repayment	Balance
	£1,000.00	£15.00	£83.33	£931.67
Jan	£931.67	£13.98	£83.33	£862.32
Feb	£862.32	£12.93	£83.33	£791.92
Mar	£791.92	£11.88	£83.33	£720.47
April	£720.47	£10.81	£83.33	£647.95
May	£647.95	£9.72	£83.33	£574.33
June	£574.33	£8.62	£83.33	£499.62
July	£499.62	£7.49	£83.33	£423.78
Aug	£423.78	£6.36	£83.33	£346.81
Sept	£346.81	£5.20	£83.33	£268.68
Oct	£268.68	£4.03	£83.33	£189.38
Nov	£189.38	£2.84	£83.33	£108.89
Dec	£108.89	£1.63	£83.33	£27.20

				1.50%
				Balance
				£930.00
				£858.95
				£786.83
				£713.64
				£639.34
				£563.93
June	£563.93	£8.46	£85.00	£487.39
July	£487.39	£7.31	£85.00	£409.70
Aug	£409.70	£6.15	£85.00	£330.85
Sept	£330.85	£4.96	£85.00	£250.81
Oct	£250.81	£3.76	£85.00	£169.57
Nov	£169.57	£2.54	£85.00	£87.12
Dec	£87.12	£1.31	£85.00	£3.42

				1.50%
				Balance
				£920.00
				£838.80
				£756.38
				£672.73
				£587.82
				£501.64
June	£501.64	£7.52	£95.00	£414.16
July	£414.16	£6.21	£95.00	£325.37
Aug	£325.37	£4.88	£95.00	£235.25
Sept	£235.25	£3.53	£95.00	£143.78
Oct	£143.78	£2.16	£95.00	£50.94
Nov	£50.94	£0.76	£95.00	−£43.30
Dec	−£43.30	£0.00	£95.00	−£138.30

				1.50%
				Balance
				£865.00
				£727.98
				£588.89
				£447.73
				£304.44
				£159.01
June	£159.01	£2.39	£150.00	£11.40
July	£11.40	£0.17	£150.00	−£138.43
Aug	−£138.43	£0.00	£150.00	−£288.43
Sept	−£288.43	£0.00	£150.00	−£438.43
Oct	−£438.43	£0.00	£150.00	−£588.43
Nov	−£588.43	£0.00	£150.00	−£738.43
Dec	−£738.43	£0.00	£150.00	−£888.43

Figure 2.22 *Spreadsheets for calculating a break-even point*

OCC

Each year, Gerry has to balance the money collected from members with that spent on the upkeep of *Overload*, the club's yacht. If Gerry knows that next year an extra £500 may be needed for mooring fees, he might suggest to Linda that she tries to recruit more members. Another option is to increase the membership fees.

If Gerry changes the data in columns C or D of the spreadsheet shown in Figure 2.13, this affects the amount shown in column E, especially the total subscriptions in cell E10. From this, using trial and improvement, Gerry could work out how many more members are needed and/or by how much to increase the annual subscription.

Yet another option is to increase the charter fee from £26 to, say, £30 per day's sailing. How could Gerry investigate this option?

A 'what if?' query is very like trial and improvement which you may remember from your maths classes. It helps if you keep a note of all your trials. Figure 2.23 shows a spreadsheet used to calculate the square root of 3 and the trials that were used to reach the 'answer'.

Activity 2.46

The formulae used in the spreadsheet shown in Figure 2.23 are listed in Table 2.6 on page 150. The formulae in cells C5, D4, E4, F4 and G4 need to be replicated down, for as many rows as you want to make guesses.

- **Enter the data but amend it to calculate the square root of 5, or 9. How many guesses does it take to get an answer correct to six decimal places?**
- **Try to amend the spreadsheet so that it will work out the square root for any number placed in a particular cell, e.g. D1.**

	A	B	C	D	E	F	G
1	Calculating the square root of			3			
2						Root is between	
3				Square it	Too big or too small?	0	3
4	First guess		1.5	2.25	too small	1.5	3
5	Next guess		2.25	5.0625	too big	1.5	2.25
6	Next guess		1.875	3.515625	too big	1.5	1.875
7	Next guess		1.6875	2.847656	too small	1.6875	1.875
8	Next guess		1.78125	3.172852	too big	1.6875	1.78125
9	Next guess		1.734375	3.008057	too big	1.6875	1.734375
10	Next guess		1.710938	2.927307	too small	1.710938	1.734375
11	Next guess		1.722656	2.967545	too small	1.722656	1.734375
12	Next guess		1.728516	2.987766	too small	1.728516	1.734375
13	Next guess		1.731445	2.997903	too small	1.731445	1.734375
14	Next guess		1.73291	3.002978	too big	1.731445	1.73291
15	Next guess		1.732178	3.00044	too big	1.731445	1.732178
16	Next guess		1.731812	2.999171	too small	1.731812	1.732178
17	Next guess		1.731995	2.999805	too small	1.731995	1.732178
18	Next guess		1.732086	3.000123	too big	1.731995	1.732086
19	Next guess		1.73204	2.999964	too small	1.73204	1.732086
20	Next guess		1.732063	3.000043	too big	1.73204	1.732063
21	Next guess		1.732052	3.000004	too big	1.73204	1.732052
22	Next guess		1.732046	2.999984	too small	1.732046	1.732052
23	Next guess		1.732049	2.999994	too small	1.732049	1.732052
24	Next guess		1.73205	2.999999	too small	1.73205	1.732052
25	Next guess		1.732051	3.000001	too big	1.73205	1.732051
26	Next guess		1.732051	3	too small	1.732051	1.732051
27	Next guess		1.732051	3.000001	too big	1.732051	1.732051

$\sqrt{3} = 1$ to the nearest whole number → 7

$\sqrt{3} = 1.7$ (correct to 1 d.p.) → 9

$\sqrt{3} = 1.73$ (correct to 2 d.p.) → 13

$\sqrt{3} = 1.732$ (correct to 3 d.p.) → 19

$\sqrt{3} = 1.7320$ (correct to 4 d.p.) → 19

$\sqrt{3} = 1.73205$ (correct to 5 d.p.) → 25

$\sqrt{3} = 1.732051$ (correct to 6 d.p.) → 27

You can carry on guessing until your answer is as accurate as you want it to be.

Figure 2.23 *Trial and improvement*

Cell reference	*Formula*
D4	C4*C4
E4	=IF(D4>3,"too big","too small")
F4	=IF(D4<3,C4,F3)
G4	=IF(D4>3,C4,G3)
C5	+(F4+G4)/2

Table 2.6 *Formulae used in the spreadsheet shown in Figure 2.23*

OCC

As the year progresses, more bookings are received. The total bookings are shown in Table 2.7.

Trip number	*Berths booked*	*Trip number*	*Berths booked*	*Trip number*	*Berths booked*
1	9	9	8	17	8
2	10	10	10	18	4
3	4	11	9	19	7
4	10	12	10	20	6
5	10	13	10	21	4
6	10	14	7	22	4
7	10	15	10	23	8
8	8	16	8	24	2

Table 2.7 *Up-to-date Sailtrip bookings*

Refer to the spreadsheet that you designed for Activity 2.41.

★ Update the spreadsheet so that the bookings to date are correct.

★ **What if** you assume that trips for which five or fewer bookings are made will not sail? What effect does this have on expected charter income?

Ideally, on average, each trip that sails should have a minimum of eight bookings.

★ Amend your spreadsheet to work out 80% occupancy for each trip, and calculate the total charter income if this were to be achieved.

★ Identify which trips should be advertised most strongly, so that trips might not be cancelled.

★ Perform a 'what if?' query to find out how many extra berths must be booked to achieve 80% occupancy.

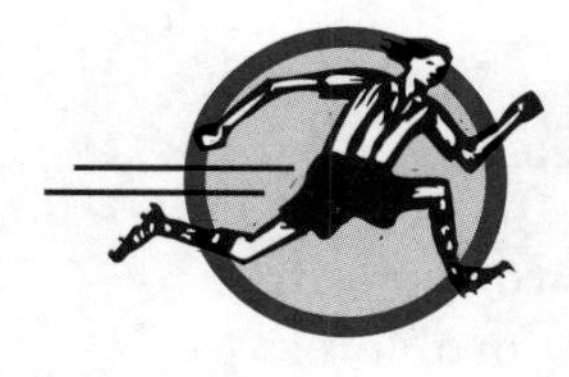

Activity 2.48

If you have not already created a spreadsheet for a third-party user, do so now. Include a description of the spreadsheet and annotated printed output demonstrating its operation and showing how it meets user needs.

★ Describe clearly the user's needs, the information to be processed and the processing required.

★ Create and use suitable spreadsheet row heights, column widths, cell formats, titles, cell references, IF ... THEN statements, arithmetic functions and formulae.

★ Use spreadsheet facilities to enter data, sort, search, calculate using absolute and relative cell references, predict results, and produce different types of charts or line graphs.

★ Annotate your printed reports so that it is clear why and how all printed items are produced.

You must also produce an evaluation of your work, so make suggestions for improvement and describe any problems experienced.

Remember to check the accuracy of your data and keep backup copies of all files.

Revision questions

1. What is the difference between data and information?
2. Name three different types of database.
3. Name six different sources of information.
4. Explain the difference between insert and overtype modes of data entry.
5. What is a pathname?
6. What is the difference between searching and sorting?
7. Explain how entries are ordered in an index.
8. Give two examples of a relational operator.
9. Give two examples of a logical operator.
10. What is a 'wildcard' search?
11. Explain these terms: table, record, field, row, column, key field, primary and secondary keys, foreign keys.
12. Explain the difference between a one-to-one relationship and a many-to-one relationship. Give an example of a many-to-one relationship.
13. Explain the difference between relative and absolute addressing.
14. Explain how to calculate a break-even point.
15. Explain how to perform a 'what-if?' query.

Hardware and Software

- Understand ICT specifications for hardware and software
- Select an ICT system and configure it to meet the needs of users
- Write a program to improve efficient use of application software (macros)
- Write a program to display hypertext information (HTML)
- Understand and develop good practice in your use of ICT

This chapter looks in detail at hardware and software, and then focuses on computer programming, including HTML programs and macros.

You should try to identify some local organisations that may give you information about the hardware and software that they use.

Several case studies and examples are used to introduce and illustrate the ideas of this chapter. Background information about these organisations is given in the Case Studies section of this book, starting on page xvi.

This unit is assessed externally only. You will have to undertake some tasks before the test and take this work into the external assessment with you. The grade on that assessment will be your grade for the unit.

Hardware

These are the five main **hardware components** of an ICT system (Figure 3.1):

- Input devices
- Output devices
- Main processing unit
- Memory devices
- Storage devices

Cables and connectors hold everything together.

Activity 3.1

Make a copy of Figure 3.1 and label it with the items of equipment in your own ICT system.

Disks (hard and floppy) store data and are used for **secondary input**. These are called **I/O devices**, i.e. they are both input *and* output devices.

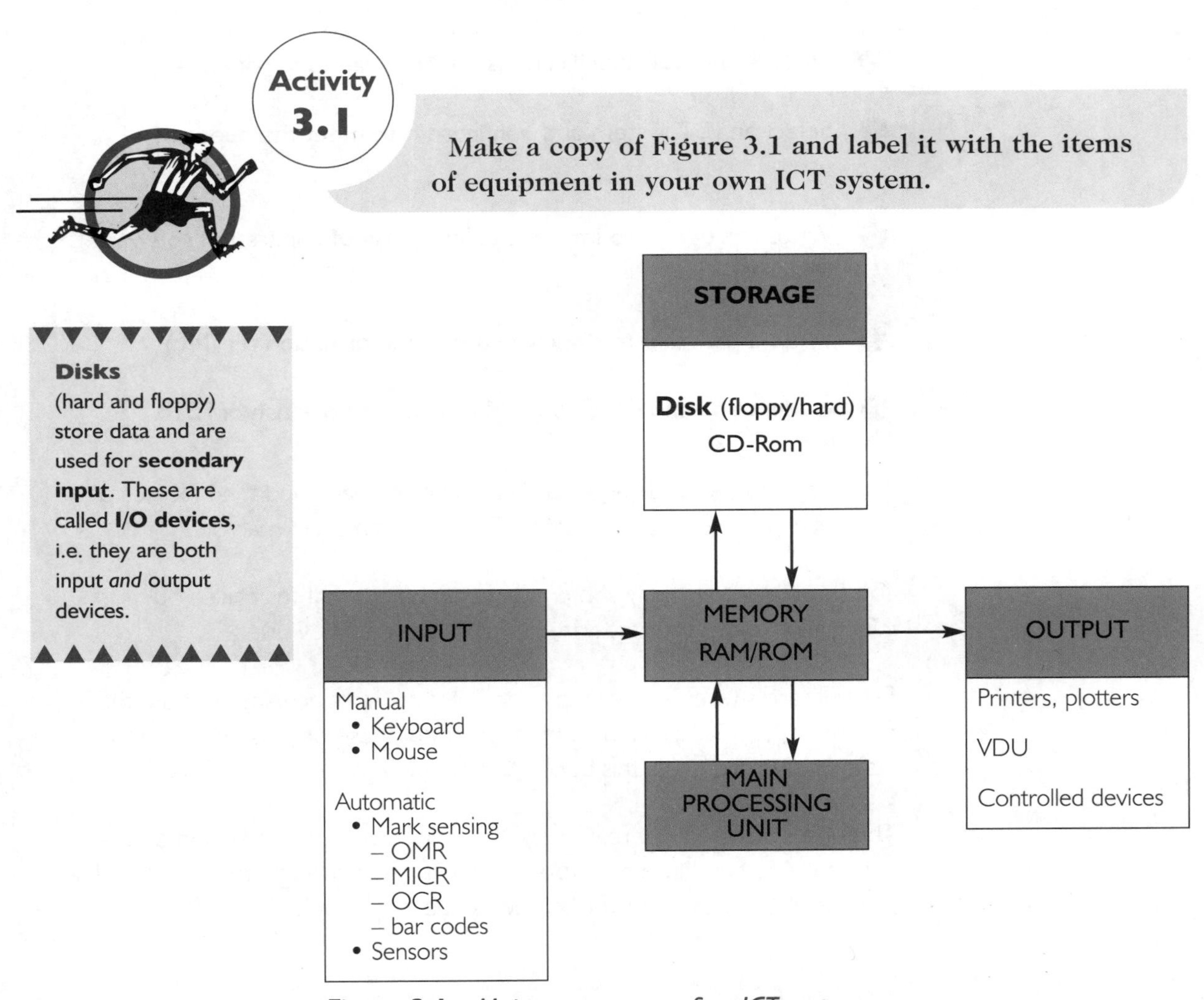

Figure 3.1 *Main components of an ICT system*

Input devices

Input devices allow data to be entered for the first time into an ICT system. This is called **primary input.**

There are two main types of input device:

- **Manual devices** involve the user's own hand, e.g. a keyboard, keypad, joystick, roller ball or mouse
- **Automatic devices** 'read' data that has been prepared beforehand, e.g. a scanner reading a barcode at a supermarket checkout

Manual data entry

This section looks at keyboards (including concept keyboards and keypads), pointing devices (mouse and trackerball), joysticks and touch screens.

Exercise 3.1

Can you think of any other manual data entry devices? If so, make notes on their features and purpose.

A **keyboard** (Figure 3.2) is the most common input device for use with general-purpose computers.

They have lots of keys, but these are not necessarily the same for all computers, nor is the arrangement of keys the same. Most keyboards have three parts.

- The main part of the keyboard is likely to be arranged as on a traditional typewriter, i.e. a **QWERTY keyboard**
- Another section may be arranged as a block of keys for the digits 0–9. It may also include the maths symbols for add, subtract, multiply and divide, and an enter key. This part of the keyboard is called a **numeric keypad**.
- There may also be special keys including, at least, enter (or return), escape (ESC), control (CTRL) and some **function keys** labelled F1 to F12. What these keys do depends on the software being used, rather than the hardware

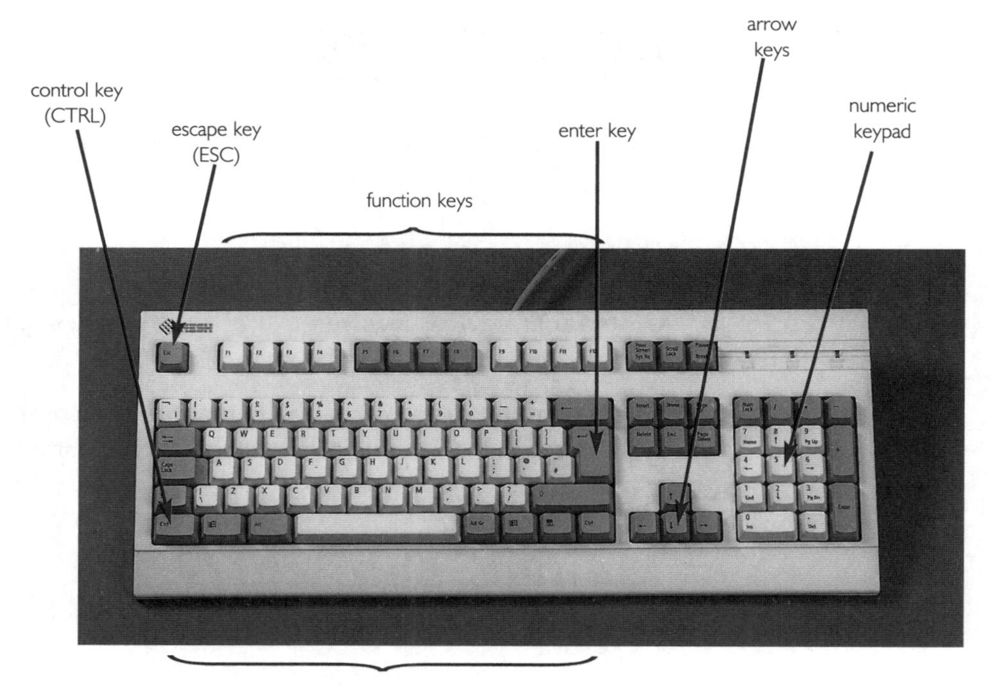

Figure 3.2 *Typical keyboard layout*

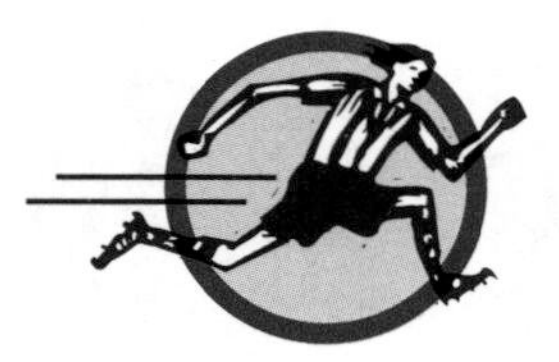

Activity 3.2

- ★ **Find out what features your word-processing software provides for users who cannot use the standard QWERTY keyboard.**
- ★ **What is the DVORAK keyboard?**
- ★ **Find out what function key operations are available with your spreadsheet software. Do these keys have the same function within your database software?**

Like a laptop computer, a **keypad** is a completely portable handheld input device often used in supermarkets to check on the price of an item. Keypads have a smaller set of keys – usually the numeric keys and a few others – and a small display area.

Keypads are used by gas-meter readers. At the start of each day data is downloaded to the keypad (e.g. the householder's address and meter number), and then at the end of the day data can be uploaded back to the computer (e.g. the gas-meter reading).

Concept keyboards were originally introduced for children (or adults) who had problems with the small keys on a QWERTY keyboard. The 'keys' were much larger and this made it easier to press the correct one. Later, the design was extended to allow a push-button choice of many options. Nowadays, concept keyboards are seen on most shop tills, especially in restaurants and bars. When a key is pressed it relates to a choice, e.g. 'large fries' or 'chocolate milkshake', and the price of the item is automatically displayed. This type of input allows the manager to preset the prices and saves the assistant remembering the cost of every item on the menu.

Chris Lane

The bar staff use a concept keyboard to record purchases, e.g. a Diet Coke and a packet of crisps. The prices are automatic, so the bar staff do not need to remember the price of any item.

During 'happy hour' prices are reduced, and the till is programmed so that, according to the time, the correct prices are charged.

Activity 3.3

- **If you already have experience of using a concept keyboard, write notes on how to program it and how to operate it.**
- **Next time you visit a local newsagent, a greengrocer's or a fast food restaurant, check whether they use a concept keyboard.**
- **When you have found a concept keyboard in use, ask the manager how complicated it is to program in the prices. Ask the shop assistant how easy it is to use.**

Some manual devices are specially adapted so that people who do not have normal hand functions can still use them. Some primary schools introduce children to a concept keyboard first, because very young children have difficulty in accurately pressing only one 'normal'-sized key. Instead, overlays are used with special software, and these may represent different colours, or different shapes for the child to choose from.

Exercise 3.2

Find out about three different ways in which input devices have been adapted to meet the needs of some users.

A **mouse** is a **pointing device** (Figure 3.3), usually connected to the computer by a thin cable. Moving the mouse across a flat surface causes a cursor, or pointer, on the display screen to move to a new insertion point.

A mouse has one or more finger-operated switches called (mouse) **buttons**.

Pressing a mouse button is called **clicking**, because it usually produces a 'click' sound.

> **Did You Know?**
>
> *If you want to, you can swap the left and right button functions on a mouse. This may help left-handed people.*

- If you **left click** the mouse in a new position on the screen, this position becomes your **insertion point** and you can start inserting text.
- If you left click when the pointer controlled by the mouse is on an icon, or a screen button, then the operation represented by that icon (or button) is **selected**.
- A **right click** may result in a menu of options, relevant to your position on the screen, being displayed. This can save time.

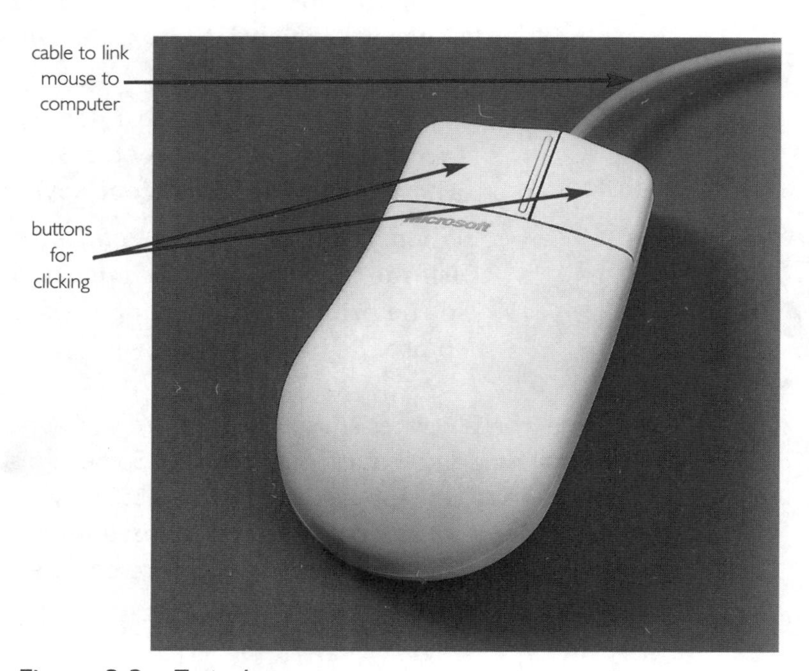

Figure 3.3 *Typical mouse*

Exercise 3.3

Modern mouse designs include a third control – a roller positioned between the two main buttons. Find out what extra features this type of mouse offers to the user.

Some software expects the mouse button to be pressed twice in quick succession. This is called **double clicking**. A single click has one effect and double clicking may have another.

Activity 3.4

- ★ **Notice how the cursor design changes as you move it around the screen in three separate software applications, such as word processing, spreadsheet and database.**
- ★ **Find out what happens when you left click, right click or double click – for each cursor design.**
- ★ **Make notes.**

Dragging – moving the mouse while holding down a button – is used to move an area of a screen display, which may be text or some part of a graphic display, from one location to another. Before such movement can take place the area concerned has to be defined, e.g. by highlighting text, or by marking the boundaries of a graphic item. Moving things around in this way is sometimes referred to as **drag-and-drop editing**. This may also be used to copy, as well as move, part of a screen display.

> **Dragging**
> the scrollbar marker slides you through the document. The **scrollbar** represents your position within a document, and allows you to jump or slide through the document. Clicking above or below the marker jumps you backwards or forwards.

Moving the icon for a file from one subdirectory to another is a way of repositioning the file within the computer's file system.

Mouse operations, such as clicking, dragging or combining these with the use of keys on the keyboard, provide a wide range of possible options at any moment. Actions such as pressing or releasing the mouse buttons are called **mouse events**.

A **trackerball** is a similar input device and is used to do the same things as a mouse. It is a ball, set into a cup, which can be made to roll in any direction by using a finger or the palm of a hand, depending on the size of the ball. The movements of the ball are mirrored on the screen by a pointer, and finger-operated switches work in the same way as mouse buttons. Trackerballs are now sometimes mounted on laptop computers, being easier to use in this position than a mouse.

Activity 3.5

Using the mouse is not the only way to move around the screen. The arrow keys can also be used. Table 3.1 shows some shortcuts keys to use instead of the mouse. Find out what other keys can be used to move quickly through a document:

- ★ **To move to the beginning or end of a line**
- ★ **To move to the beginning or end of the document**

To move	*Press this key*
One character to the right	RIGHT ARROW
One word to the right	CTRL + RIGHT ARROW
Down one line	DOWN ARROW
Down one screen	PAGE DOWN
Down one page	ALT+ CTRL + PAGE DOWN

Table 3.1 *Shortcuts for moving around a document*

A **joystick** is most often found on PCs that are used mostly for playing games. Like the gearstick in a car it has 'directions' – forward, backward, left or right – and a button that can be pressed, e.g. to mean 'fire'. It is easier to use than a keyboard or mouse for games. Joysticks – or something very similar – are also used in training situations where the person being trained would have a similar device to use in real life, e.g. a pilot.

A **touch screen** looks just like a normal **VDU** screen. The difference is that, if you place your finger (or a pen) near the screen, the surface can detect exactly where your finger (or the pen) is. There are two ways such a screen might work:

- **The screen may contain a grid of wires, running horizontally and vertically, which can sense the 'coordinate' position of the finger**

- **Infra-red beams may be directed horizontally and vertically across the screen, which are broken by the presence of your finger**

Whichever method is used for the 'physics' of the hardware, the software can work out where your finger is. Touch screens are used in situations where having a keyboard may be impractical, e.g. in information systems where the user cannot be given access to the system, apart from the screen.

Exercise 3.4

List three examples of ICT systems that use touch screens.

Automatic data entry

This section looks at scanners, including flat-bed scanners, barcode readers, mark sensing, other sensors such as light sensors and heat sensors, and data-logging devices such as digital cameras.

Exercise 3.5

Can you think of any other automatic data-entry devices? If so, make notes on their features and purpose.

Automatic data entry is used for data that has been prepared in some way, e.g. scanning directly from an original document or inputting computer-readable codes such as barcodes. Automatic data-entry methods provide quicker ways of capturing data and can reduce the number of errors made. They do involve some extra work, e.g. setting up barcodes initially, but the whole process then becomes automatic, saving both time and money.

A **flat-bed scanner** is an input device that allows you to transfer data from a sheet of paper straight to the computer. It looks and works very much like a photocopier. It shines a light across the paper and measures the reflected light. This data is turned into a bitmap file and can then be processed using graphics software.

Hawkes Design

Peter has a scanner with a transparency adaptor. It scans prints up to A4 size. It also scans slides and transparencies.

A **barcode reader** works in the same way. A laser beam is shone across the code and interprets the patterns reflected by the barcode. Sometimes the reader is built into equipment such as a supermarket checkout till. Sometimes the barcode reader is handheld: then it is called a **wand** (Figure 3.4).

Figure 3.4 *Typical barcode scanner used in libraries*

A **mark sense reader** is an input device that reads special forms (or cards) by detecting the marks made on the form in predetermined positions. The marks may be handwritten or they may be printed in some way. There are three main types of mark sensing:

- An **optical mark reader** (OMR) reads marks made in predetermined positions on special forms (or cards) by a light-sensing method, for example the numbers recorded on a National Lottery ticket, or a multiple-choice test answer sheet (Figure 3.5).

The document is scanned but extra checks are made to ensure the form is placed in the scanner the correct way round. For this, extra marks are printed on the form, called time tracks.

MULTIPLE CHOICE TEST

Answer Sheet

Name ....

Question					
1	[a]	[b]	[c]	[d]	■
2	[a]	[b]	[c]	[d]	■
3	[a]	[b]	[c]	[d]	■
4	[a]	[b]	[c]	[d]	■
5	[a]	[b]	[c]	[d]	■
6	[a]	[b]	[c]	[d]	■
7	[a]	[b]	[c]	[d]	■
8	[a]	[b]	[c]	[d]	■
9	[a]	[b]	[c]	[d]	■
10	[a]	[b]	[c]	[d]	■

Candidate uses pencil to shade area between [and]

Time tracks

Figure 3.5 *OMR data entry*

Chris Lane

The Chris Lane membership card has a barcode on the reverse side. This card is used to gain entry to the club. Members swipe the card through a reader, which is on the wall next to a turnstile. If the card is recognised, the turnstile lets one person through.

The switch card system means the club can also keep a record of each time a member visits the club – or more importantly, a list can be printed of any members who have *not* visited the club for a long time, e.g. one month. The membership department can then telephone these members and invite them to a forthcoming event, e.g. a quiz evening, so as to encourage them to return to the club.

Exercise 3.6

Look at the National Lottery data entry form. Notice where the time tracks are.

- **Magnetic ink character recognition** (MICR) is machine recognition of style characters printed in magnetic ink. The commonest application is the data printed on a cheque: this usually includes the cheque number, the branch number and the account number. These characters are both machine and human readable (Figure 3.6).

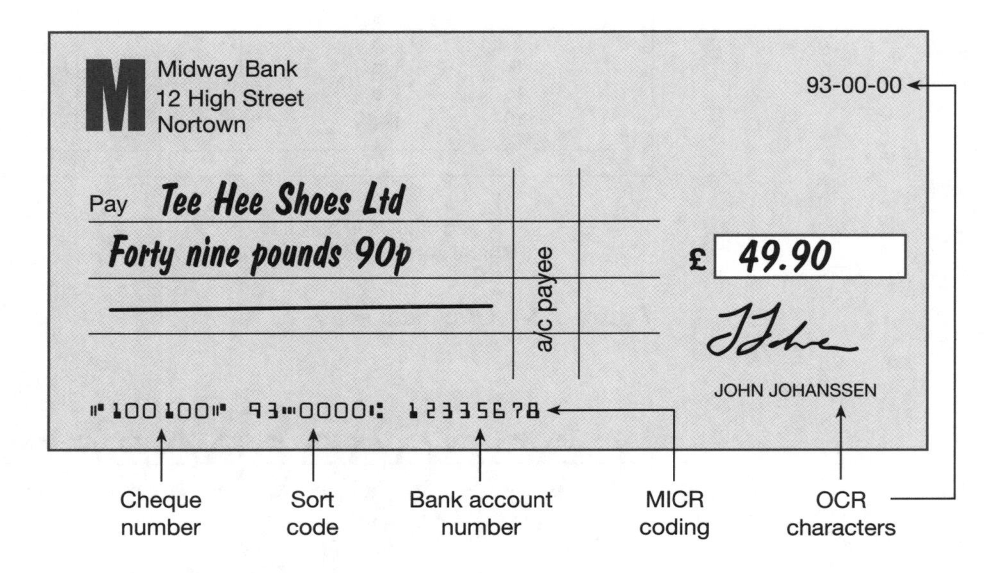

Figure 3.6 *A cheque with MICR markings*

- **Optical character recognition** (OCR) is machine recognition of printed characters by light-sensing methods, e.g. the reading of typed postcodes when mail is sorted automatically, or the machine-readable section of a European Community passport (Figure 3.7).

Many automatic devices are called **sensors**. Like human sensors, such as eyes or ears, they can receive data in many ways:

> **Did You Know?**
>
> **Illuminance** is measured in lux.

- **Light sensors** sense the brightness of light – the illuminance
- **Heat sensors** sense how hot the surroundings are

BURLEYWOODS

STATEMENT OF ACCOUNT
Registered Office:
100, Old Street, Manchester
Registered Number: 470484 London

Account Number	550464-2
Statement Number	2
Statement prepared on	04/08/99

1 00100

MS P BOWERS
12 ROWENS CLOSE
WOKINGHAM

7161

Date	Description	Quantity	Value
	Balance brought forward from last statement - number 1		32.97
18 JUL	Payment Received - Thank You		10.00-

PLEASE PAY BY 24th AUG

Current balance	22.97
CREDIT LIMIT	750.00
AVAILABLE TO SPEND	727.00

YOU SHOULD PAY AT LEAST £3.20

67/1240223

Girobank Trans cash
Girobank plc Bootle Merseyside GIR 0AA

BURLEYWOODS

bank giro credit

135
205

Reference	Credit account number	Amount (Cheque Acceptable)	By transfer from Girobank a/c number
550464-2	257 180	£	

STANDARD FEE PAYABLE AT PO

Cashier's stamp and initials

Signature

MS P BOWERS

Date

57-18-03

NATIONAL WESTMINSTER
HEAD OFFICE
COLLECTION ACCOUNT

CASH
CHEQUE
TOTAL £

Items Fees

Please do not write or mark below this line and do not fold this counterfoil

5504642 &4002571803 91 X

Figure 3.7 *OCR data entry – the bottom section contains the OCR data*

Did You Know?

Microphones are now commonplace on modern PCs since the facility to use the PC as a complete workstation, including making voice telephone calls, was introduced. These microphones are very small and work just like 'normal' microphones.

- **Sound recognition** systems take in data using a microphone
- **Contact sensors** 'know' when a circuit is completed – when two things are touching
- **Proximity sensors** can tell when two objects are close to each other but not yet touching

Exercise 3.7

Think about ways microphones can be used with PCs.

Sensors are used in many situations, usually without people realising

- When you use a lift, many sensors control the opening and closing of the doors and the movement between floors
- In a car wash, sensors detect the position of the car
- When you leave a supermarket, the doors open automatically for you
- Security systems use sensors to detect movement, so that at night, lights turn on when someone approaches a security sensor
- Greenhouse control systems use sensors to find out the temperature within the greenhouse and the humidity level of the air (how much moisture it holds)
- A quality control system may use a spring gauge to sense the weight of a finished item (so that it can be rejected if it is too heavy or too light)
- An environmental control system may use a sensor to analyse exhaust fumes from a furnace for the concentration of pollutants within the air
- A weather station uses many sensors to record all aspects of the weather: rainfall, wind speed and humidity

The Met Office

In 1992 the Met Office installed a sophisticated, computer-based building management system (BMS) which – among other things – detects and monitors smoke detectors and fire alarms.

In the UK there is a network of 40 flood-level gauges at strategic points around the coast that are linked to the main computers by modem. This system gives a comprehensive overview of tides and tidal surges as they move around the coast.

In addition, the Met Office collects data from a wide range of UK, European and international sources, either directly or via other national and international weather services. Satellites, sondes (high-altitude balloons), ground stations (some automatic), ships' captains and airline pilots all report on conditions such as turbulence, air pressure and temperature, wind speed, sea state and so on.

Sailing Breaks

John Hore has a yacht called *Half Nelson*. On his boat, John has a two-headed gas detector and shut-off valve. Because gas is heavier than air, it is important that any gas leaks are detected before the concentration builds to a dangerous level.

John's GPS (global positioning system) relies on information from satellites to determine his position.

His on-board equipment includes an electronic depth-measuring device. This device works by sending a signal down through the water and then seeing how long it takes to receive a 'reply' signal. In very deep water the signal may not return, so the equipment shows an error signal, but this is not a problem. It is more important to be aware of the clearance below the keel in shallow water (so he can avoid going aground!).

Activity 3.6

Systems similar to GPS have been considered to keep track of buses, and nowadays some car models incorporate GPS to provide a route finder for the driver. Find out as much as you can about this type of system. What sensors are involved?

A sensor is a device that outputs electrical signals according to conditions in its environment. For example, a sensor records heat, light, pH (acidity), sound or movement. If sensor readings are **sampled** frequently, a change in the environment – even very small changes – can be monitored.

- A **transducer** is an electronic component that converts one form of energy to another
- A **thermistor** converts a temperature into electrical energy with a varying voltage
- A **photo cell** converts the brightness of illuminations into a voltage

The term transducer is generally used to describe devices that produce electricity, rather than those that convert electricity into another form of energy. A sensor is therefore a transducer that responds to a physical property, such as pressure, rate of flow, humidity, or the proximity of ferrous metal.

The sensor produces an electrical output which is either **analogue** or **digital**. Some sensors, called **passive devices**, require no external electrical source. Those that require an external voltage are called **active devices**.

Activity 3.7

- ★ **Check that you know the difference between the terms analogue and digital.**
- ★ **List 10 types of sensor and, for each one, decide what type it is: passive or active, digital or analogue.**

Data capture describes the method used to transfer data into an ICT system.

When entering data manually, the user may be creating a letter from new or copying information from a source document, e.g. an order form. The blank order form is designed so that, when completed, it will hold all the information needed. This may include some special coding, e.g. M/F for male/female, S/M/L/XL for the size of a coat. Filling in the form is the data capture stage of input.

Some automatic devices are special **data-capture devices.** They are not physically attached to the computer that is to process the data after it has been captured. This may be because conditions at the sensor are not suitable for a computer, e.g. in measuring an earthquake it does not make sense to site a computer installation where you know an earthquake is likely to happen. It may just be inconvenient, e.g. for a photographer taking wedding photos, or it may be that what is being logged is too far away, e.g. in space.

The Met Office

The Met Office has weather stations all over the UK. These are used to collect lots of different information: wind speed and direction, temperature and rainfall.

Satellites are also used to capture information (signals) and to 'bounce' them back to Earth.

These 'snapshots' of the weather are fed into the Met Office's computer system and used to forecast the weather for the next day, week, month, or even longer.

When the data is captured and kept until needed later, the data-capture device is also called a **data-logging device**. The data is captured, and then later it is input (or uploaded) to the computer for processing.

Digital camera is just like a normal camera in that it takes still pictures. However, instead of recording the image on film which then has to be processed, the image is stored digitally.

Hawkes Design

Peter Hawkes has a digital camera which he uses to 'capture' a picture digitally. This digital image can then be loaded into his computer for processing.

Output devices

Data display is the purpose of most output devices, the screen and printer in particular.

- Display of data is an important part of data entry: it shows the operator what has been keyed, so that it can be checked against the original input document. This is called **screen verification**.
- Display is also necessary for **interaction** between the operator and the ICT system. **Menus** are displayed and the operator makes a choice; **messages** are displayed if the operator does something strange, or if the equipment does not perform as expected.

Printed output – called **hardcopy** – is often a main product of an ICT system: invoices, payslips, management reports, letters to clients and so on.

- Printed output provides a permanent record of data that you no longer need to keep on the ICT system. This is called **archiving**.
- A hardcopy of data is **portable**. It can be taken away from the computer area or passed on to someone else. This may be more suitable than giving them a copy of the data on disk.
- When interrogating a database the number of matches may be one or two, and you could copy this information from the screen, or just remember it. If the query resulted in 200 matches it would make more sense to have a printout of the records.

This section looks at VDUs, printers and plotters.

Exercise 3.8

Can you think of any other output devices? If so, make notes on their features and purpose.

Output devices present the data that has been processed within the computer as information for the user. There are many different forms of output. Three common forms allow the user to hold, see or hear the output. Another involves controlled devices.

- Visual output is presented on a screen
- Printed output – called hardcopy – is produced on a printer or a plotter
- Aural output is presented using a loudspeaker, e.g. an alarm bell ringing in a security system
- Controlled devices such as motors and buzzers are common in monitoring and control systems

VDU

VDU stands for **visual display unit**. Sometimes it is more simply called a **screen** or **monitor**.

The screen displays information using a cathode ray tube. This is similar to a TV except it cannot receive TV signals. Instead, signals are sent from the computer for display on the screen. The **size** of screen is its diagonal length (Figure 3.8).

The **VDU control panel** allows you to adjust the brightness and contrast of the display.

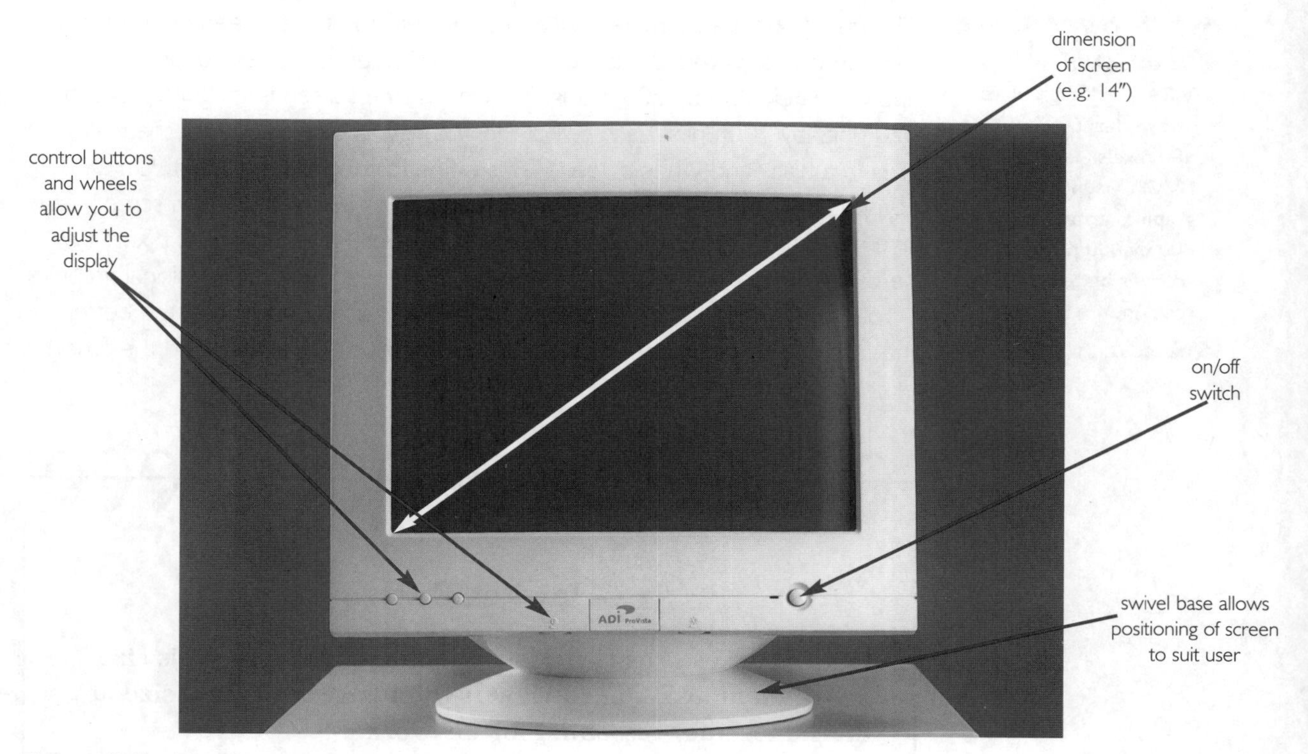

Figure 3.8 *Typical monitor or display*

Did You Know?

A VGA monitor has a vertical refresh rate of 60–70 scans per second. For SVGA monitors, the rate is 72 scans per second.

The screen is continuously energised so that the image remains visible to the user. An electron beam passes across the display, and hence the whole screen is continuously 'repainted'. The rate at which the whole screen is repainted is called the **vertical refresh rate**. A low rate causes flicker, and flickering can be harmful to some users.

Exercise 3.9

- ★ **Why were screen savers invented? What is their purpose?**
- ★ **What is a screen filter? What is its purpose?**

Monitors can be **monochrome**, displaying one colour, e.g. white, green or orange on a dark (usually black) background. **Colour monitors** display in many different colours according to the type of screen and computer being used.

The **prompt** is a character (or sometimes a message) displayed on a screen to indicate that the operator is expected to do something, e.g. to input data into the system. Sometimes, this visual prompt is emphasised by a sound, such as a beep.

Resolution
VGA – video graphics array – has 640 by 480 pixels.
SVGA – super video graphics array – has 800 by 600 pixels, and so gives better resolution.

The **resolution** (or apparent clearness or quality) of the screen depends on the number of **pixels** displayed on it. On TV screens the resolution is approximately 320 by 200 pixels. This means the screen is split into a grid of 320 units by 200 units, each cell of the grid having one colour (or shade of grey in a black and white screen). This is fine for displaying teletext. On a computer screen better resolution is needed. For a low-resolution screen, say one measuring 36 centimetres across the diagonal, the number of pixels may be 640 by 400. For a high-resolution screen – needed for professional graphics – you would need 1024 by 768 pixels. The higher the resolution the better the quality of the picture, and the higher the cost of the screen and the amount of computer memory the display needs.

Hawkes Design

Peter Hawkes uses two 21-inch colour monitors. This size of screen allows him to view two A4 pages at actual size at the same time – essential for his work.

The Met Office

The Met Office has in excess of 500 terminals and PCs attached to a system called COSMOS. At any one time 170 of these terminals can be in use. The terminals are of various types, including an increasing number with alphanumeric and graphical VDUs, as well as nine with powerful high-resolution colour graphics displays.

Laptop computers (Figure 3.9) have built-in screens, which are usually quite small and flat. Some screens are made from two thin sheets of glass with liquid crystals between them; these are called **liquid crystal displays**. The resolution is not good, but may suit the user of a portable computer.

Figure 3.9 *Laptop computer with a thin liquid crystal display*

Activity
3.8

* What size screens are available for a standalone PC? What are the advantages and disadvantages of the various sizes?
* Find out what screen types are available on laptop computers.
* Find out how much the larger screens cost to buy, compared to smaller screens.

Printers

Printers are used to produce **hardcopy** of data as a permanent record. Printed output can be produced on any type of printer: dot matrix, inkjet or laser. The type of printer used depends on the quality of output required, the speed of printing needed and the cost.

The Met Office

The Met Office use line printers which print up to 150 characters per line at speeds of 2800 lines per minute. These are a centralised resource used for small/moderate printing requirements. In addition, several 'slow' printers are distributed around the HQ buildings to enable programmers to print a few pages at a time. If multiple copies are to be printed, e.g. the Met Office's Annual Report and Accounts, these are done by the Stationery Office Ltd (a professional printing organisation).

Plotter
is a special type of printer, which is used to prepare technical drawings or other output on paper larger than A4 size.

Exercise 3.10

Using a source such as the British Computer Society *Glossary of Computing Terms*, or the Internet, find out how a **plotter** works.

Impact printers, e.g. dot matrix printers, involve a printhead hitting the paper through an inked tape. Impact printers are noisy and slow, but are needed if the output is a multipart form.

Dot matrix printers (Figure 3.10) form each character from a grid of pins. The more pins that are used, the greater the resolution and therefore the quality of printing. Most dot matrix printers also offer two modes: draft and 'near-letter quality' (NLQ). NLQ printing involves printing the same character twice, close to each other; this gives a better printed effect, but takes twice as long and uses up the ribbon twice as quickly.

Inkjet printers (Figure 3.11) 'squirt' small bubbles of ink at the page and so they are much quieter. They are sometimes called **bubble-jet printers**. The paper must be a good quality, otherwise the printing may 'bleed' and the end result can be poor. Colour printing is possible, which offers good opportunities to produce excellent artwork and designs. Inkjet printers are inexpensive to buy but the ink cartridges can prove expensive.

Laser printers (Figure 3.12) work on the same kind of principles as a photocopier. A laser beam is used to 'draw' the shape on to a light-sensitive electrostatically charged drum. This drum then rotates over a source of toner – powdered ink – which sticks to the parts of the drum that have been affected by the laser beam. Finally, the drum rotates over a sheet of paper and the

***Figure 3.10** Dot matrix printer*

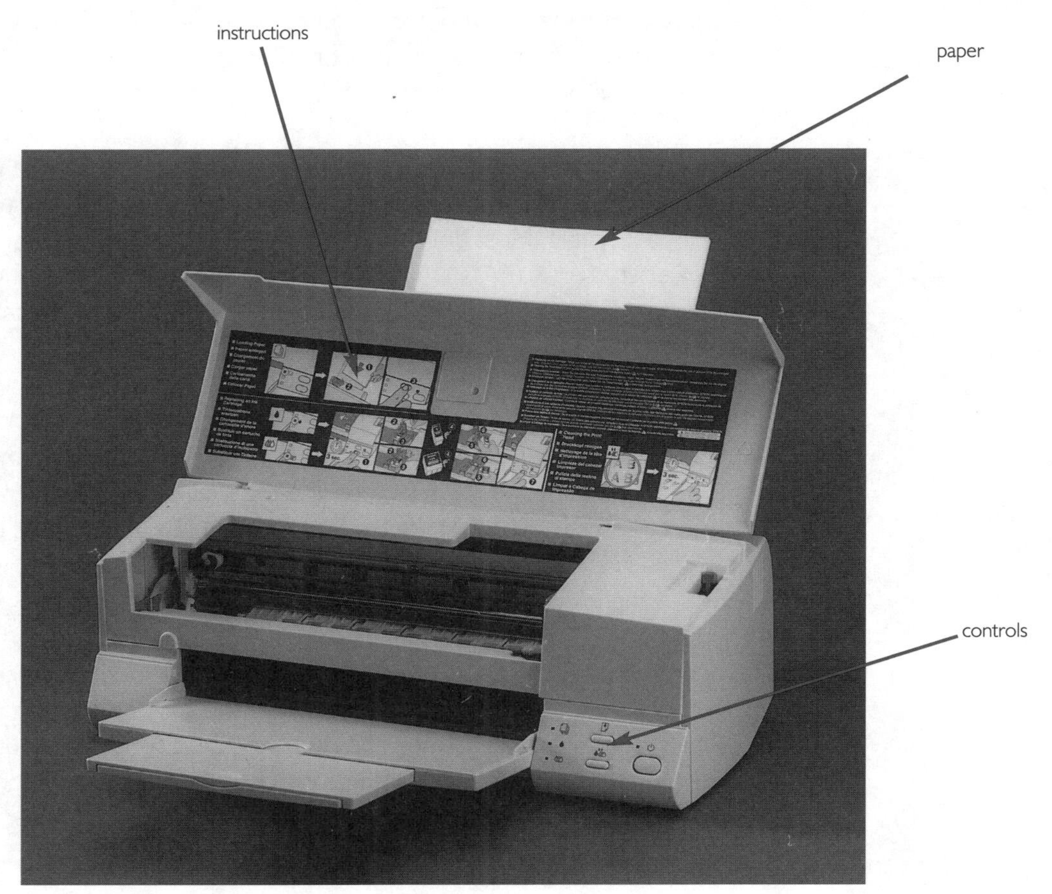

Figure 3.11 *Inkjet printer*

image is transferred from the drum to the paper. The paper is heated as the drum rotates and this makes the toner stick to the paper as it passes.

Laser printers offer good **resolution** but they are expensive to buy and to run. Toner cartridges need replacing frequently, and the running costs can be high.

Sailing Breaks

John Hore has a combined scanner, copier and inkjet printer. John works from home and he chose an all-in-one device so as to reduce space used on his desk.

He also has a laser printer which he uses for quality printing of his course notes for the RYA shore-based course that he teaches.

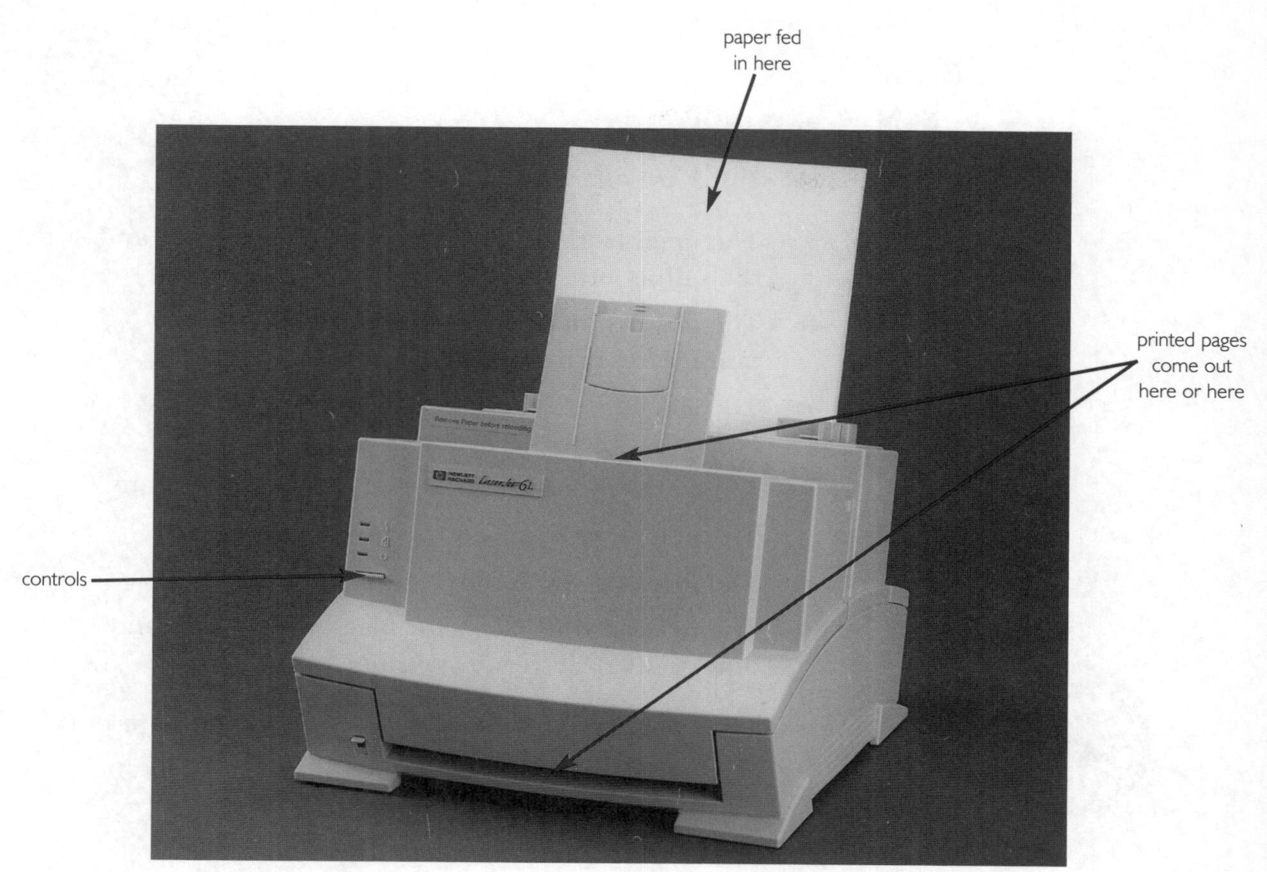

Figure 3.12 *Laser printer*

Hawkes Design

Peter has a B&W (greyscale) laser printer which prints to A4 and A3 edge-to-edge, i.e. with no white space border. Peter also has a colour inkjet printer which prints up to super A3 size, i.e. A3 plus the crop marks which are used to position the pages correctly when they go to a professional printer for publication.

For each of six different printers, find out what features are offered and at what price:

- ★ **The manufacturer's name, the model number and the selling price**
- ★ **The dimensions (width, height and depth in millimetres) and weight**
- ★ **The size of paper that can be printed (smallest and largest)**
- ★ **The monochrome print speed (pages per minute)**
- ★ **The colour print speed (pages per minute)**
- ★ **The printing resolution**
- ★ **The ink cartridge costs for black and colour, and how many pages each cartridge prints**

Include laser printers as well as inkjet printers, and present your findings as a table or chart.

Loudspeaker

Nowadays PCs are used with multimedia systems, and you are as likely to listen to a music CD on a PC while working as on a music system. For the loudspeaker to give out music (or any other sounds), a **sound card** is needed with the computer. Sound is also used as output in a number of other situations.

- *On some tube trains information is given on an information board within the carriage, and is also relayed electronically as a voice: 'The next stop is Victoria.' Similar systems are used on mainline stations to warn waiting passengers of a fast train coming through the station: 'Stand clear on Platform 7. Fast train approaching.'*

- *Some banks allow you to make enquiries about the balance in your account using touch-tone technology. After you have successfully passed all the security checks, your balance is 'read' back to you. You can also find out what amounts have been paid into and withdrawn from your account.*

Sailing Breaks

John Hore's gas detection system sets off a bleeper when the gas concentration reaches too high a level. His echo sounder (which measures the clearance beneath his yacht) also bleeps if the clearance is less than a certain amount. John can control the 'trigger value' so he can keep a careful watch on clearance, e.g. if motoring up a channel near low tide.

Exercise 3.11

We are promised in-car sound systems in the future. What kinds of messages might be given to the driver and passengers?

Controlled devices

If the output from a computer is to go to another machine rather than to a human, a controlling device is used instead of the usual output device. There are two main types of controlling device: relays and actuators. A **relay** is a switch that can be turned on or off by an electrical signal from the computer. This relay can then be used to control lights or motors, turning them on or off. An **actuator** is any device that results in a movement when it receives an electrical signal. It therefore transfers the electrical signal into a movement and makes something happen.

In control systems a variety of output devices are used:

- In a burglar alarm system the output may be an automatic telephone call to the police
- In a shop's security system a buzzer may sound if a customer tries to leave without paying for an item that still has a security tag on it

- In a fire alarm system the output may result in sprinklers being turned on
- In a greenhouse ventilation system the output may involve a window being opened or closed

It is not necessary for you to understand exactly how all specialist devices work, but you do need to know what type of device they are: input or output.

Exercise 3.12

List 10 different control systems and identify the controlling device being used.

OCR's and AQA's Unit 9 concentrates on monitoring and control systems, so at this stage you need only look at this topic briefly.

Input/output devices – memory and storage devices

Some devices are used for both input *and* output. These are called storage devices. Storage devices are an essential part of an IT system. There are two main types: internal and external devices.

- Internal devices – within the computer itself – are called **memory** devices
- External devices – connected to the computer by cables from the I/O ports – are called **storage** devices

Memory is where data is held. This data is made up of files, either program files or data files.

Did You Know?

Kb is short for kilobyte. Mb is short for megabyte. Gb is short for gigabyte. Tb is short for terabyte.

Memory is measured in bits (binary digits). One bit can hold 0 or 1. Bits are grouped into bytes (8 bits = 1 byte). A byte has enough bits to represent numbers from 1 to 256, and these are used to represent characters.

Exercise 3.13

How many bytes are there in a kilobyte? How many bytes are there in a megabyte? In a gigabyte? In a terabyte?

Did You Know?

Immediate-access memory is usually about 1000 times as fast as backing store.

Computer memory serves two purposes:

- To hold programs or data that the processor needs immediately – in the **immediate-access store (IAS)**
- To hold data that may be needed at some time – in the **backing store**

IAS memory must be able to read (and be written to) very quickly, but backup memory can have much slower reading and writing times.

The IAS memory is located very close to the processor, so that signals take the shortest possible time in coming from and going to the processor; but backing store can be in separate units connected to the processor by cables. Note that memory is different from storage:

- In memory, data is immediately available. This is the **primary** memory, but may also be called main memory, or the store.
- From storage, data has to be retrieved, e.g. from a floppy disk or the hard disk drive. This is called **secondary** storage, but is sometimes called offline storage, auxiliary store or – more usually – the **backing store**.

Portable
For files to be portable they are usually stored on a floppy disk or CD. The file can be output from one ICT system, and then input to another one. Nowadays, files may also be sent electronically from one system to another as files attached to an e-mail.

The **backing store** provides long-term storage on disk or tape, and when you **back up** your data files you do so on to a backing store. It is a permanent store on a device attached to the IT system, e.g. the hard disk, a Zip drive or a rewritable CD.

The auxiliary store allows you to access data files which are much larger than the capacity of your computer memory. It also allows data and programs to be **portable**, i.e. they can be moved from one computer to another.

Exercise 3.14

What device is used to backup your ICT system? What alternative devices could be used? What are the advantages and disadvantages of your backup system, compared with an alternative system?

Memory is either **volatile** or **non-volatile**. Temporary (RAM) and permanent (ROM) stores exist within the computer housing itself. The difference between them is the type of storage used:

- **Volatile** memory is a form of storage that holds data only while power is supplied. This is therefore a **temporary** store.
- **Non-volatile** memory keeps its contents even when the system is switched off. This **permanent memory** retains its contents regardless of power supply, and cannot be erased or altered.

All auxiliary stores (e.g. CDs, disks and tapes) are non-volatile and hence provide a permanent storage for data and programs. Some internal storage – read-only memory (ROM) – must also be permanent so that it can hold the operating system that you need on start-up. This information cannot be changed, and must not be lost when the power is turned off.

Some internal storage is temporary – random-access memory (RAM) – and this holds data which is used during the running of your programs, and which may change. RAM may be either **static**, which holds its memory while there is a power supply, or **dynamic**, which has to be refreshed by reading and rewriting the contents very frequently (about every 2 milliseconds). Dynamic RAM (DRAM) is more widely used than static RAM because it needs less power.

Because of the different requirements for these two functions of memory – permanent and temporary storage – completely different kinds of technology are used in a particular computer system. For IAS memory most computers use random-access memory integrated circuits (RAM ICs), in which very large amounts of data are stored in a single chip. For backing store, magnetic storage, such as disks or tapes, is used instead.

> **Did You Know?**
>
> IAS memory is sometimes in two parts. One part, the **cache** memory, is made up of a small-capacity but exceedingly fast memory and is located next to the processor.

Memory is often described by the type of **access** that is possible. For example:

- All the storage locations in IAS memory can be accessed directly and the access time for all locations is the same. Because all storage locations are equally quickly accessed, this is described as **random-access** memory (RAM)

- Data stored on a tape can only be reached by going through the tape, in sequence, until the right place is found; this is described as **serial access**
- Storage on a disk is in concentric rings and is a collection of small sequential lengths of storage. Because disk storage can be so quickly accessed, it is generally thought of as **direct (random)-access** storage.

Some memory, e.g. **ROM** (read-only memory) is **read-only**: it cannot be written to except during manufacture. This is used for both data and programs.

There are optical ROM systems and semiconductor (integrated circuit) ROM systems. Software in ROM is fixed during manufacture, but there are other ways of putting programs and data into ROM. Some chips are manufactured as a blank memory array that can have data 'programmed' into it at a later time (e.g. by exposure to ultraviolet radiation): these are called **PROMs** (programmable ROMs). One advantage is that some of these PROM chips can be reused.

Did You Know?

PROM chips are used for programs that control traffic lights or lifts, and for computer games programs.

When they were first introduced CD-Roms were (as the name suggests) read-only. Nowadays, recordable and rewritable CDs are available. **Write-once, read-many (WORM)** devices use a laser system to etch data on to a blank disk; the recorded data can then be read as often as needed, but cannot be rewritten.

Activity 3.10

For an ICT system that you use, compare the different types of storage for:

- ★ **storage capacity**
- ★ **read capability**
- ★ **write capability**
- ★ **cost**

Disk

A **magnetic disk**, usually made of plastic, is coated with a layer of magnetic material on which data can be stored by magnetically setting the arrangement of the magnetic material. This is done by electromagnetic read/write heads. To use disk storage, you need these two things:

- The **device** – the hardware machine to write to or read from the disk – which is called the **drive**
- The **medium** – the disk on which you write (or read from)

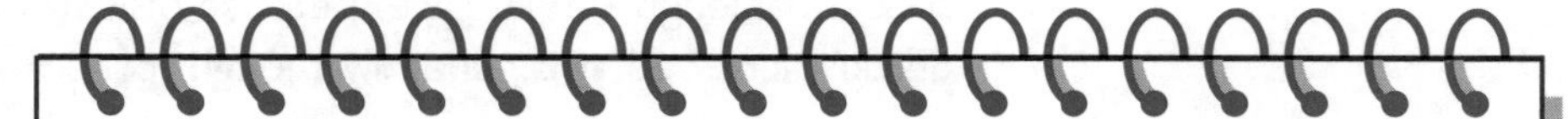

Peter Hawkes

Peter has an external CD drive and an external hard drive – for writing to 650 Mb CD (for archive purposes). He has a Zip drive for writing to a 100 Mb Zip disk – for backup and file transfer to clients. He also has a Syquest, but that is now relatively obsolete. For small files Peter uses floppy disks.

A **disk drive** is the device or unit made up of the mechanism that rotates the disks between the read/write heads, and the mechanism that controls these heads. Most disk drives have one set of read/write heads for each surface, which have to be moved to the required track. A disk unit with one set of heads for each disk track is called a **fixed-head disk unit**. This arrangement gives much faster access to data on the disk(s), but at increased cost.

A **hard disk drive** uses rigid magnetic disk(s) enclosed in a sealed container. It has the advantage of allowing high recording density because the recording heads can be very close to the magnetic material on the disk.

Floppy disk drives use flexible disks which can be removed from their drives by the user, unlike hard disks which are permanently mounted within the computer (Figure 3.13).

A **CD-Rom drive** (sometimes called a CD-Rom player) is very similar to an audio CD player and is used to read CD-Roms. A CD-Rom jukebox is a CD-Rom drive with a mechanism for automatically changing the current disk for another selected disk.

Disks may have data stored on one side only (single-sided) or on both sides (double-sided). The disk may be rigid (a hard disk) or flexible (a floppy disk). Where a disk drive has multiple disks (a disk pack) these are generally rigid hard disks on a common spindle, with read/write heads for each disk. If the disk pack is removable so that it can be exchanged for another complete pack, it is called an **exchangeable disk pack**.

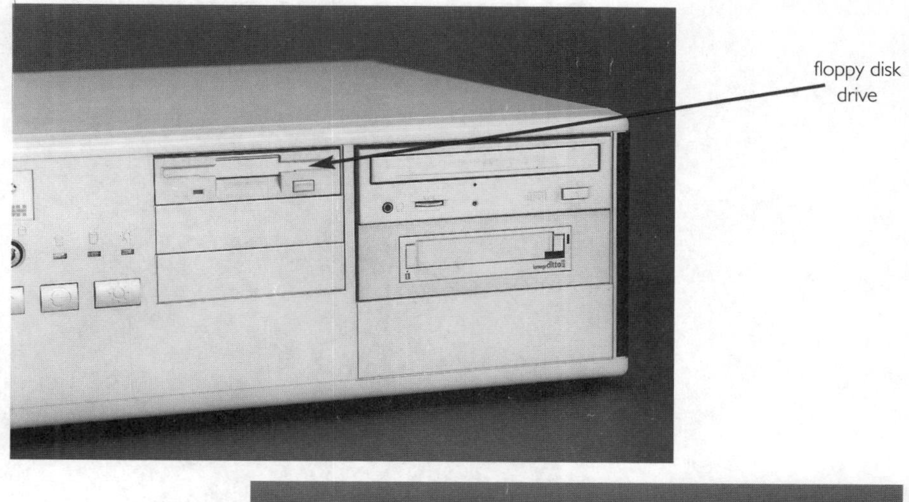

Figure 3.13 *Floppy and hard disk drive*

A **floppy disk** (sometimes called a diskette) is protected by an outer covering which prevents the magnetic coating from being damaged and keeps out dirt. Floppy disks are made to agreed standard designs and so can be used on any drive for the same size disk. The commonest size is 3½ inch, but the earlier 5¼ inch standard is also still used (Figure 3.14).

Floppy disks need to have some way of showing where the tracks start. In 5¼ inch disks this is done by an index hole – a small hole near the central hole – which lines up with a gap in the casing once every revolution. In 3½ inch disks it is only possible to fit the disk into the drive in one position.

Main processing unit

Data processing is the main objective of an ICT system and the processor is the most important part of the hardware. Programs are stored within the

Figure 3.14 *Types of floppy disks and a CD*

computer; they are run by the processor and data is processed to give the result required. Data, stored in memory and on backing storage devices, is processed by the main processing unit – also called the **central processing unit** (CPU) – and this processing may involve calculations, sorting records into an order or searching for a particular record.

The **CPU** controls every piece of hardware attached to it, and all software running in it (Figure 3.15).

- **It controls the running of software programs**
- **It controls the movement of data to and from peripherals**
- **It does all calculations and all tests, and makes all decisions**
- **It controls the timing of the machine**

The ability of a CPU is measured in terms of its speed of processing: the faster the processor, the more powerful the system. The amount of memory (RAM and ROM – see page 183–5) is also important. Generally speaking, the more powerful machines are more expensive, although as time passes newer machines are far more powerful than their predecessors and yet the prices do not rise at the same rate.

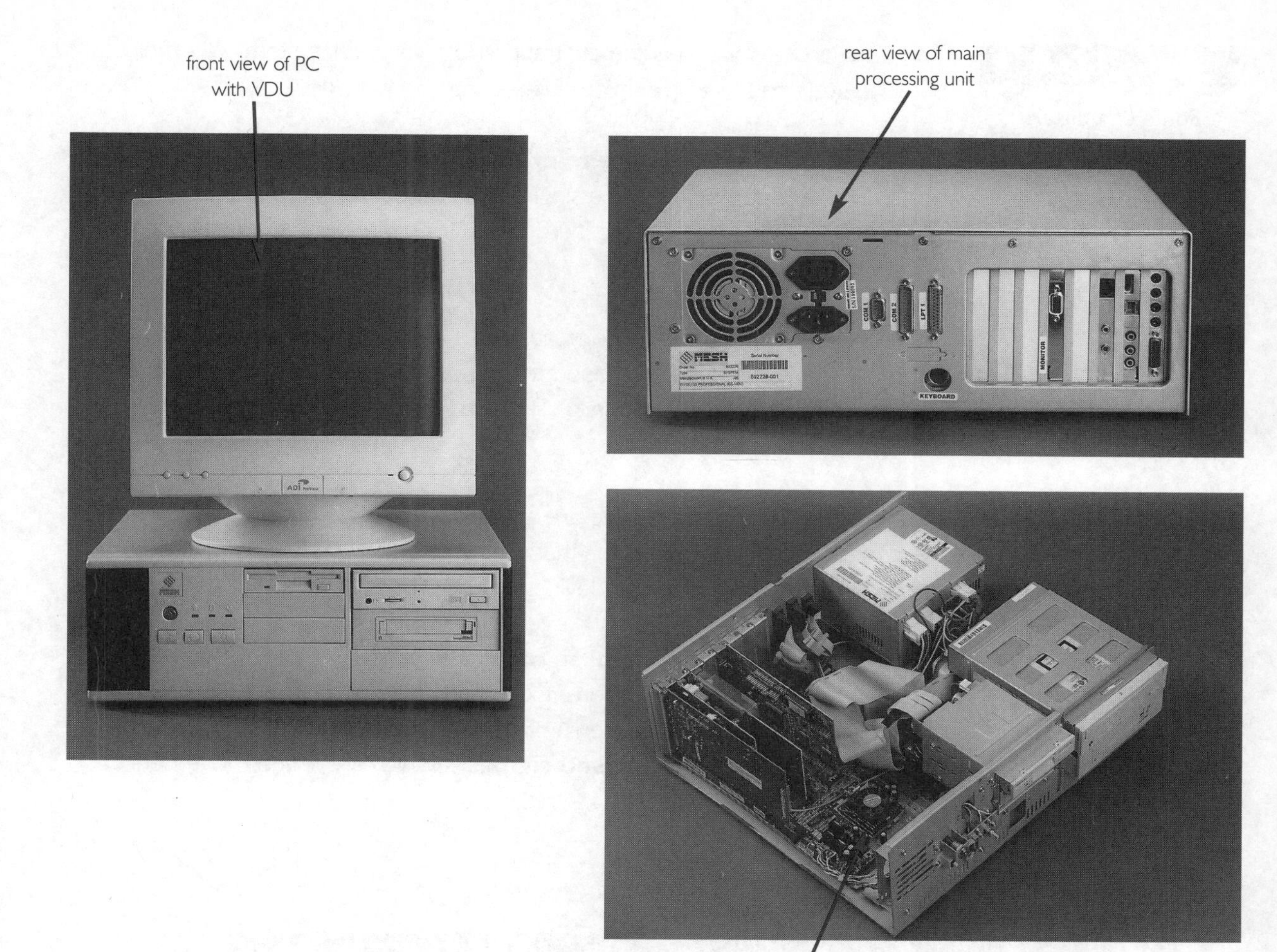

Figure 3.15 *Front, rear and inside views of a typical PC*

Sailing Breaks

John Hore's ICT system is based on a Pentium III processor.

The main processing unit contains the decision-making part of the ICT system:

- **Central processing unit (CPU)**
- **Memory (RAM** and **ROM)**
- **Ports** (input and output connectors)
- **Motherboard**

Did You Know?

Some computers have more than one processor.

The main processor unit is the central part of every ICT system. All other items are referred to as **peripherals** – things on the side.

One special form of CPU is the **microprocessor,** in which the components of the CPU are combined into a single unit. Microprocessors are used in microcomputers and computerised devices, for example the control circuits of washing machines.

Additional devices are required for networks and to provide access to the Internet. These devices are needed to support communications. Examples are the network card and the modem. These are usually fitted inside the main processing unit.

At the back of a computer there are a number of **ports** (Figure 3.16). These are connection points or sockets that allow the internal circuits of a computer to be connected to peripheral devices, e.g. a printer.

The output ports allow **control signals** to be sent from the computer, and different kinds of port allow different kinds of signals (continuous or pulsed) along different types of cable (serial or parallel). **Continuous signals** are sent in a steady voltage stream; **pulsed signals** – which allow fine movement

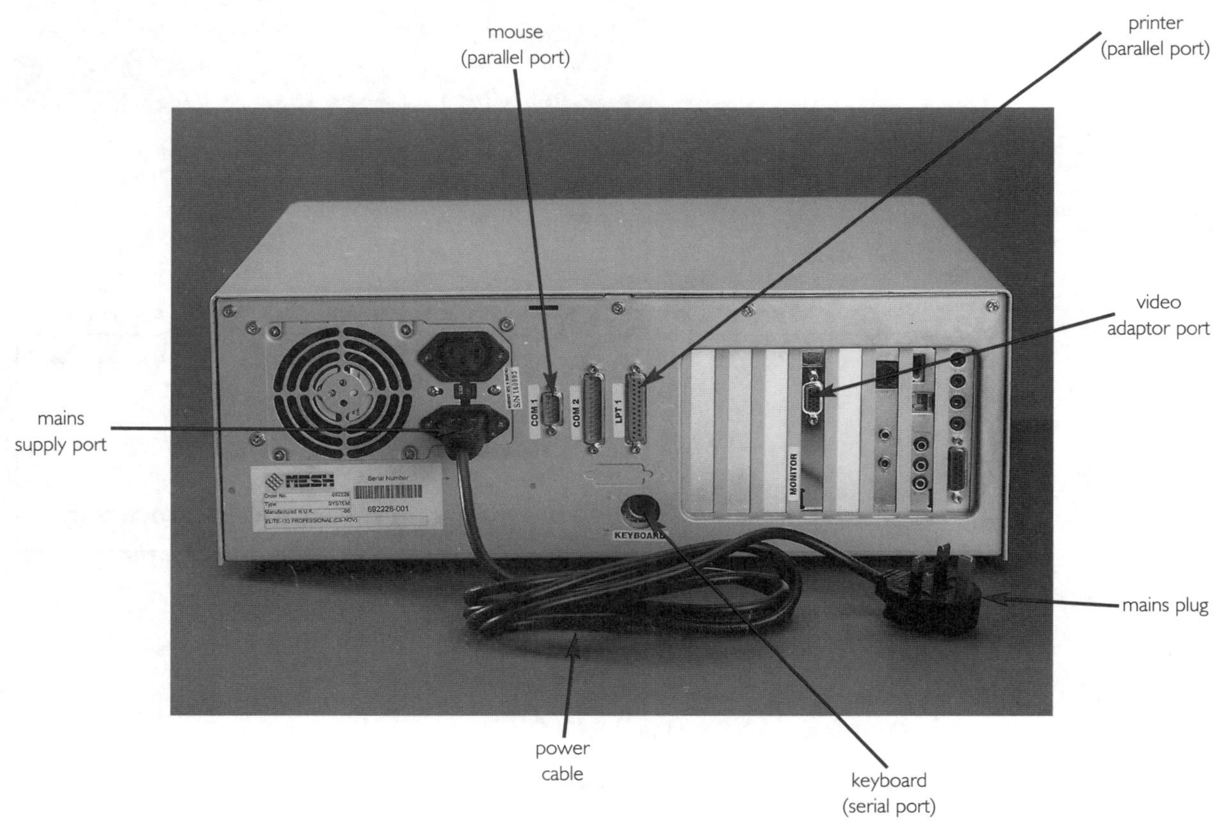

Figure 3.16 Ports in the back of a typical PC

> **Did You Know?**
>
> On the latest PCs ports are coloured, as are the connectors on the cables, so that matching the correct cable to the correct port – red to red, blue to blue – is easier.

control, e.g. of a robot arm – are sent as a series of signals broken by gaps in time.

A **printer port** is the connection point for a printer. Within the computer an interface provides the electronic link between the processor and the printer. When the computer prints, a **software utility** called a **printer driver** changes the font and layout codes used in the computer into a form that the printer understands. Although several different printers may use the same port, each one may require a different driver.

Exercise 3.15

Make a list of the printers that are connected to the systems you use (at school, home and work). Which ones are serial printers? Which are parallel printers? What printer drivers are available?

Cables and connectors

There are two main types of cable: serial and parallel. **Serial** cables can only take one bit of information at a time; **parallel** cable looks like a ribbon and can take several bits of information at the same time. Parallel connections allow faster information transfer.

Wire is a standard form of cable used to provide the connections in a network.

- **Copper cables** tend to be used in local area networks (LANs), since they are readily available and have suitable electrical characteristics
- **Coaxial cable** is the same kind of cable that is used for connecting a TV aerial to a TV set. It has two conductors: one wire down the centre of the cable, which may be a single strand, insulated from a second wire which is made up of many strands braided around the insulation for the inner wire.
- **Twisted pair (TP) cable** is a pair of insulated copper wires twisted together and surrounded by a copper braid and external insulation. Used in the correct situation, these cables provide minimum interference data transmission. **Unshielded twisted pair (UTP)** is similar to the twisted pair cables described above, but has no earth shield.
- **Fibreoptic cable** (or optical fibre) – a very fine glass strand –

allows rapid data transmission using light beams. Fibreoptic cable provides interference-free, secure data transmission and, unlike metal wires, will not corrode.

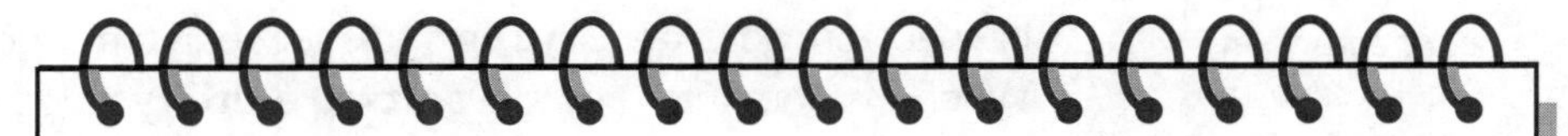

Sailing Breaks

John Hore's BT Home Highway connection gives him two high-speed data connections for the Internet plus two analogue lines, one for voice and the other for fax.

Software

The software – the elements of the system that are not hardware – is what makes the ICT system do what you, the user, want it to do.

All makes of computers are different, and the manufacturers design them to have different features. This is a good selling point for the manufacturer, but means that each type of computer has different software needs. However, all ICT systems have these four types of software:

- **BIOS** (start up)
- **Operating systems**
- **Programming languages**
- **Applications software**

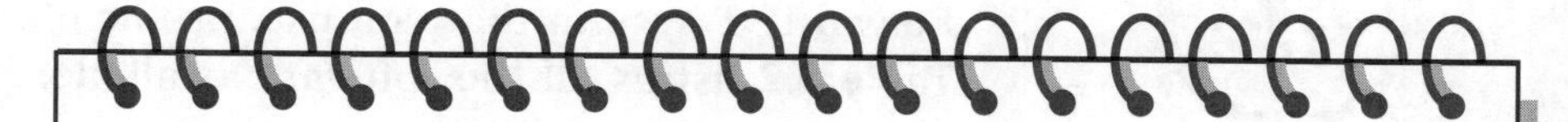

Hawkes Design

Peter has two Apple Macintosh computers – as used by most graphic designers. The latest model is the G4, but Peter has the G3 (1999) and a PowerMac 8500/180 from 1996. Table 3.2 shows the software Peter Hawkes has on his system.

Type of software	*Software installed on Peter Hawke's system*
Operating systems	Mac OS8.5
Applications software	Quark XPress – for page layout and design, typography Adobe Illustrator – for line graphs, diagrams and charts Adobe Photoshop – for image manipulation, dealing with scanned images Microsoft Word – for text editing, translating text from PCs Xerox Textbridge – for OCR Adobe Streamline – for translating bitmap images to vector graphics Binuscan Photoperfect – for automatic colour balancing of scanned images Adobe Acrobat – for creating PDF files for transfer to various computer systems

Table 3.2 *Software on Peter Hawkes' system*

Sailing Breaks

John Hore uses a Windows ICT system: Windows 98 with MS Office – Word for writing and Excel for accounting. He also has Publisher 98, which is used to design brochures and his website.

To scan in graphics John has Corel Photo House 2, and for scanning OCR documents he uses OmniPage Pro 10.

Exercise 3.16

For an ICT system that you use, produce a table similar to Table 3.2 listing all the software available.

BIOS (start-up)

BIOS
stands for basic input–output system.

The BIOS is the part of the operating system that handles all the input and output of the computer. It is stored on ROM, and so is available as soon as the computer is switched on (at start-up).

On power-up a **boot-strapping** procedure is actioned. The main operating system (like DOS – disk-operating system) is loaded as part of this procedure, and then the user interface (such as Windows) is activated. Communication with the user is then via this interface.

During start-up two files are used:

- **CONFIG.SYS** contains information about the hardware connected to the system, e.g. which language the user wants to use
- **AUTOEXEC.BAT** is a special purpose batch file which, when executed, loads the various software, e.g. it sets the keyboard as

being UK, and initialises a sound card before activating Windows. The batch file contains basic start-up commands that help to configure the system of installed devices and thus suits the user.

At start-up the system knows what kind of mouse you are using, what type of monitor etc.

During start-up there is also a self-test to make sure all hardware, including peripherals, is working properly.

Depending on how a system is set up, some of the commands that are executed during start-up are displayed on the screen.

Activity 3.11

Next time you turn on a computer, watch the screen very carefully. Note the commands that appear on the screen, if any. Ask the technician responsible for your computer system (or your teacher) to explain what the messages mean.

Operating system

Each ICT system is controlled by its operating system. Without an operating system the computer can do very little. The operating system – a program resident in the computer (usually, at least in part, in ROM) – is built from lots of small programs, each of which controls some part of the hardware. Together, these programs allow the operator to use the computer. Operating systems are very complex, even those that control a simple standalone computer.

There are two main types of operating system: **command-driven** and those with a **graphic user interface (GUI)**.

- With a command-driven operating system all communication with the user – the man–machine interface, or human–computer interface (HCI) – is done by the user entering commands via the keyboard
- With a GUI the user is presented with a screen on which icons appear: communication will include the keyboard for text input, but a mouse is used most of the time, especially for selecting options. This is called a **WIMP environment**.

WIMP
stands for window, icon, mouse, pointer.

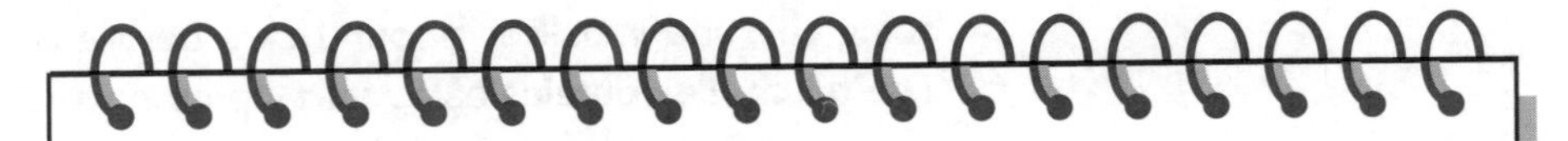

Sailing Breaks

John Hore works in a WIMP environment.

Chris Lane

The networked computers at Chris Lane – 30 in total – are running under Windows 98. There are three main systems in operation: Microcache (a database to track membership) which operates under DOS, ACT 4.0 (a sales database used to ensure smooth processing of potential members through their induction programme) and Sage Sovereign (an accounting package used to control all monies coming in and going out of the club). However, a Windows-based upgrade of the Microcache software is now available, so plans are afoot to replace the current software with more up-to-date systems. These will provide more integrated systems, which will improve the day-to-day efficiency of the Chris Lane team.

Activity 3.12

Find out which type of operating system is used on your computer. Use your computer system and another which has the other type of operating system.

- ★ For a command-driven operating system, list some commands that are used and explain their effect.
- ★ For a system with a GUI, copy some of the icons that are presented on the screen and explain what happens when you select them.

Which type of operating system do you prefer to use? Why? Discuss this with others in your group.

Did You Know?

When you change something on the control panel (to customise your PC), the system automatically amends the CONFIG.SYS file (and other initialisation files used during start-up) so that the change is 'permanent' (until you change it again, of course!). When you install a program, e.g. virus detection software, the software automatically amends your AUTOEXEC.BAT file so that virus detection is enabled every time you switch on the computer.

Table 3.3 lists the main functions of an operating system.

Function	***Purpose***
Start-up	Checking that all the peripherals are working and properly connected
Security	Logging on procedures, controlling user access, checking passwords
Communication	Receiving commands from the user (e.g. from the keyboard), displaying messages to the user (e.g. on the screen)
Control of peripherals	Sending data to a printer and communicating with the printer so that all data is printed, even though the printer and computer work at different speeds
Control of memory	Keeping track of what is held on a disk by updating the disk directory
Error control	Checking data on entry and displaying messages if anything is wrong, e.g. a letter keyed into a numeric field

Table 3.3 *The main functions of an operating system.*

Default values are the values assumed by the manufacturer when you first buy an ICT system, e.g. the language which you will expect to use, and the type of hardware you will connect to the computer. These default values can be **customised** to suit the user.
Configuration of an ICT system is the combination of hardware and software used.

Exercise 3.17

Make a list of operating systems currently on the market. Which ones are for standalone ICT systems? Which ones are for networked ICT systems?

Configuring/customising an operating system

When an operating system is first installed a number of settings are preset at **default values**, and one of these is the **configuration**.

If the system assumes a standard keyboard, standard mouse etc., and the user wants to use a special mouse or a higher-resolution screen, telling the operating system this is called **configuring**. (Some of the lastest operating systems can do this automatically.)

Other default values relate to how the interface between the user and the

Customising an operating system means making decisions about how you want it to present information to you, i.e. controlling the user interface.

Password is a word or code that a user keeps secret, and is used to gain access to an ICT system.

machine will operate, e.g. the background colour on the screen, or security options such as passwords.

All operating systems also allow the user to **customise** settings, i.e. to set up new default settings which will apply every time the system is powered up:

- Set up security passwords
- Include antivirus checks
- Change the screen prompts or desktop appearance
- Decide mouse settings (speed, pointer style)
- Set up directory structures (folders)
- Provide icons or menus to start software and open specific files
- Select appropriate printer drivers

Did You Know?

On some systems it is possible to include the user's name on printouts. This is particularly helpful if the workstations are situated in a different room from the printers and everyone is sending output to the printer.

It is unlikely that you would have access to your school, college or work facility to set up **security passwords**! However, if you have your own ICT system at home, this may be one of the first things you would do.

If a system is used by more than one person, each person can be assigned a unique **user ID** (identity number). A record can then be kept of who has used the ICT system.

It makes a lot of sense to include **antivirus checks** on an ICT system.

Sometimes **viruses** are date dependent, i.e. they have no effect until a certain date, and then they activate, for example filling your screen with daft messages or images.

Virus is a program that is designed to copy itself, so that the end result is the failure (crash) of an ICT system.

Viruses can infect your ICT system if you allow them to be introduced. They transfer from machine to machine via disk files, so if you accept a floppy disk from someone else that disk may be infected.

Exercise 3.18

Find out what antivirus software is used on your school or college system.

What is a 'parasitic virus'? What is a 'worm'?

The BCS Glossary is a useful source of information about ICT terms.

Antivirus software is produced to prevent virus infection. It scans files and warns you if a virus is found. It can then try to 'clean' the disk file. New viruses are being invented all the time, and so the virus protection industry is thriving.

If you like, you can change the screen prompts or **desktop appearance** of your system. You may decide it is useful to have a clock and today's date visible on your screen at all times. In the latest systems you can arrange for today's newspaper to appear (downloaded from the Internet) as soon as you power up.

Activity 3.13

Explore the options available to you to change the desktop appearance on your ICT system. Make notes on the options and list the current default values.

Mouse settings such as the speed at which the pointer moves across the screen (and keyboard reaction times), can be controlled, usually using the Control Panel Utility.

Exercise 3.19

Find out the current default value for the mouse speed on your ICT system.

Activity 3.14

Change the mouse settings so that the right and left buttons are interchanged. Use the mouse like this, and then change the settings back to how they were originally. Find out what 'pointer style' is used. Does your system allow you to change this?

Quite soon after using an ICT system for the first time the number of files increase to the point that, unless you set up **directory structures** (folders) you will have great difficulty in finding anything at all. The structure is like a tree, except that it is upside down! At the top there is the **root directory**. Beneath this, the first level of files or **subdirectories** leads on to further subdirectories.

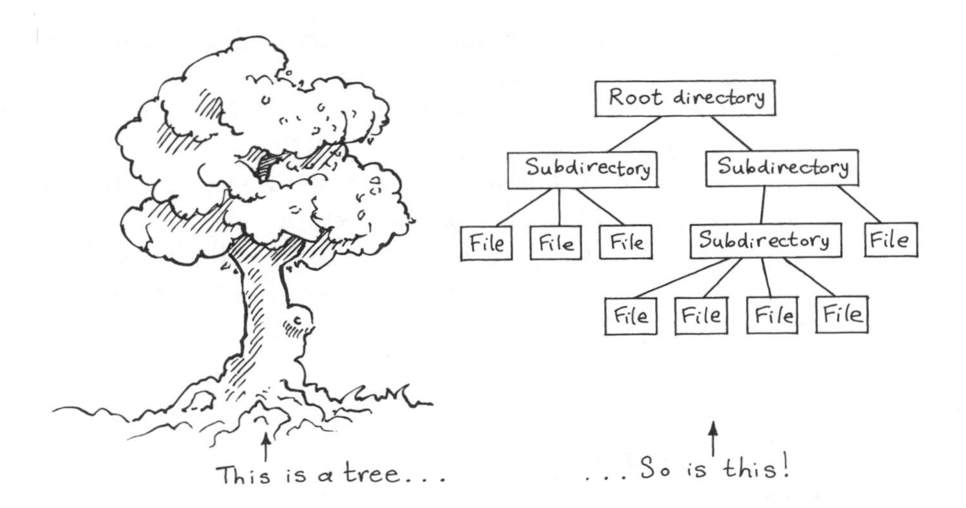

Activity 3.15

Find out what directories already exist on your ICT system. Find out how to create a new directory (folder).

When installing new applications software in a WIMP environment, often the software automatically provides icons or menus to start the software and open specific files. This then allows you, as the user, to just click on the icon to start the software.

Exercise 3.20

Identify icons that automatically start software applications.

Activity 3.16

Find out how many different ways you could start an application *without* using the icons provided.

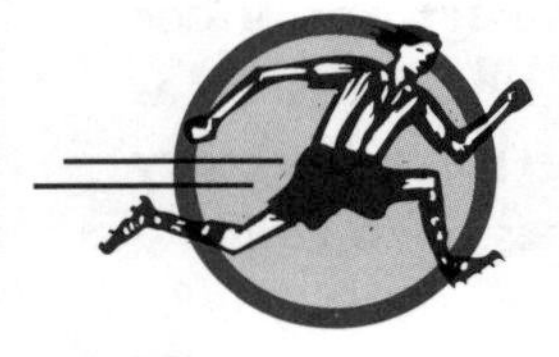

> Your online help may offer several ways of starting software.

As noted on page 191, all printers may connect to the printer port on an ICT system, but you have to select an appropriate printer driver so that the codes sent by the computer are understood correctly by the printer.

Activity 3.17

Find out which printer drivers are available on your ICT system.

- ★ **Choose a one-page document (or one page from a longer document) that includes more than one font.**
- ★ **Change the printer driver for a completely different make of printer and print the document.**
- ★ **Change the printer driver to one for the same make of printer but for a different model and see what effect that has on printing a document.**

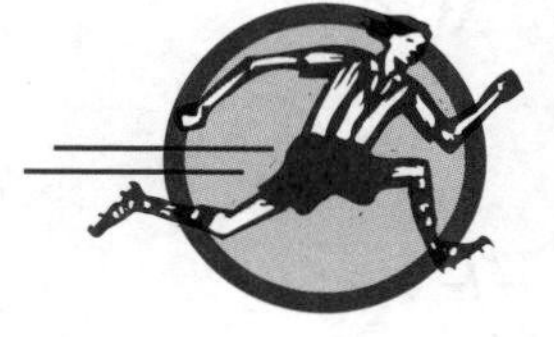

Changing to an 'older' or 'newer' driver than your actual printer may produce interesting effects.

Activity 3.18

With a particular user in mind, describe basic specifications for input and output devices, the main processing unit, and software and configuration requirements to meet your user's needs by identifying their purpose and properties.

For a different user, provide detailed definitions of input and output devices and accurate descriptions of the main processing unit, software and configuration requirements to meet this second user's needs, including their purpose and properties.

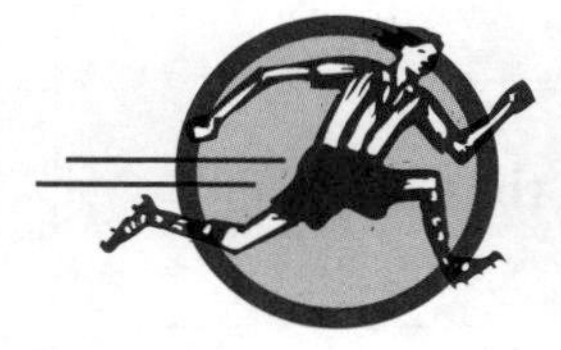

Choose your two users to be as different as possible. Choose people whose jobs – and hence their day-to-day use of ICT – are very different, even if they are in a similar industry: e.g. someone on the move all day, such as a reporter, and someone based in an office or at home, e.g. an author.

Programming languages

In the same way that English people speak to each other in English, and French people use French, computer users 'speak' to a computer in a **computer language**.

Although we are promised that, before long, we will be able to talk to a computer rather than using the keyboard, that technology is not quite up to speed yet.

Meanwhile, all instructions given to a computer are written in a computer language.

Exercise 3.21

Make a list of all the programming languages that are available to you.

Hot link
is a function key (or a combination of keys) which, when pressed, make something happen straight away. They are called 'hot' to stress the urgency of the action.

Wizard
is a feature of online help which takes you step by step through a complex procedure, asking you questions along the way, so that the net result is exactly what you want without all the headaches of doing things from scratch.

In this chapter you will do a little bit of 'programming', creating pages of information to be browsed using **hot links** (page 209), and writing **macros** to automate actions in applications software (page 216).

For both of these you can use **wizards**, so you will not have to learn the programming languages at all. However, Unit 11 is dedicated to programming, so if you enjoy writing programs, Unit 11 will give you lots of practical experience.

Applications software

Once the computer has an operating system, you can load applications software to do a particular task, such as word processing or payroll.

There are various types of application software to meet user needs:

- **Document (word) processing**, and **desktop publishing (DTP)**
- **Databases**, **spreadsheets** and **graphics**
- **Programming languages**, and **utilities** such as **virus checkers**
- **Communications software** such as **e-mail**
- Personal organisers and other accessories

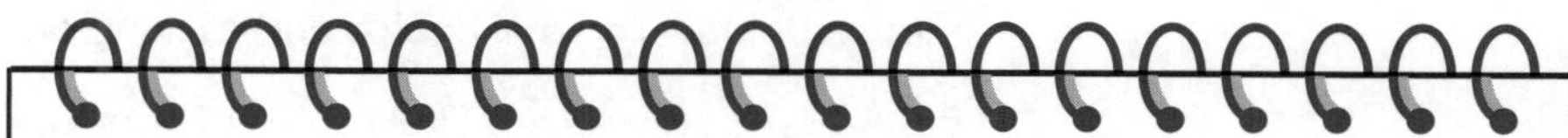

Hawkes Design

Peter Hawkes has several applications packages (see Table 3.2 on page 194).

Chris Lane

For the management team at Chris Lane, PCs are provided with Microsoft Office 97 using Windows 98. They use Excel spreadsheet software, and Microsoft Outlook for e-mail. The Internet is used extensively to keep up to date with current legislation, e.g. on health and safety, and for research into possible opportunities for development.

Did You Know?

When you buy an application you must choose a version that runs on your particular IT system, including your operating system. These are called **platforms**.

Many of these applications are considered elsewhere in this course:

- Unit 1 includes presentation of information using word processing
- Unit 2 introduces spreadsheets and databases
- Unit 6 looks at graphics and DTP

Other units concentrate on single applications like **multimedia**, spreadsheets for numerical **modelling** and databases. So, you will have lots of opportunities to use applications software during your course.

You must learn how to match applications software to users' processing needs. For this, you need to recognise the main features of the applications. *All* applications share these features:

- Programs are grouped to form a **package** or suite of programs which together perform a particular function, e.g. invoicing or database management
- A manufacturer of software will tend to use the same operating methods for all their software, which makes it easier for a user to learn new packages – the emphasis is on **user-friendly software**
- Most software packages are **menu driven**: you might select using arrow keys and pressing enter, or by pressing the initial letter of your choice (P for print, S for save, and so on) or by moving the mouse pointer to your choice and clicking on it
- DOS-based software is likely to use **functions keys** or **multiple keystrokes** to make special things happen; Windows-based software will involve using the **mouse** to click, or double click, on **icons**
- **On-screen help** will be available, so if you get stuck you can press the help key and find out what to do next

Table 3.4 lists the applications and gives brief details of their particular features.

Application	***Features***
Document (word) processing	Processes text; features include 'find and replace', spellcheck and grammar check; styles allow consistent presentation; choice of fonts (typefaces and point sizes)
Desktop publishing (DTP)	Integrates text and images to create paged layouts
Databases	Record-structured data; relational databases allow links between tables; sorting of records based on key fields; searching of records to match a criteria; selection of fields to present in a report
Spreadsheets	Number-structured database; rows and columns of cells; cells contain text, number, a formula or blank; formulae allow automatic calculations; what if? queries
Graphics	Creation of images; editing; bit map and vector graphics
Programming languages	Facilities to write programs
Utilities such as virus checkers	Standalone applications that can be enabled to run while you work
Communication	Uses modem link (or ISDN line) for e-mail and Internet connection; can send/download files to/from other computers
Personal organisers	Standalone applications designed to make everyday working easier; diary, clock, calendar etc.

Table 3.4 *Features of applications software*

Customising applications software

In the same way that operating systems can be customised, so too can applications software.

Users often know little about their applications software. To enable your users to make immediate and effective use of the software, you must be able to customise it to meet their needs:

- Setting spelling and grammar checks
- **Setting/modifying default templates** and creating simple macros
- Setting backup method/timing
- Setting suitable printer drivers

- Setting display parameters, toolbar display and layout, including scrollbars and status bars
- Setting use of key-operated commands and macros
- Setting default file locations

When applications software is first installed the manufacturer's default setting will apply. So, for example, the **default language** may be English (USA). If you want to use the spelling and grammar checks you need to ensure that these are changed to the language you are actually using – probably English (UK) – otherwise the spellchecker will not trap all the errors you would like it to, and it may flag words which you think are correctly spelt.

Activity 3.19

- ★ Key these two sentences into a blank document (mistakes included!):

  The colour chosen for this organisation's logo are grey. The design was modelled using graphic softwear.
- ★ Perform a spellcheck and note any words that are flagged as incorrect (but do not change them).
- ★ Change the language from English (UK) to English (USA) – or vice versa, depending on your current setting.
- ★ Perform another spellcheck. Compare the results with the previous spellcheck.
- ★ Which words were rejected by both?
- ★ What words were accepted in one language but not in the other?
- ★ Were all errors flagged?
- ★ Does the grammar checker (for either language) find the grammatical error?

Backup
is a separate copy of a file – usually stored away from the computer, in a fireproof safe.

Setting/modifying default templates is covered in Chapter 1, and **creating simple macros** is covered elsewhere in this chapter (page 216).

Backups are discussed on pages 90 and 183.

It is important to schedule backups so that possible data loss is minimised. Backups should be taken regularly, e.g. at the end of each day or week. Your

Autosave is an option to resave your files regularly. It overwrites the current version of your file. An **archive** copy of files is taken when they are no longer needed on an ICT system. They are simply put to one side, but are available should anyone need to retrieve them.

backup utility should allow you to schedule these to take place at the same time, e.g. at 5 pm every Wednesday. Your backup utility may also offer options like 'new and changed files' only. This means that only material that has been worked on since the last backup will be backed up, and this will not take very long. Full backups may take an hour or more, and may disrupt normal working. If there is a disaster and you need to recover or **restore** backup files, your software should provide this option and lead you through the necessary steps.

Regular saving of your work is also sensible, and the timing should reflect how quickly you make changes and how crucial the text is to you.

Exercise 3.22

What is the difference between autosaving and backing up?

Printer drivers are discussed on page 201 and explored in Activity 3.17.

Display parameters control the choices you make about what appears on your screen. These include the enlargement (zoom control), show/hide of paragraph marks, toolbars, scrollbars, etc.

Activity 3.20

- **Compare the display options available on at least two applications.**
- **How do you switch on/off the show/hide option? What is the benefit of having this on?**
- **Change the enlargement from 100% to 50%. What is the benefit of this option?**
- **Explore the Options menu to discover what default options are current.**

It will speed up processing, e.g. editing text, if you customise applications software by setting up key-operated commands and macros. **Macros** are discussed on page 216, and the method for setting up key-operated commands is dealt with at the same time because they are so similar.

When applications software is installed, often a **default file location** (directory or folder) setting specifies where all documents created by that application are to be filed. It may suit you to save your files in a different location. If so, changing this default setting will save you having to respecify the desired location every time you save a file.

Activity 3.21

★ Explore one software application to find out what default settings exist.

★ Check another application to see if the same settings are in operation.

★ Find out how to change the default setting for saving files.

When the operating system and applications software is configured to suit user needs, you must test that it works. A typical test will include these stages:

- Power up
- Use the operating system
- Access the application software
- Use the macros and templates you have created
- Enter and save information
- Retrieve and print information

Activity 3.22

★ With a particular user in mind, configure the operating system and applications software appropriately to meet the user's needs.

★ Fully test your system, producing actual screen prints.

★ Annotate your screen prints accurately and clearly to show how you configured the operating system and software.

Computer programming

Most computer users never write programs; they do not need to because commercially available software helps them to do what they want. The main advantage of programming, though, is the control it can give you. For this unit you will learn about two particular purposes of programming:

- **To display pages of information that can be browsed using hot links – for this you will use hypertext mark-up language (HTML)**
- **To automate actions in applications software using macros – for this you will use a macro programming language (available in most application software).**

You will use automated techniques to create program code, and then look at and make minor modifications to the code created.

HTML programs

Hypertext systems provide what may seem to be a rather unstructured way of browsing through or searching for information. Each 'page' of information may be linked to one or more other pages. In a similar way, a cross-reference on this page may suggest you look at more information on page 72, for example. All the pages in the book are numbered so you can leaf through until you find the right one. In a hypertext system the pages are screens, and if you click on a **hot spot** (a cross-reference) the system jumps to another page. This is much quicker than leafing through a book!

> **Hot links**
> are used to jump from one page in a hypertext system to another.
> Clicking on the **hot spot** jumps you to the new page.

Hot links may be highlighted text which, when the cursor moves near it, turns the cursor into a hand pointing at the text. Hot links may also be buttons, on which you can write a message, or buttons with standard symbols (like arrow left, meaning go back to the previous page).

Activity 3.23

Visit a web page and notice any hot-link buttons that offer you the option of moving to another page. What is written on these buttons? What happens to the cursor when you get close to a button?

Home page
is the first page that you see for any particular website. It should be like a contents page, offering the user a route to the other pages within that website.

Hit
each time you visit a website it is noted as a **hit**.

Penhaven

If you visit the Penhaven website (http://www.penhaven.co.uk) the **home page** offers you a choice of visiting four other pages: Penhaven, Directions, Tariff and Specials. Notice that the text on the Penhaven buttons is in a particular font.

Altogether, there are five pages on this website. Each one gives you the option of moving to any of the others, so all are fully interlinked.

Notice also that the home page records how many **hits** this page has had.

Tag
within a web page is a special instruction that controls how the next piece of text appears (e.g. its point size), or inserts a picture, or jumps to another page.

HTML (hypertext mark-up language) is a computer language used to create multimedia pages for a hypertext system, such as those on the Internet. Each page consists of text and **tags**.

The text can be prepared using a number of different applications, e.g. a word processing package or a desktop publishing package.

Activity 3.24

- ★ Find out which applications have the option to save material as web pages.
- ★ Choose one of these applications and create two pages which will be used as your web pages.
- ★ Save them as web pages.
- ★ Check how the same process would be done using another application. Is one any easier to use than the other? If so, why?

At this stage, any two pages of text will do (see Figure 3.18, on page 212). Later, you will design pages.

Did You Know?

Some more modern versions of software applications, e.g. PowerPoint, have the option SAVE AS WEB PAGE. This creates the HTML language automatically.

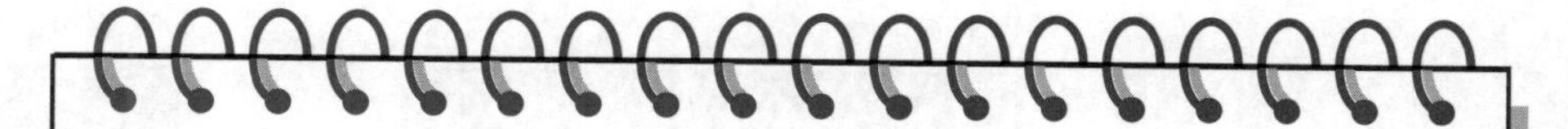

Sailing Breaks

John Hore used Publisher 98 to create his web pages (Figure 3.17).

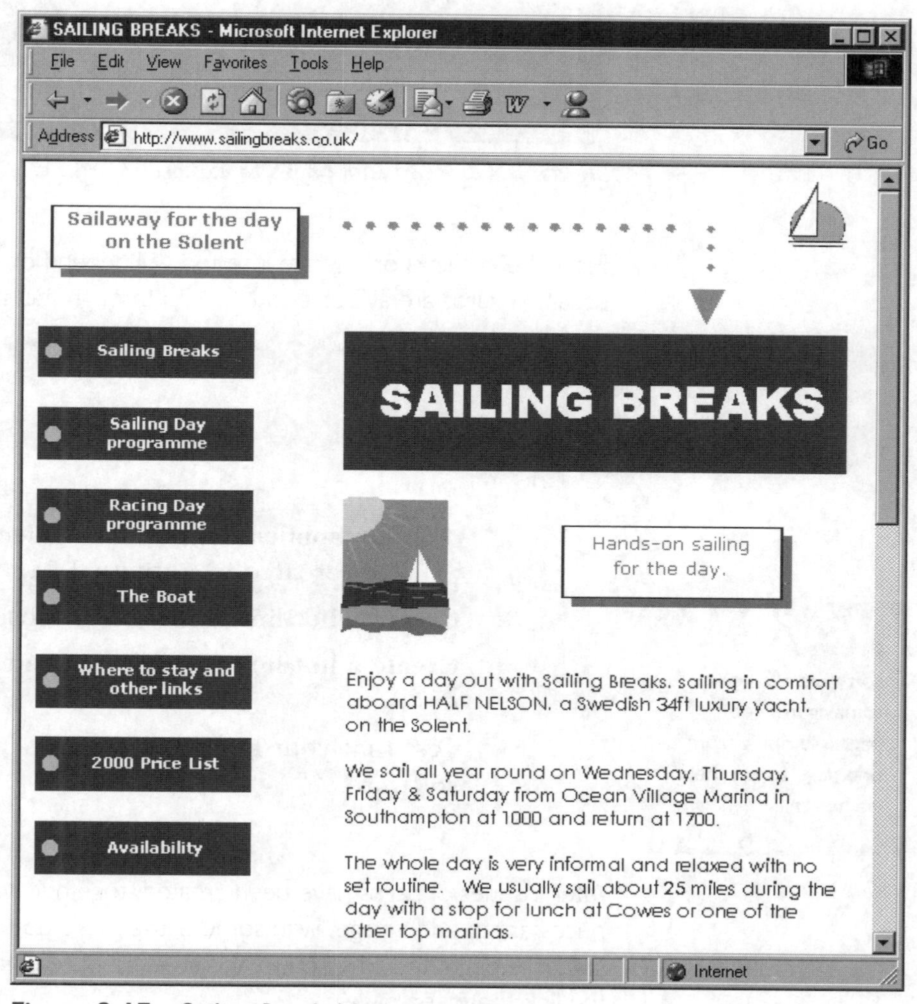

Figure 3.17 *Sailing Breaks' home page*
Courtesy of John Hore, Sailing Breaks

Page 1 – Home Page

Page 2

Figure 3.18 *Two trial pages to explore HTML*

How the hot links or tags are inserted will depend on your software, but usually wizards are available to take you through this step by step.

Activity 3.25

- ★ In an application of your choice, retrieve the two pages created in Activity 3.24.
- ★ Create a hot link from the first page to the second.
- ★ Create a hot link from the second page back to the first.
- ★ Test that your hot links work by using **browser** software.

Browser software allows you to navigate web pages, jumping from one page to another via hot links.

After a series of pages have been created, together with their links, it may be necessary to add a page, with some extra, more up-to-date information. Your software ought to allow you to add an extra page of information, and to amend the links between pages.

- ★ Retrieve the two pages created in Activity 3.25.
- ★ Create a third page.
- ★ Change the links so that page 1 links to 2 and 3, page 2 links to page 3, and page 3 links to page 1 (see Figure 3.19).
- ★ Test that your hot links work by using browser software.

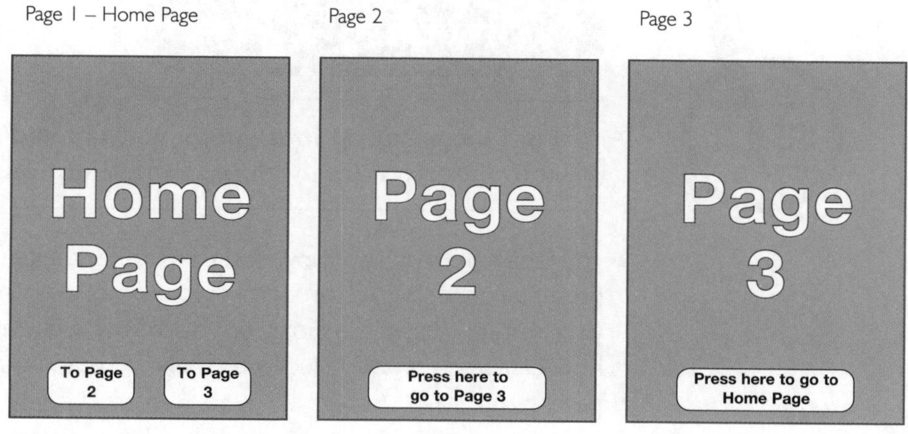

Figure 3.19 *A three-page linked design*

Hypertext systems can be used to display text and graphics, and may play sound files. For this you may find a multimedia authoring application is most useful, but other applications may also allow you to embed sound sequences.

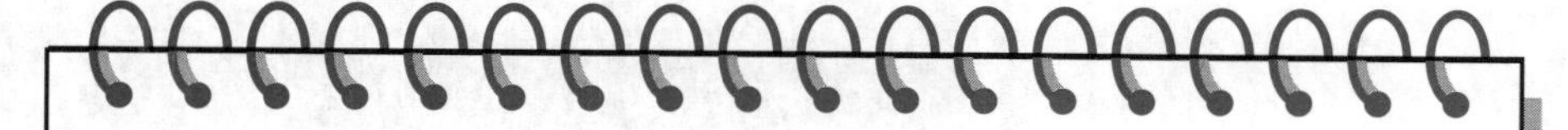

Sailing Breaks

John Hore's web pages include a picture of his yacht *Half Nelson*, and himself – looking a bit windswept!

Activity 3.27

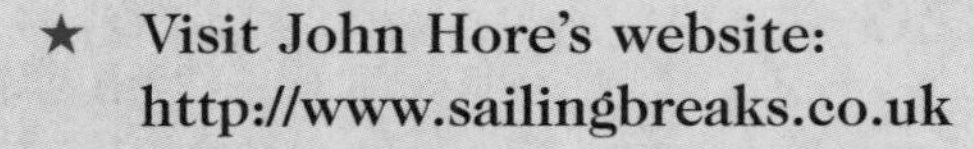

- ★ Visit John Hore's website: http://www.sailingbreaks.co.uk
- ★ Navigate all the pages and test out that all the hot links work. Notice that John has used icons, e.g. the sun shining behind a cloud, to brighten up his web pages.
- ★ Visit one or two of the other sites that his website recommends to you.

Exercise 3.23

Find out what options you have to include graphics, sound and pictures into a web page presentation.

Your software may also allow you to do other things that would improve the presentation, and if you are keen to do some 'real' programming you may find your software has the options for you to use VisualBasic. In a similar way to how database reports include **controls**, you can place controls on your web pages.

Activity 3.28

Make a note of the best and worst sites that you visit. Compare notes with others in your group. What makes a 'good' site? What makes a poor site?

The Red Letter Day site at http://www.redletterdays.co.uk is particularly colourful (red!), but the design is simple and yet very effective. This website uses a flashing and alternating message which is eye-catching. Because the design is so simple, this site also downloads very quickly. You might also decide that you want to include the number of hits (like Penhaven). For complexity of information you can look at almost any site! Most banks have sites which are packed with messages and flashing boxes.

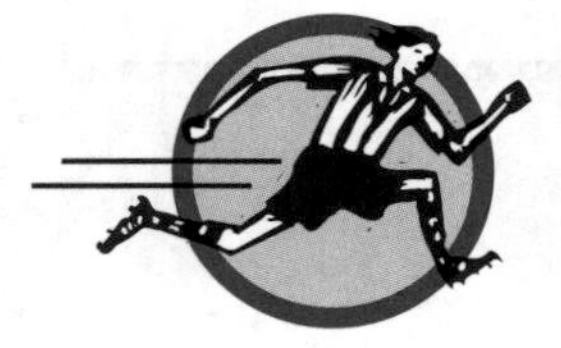

Activity 3.29

- Working within the software available to you, plan a multipage presentation with several linked HTML pages of information to suit a particular audience.
- Decide what information you will present on each page, and what links you will need between pages.
- Sketch your basic design for the HTML program and create suitable text, images, sound, control buttons and hot spots to link the pages.
- Check the appearance of the presentation using a browser.

The presentation techniques that you need appear in Chapter 1: Presenting information. Make sure you use presentation techniques effectively. For artworks you could scan and edit pictures and/or use images you create, or use clip-art. You could also identify and use suitable sound clips.

If you were creating a series of web pages for a client, at this stage you would show this to your client and ask for feedback. Your client might feel that you have not included all the information that is necessary, or that your pages are too cluttered, or that the movement within the site is not as good as it should be.

Activity 3.30

With others in your group, review your presentation. Make notes on how it could be improved.

Edit the presentation so that it meets the requirements of your intended audience.

When your presentation design is finalised, create detailed plans of your HTML program.

Your aim is to provide several attractive, easy-to-read, easy-to-use HTML pages of information that make good use of text, sound and graphics, and enable the user to move easily between the pages using button, graphic and textual hot spots.

Many programming languages enable you to place comments in the program. These help you and others to understand (or remember) the purpose of small parts of the program.

If you are using Powerpoint, each slide can have its own notes. This is very useful when preparing a presentation. The notes can include reminders to the speaker about handing out material, or examples that are needed to explain what appears on the slide. It may include the expected time for this particular slide, so that the speaker can check if the talk is progressing according to plan. The print options include 'Print notes' so a hardcopy can be used by the speaker while the audience is looking at the slides.

Activity 3.31

Document your presentation by adding comments to explain what you have done and how the presentation works.

If your software does not have an option for you to annotate the pages, you may need to print them out and handwrite your explanation.

Macro programs

Programs that are used to automate actions in applications software are called **macros**.

Macro
is a sequence of instructions which are defined by a single element, called the **identifier**.

Macros can be produced by simply recording the keys that a user presses, or by using a routine or 'wizard' that guides the user through a sequence of operations and records the result. Macros can be used in a number of situations, but essentially they are used to **replace multiple key strokes**. When you '**call**' a macro, the sequence of instructions is used. Macros save time and can reduce errors.

- ★ **Using your word-processing software, look in your online help for 'macro'.**
- ★ **Read the material supplied and then go through any demonstration that is provided.**
- ★ **Check that you understand how to create a macro by recording a macro to add a box around the paragraph where your cursor is positioned. Call the macro 'BOX'.**

You could create macros for any other sequences of keystrokes that you find you have to do over and over again. This will save you time.

The code created (using an early version of Microsoft Word and a more recent version) is shown in Figure 3.20.

Activity 3.33

Assign the macro BOX to a toolbar button.

If you are using Word 6, choose TOOLS/CUSTOMISE/TOOLBARS and select the Macro BOX. Then drag the cursor to wherever you would like the button to appear within your toolbars. You will then see the Custom window, and choosing Edit will allow you to draw a suitable picture for the button.

If you are using a more recent version of Word, choose TOOLS/CUSTOMISE/COMMANDS and select macro BOX. You can then drag the button to wherever you want it. It appears with text 'Normal.New.Macros.BOX' but you can edit this (choose default style and draw a picture instead) and this reduces the size of the button.

If you are using another word processing application, ask your teacher to explain anything you do not understand about generating macros on your system.

```
Word 6 version of BOX macro:

Sub MAIN
FormatBordersAndShading .ApplyTo = 0, .Shadow = 0, .TopBorder = 1, .LeftBorder
= 1, .BottomBorder = 1, .RightBorder = 1, .HorizBorder = 0, .VertBorder = 0,
.TopColor = 0, .LeftColor = 0, .BottomColor = 0, .RightColor = 0, .HorizColor = 0,
.VertColor = 0, .FromText = "1 pt", .Shading = 0, .Foreground = 0, .Background = 0,
.Tab = "0", .FineShading = -1
End Sub

A later version of word produced this macro (using the same key depressions).

BOX Macro
Macro recorded 11/04/00 by jenny

  With Selection.ParagraphFormat
    With .Borders(wdBorderLeft)
      .LineStyle = wdLineStyleSingle
      .LineWidth = wdLineWidth050pt
      .Color = wdColorAutomatic
    End With
    With .Borders(wdBorderRight)
      .LineStyle = wdLineStyleSingle
      .LineWidth = wdLineWidth050pt
      .Color = wdColorAutomatic
    End With
    With .Borders(wdBorderTop)
      .LineStyle = wdLineStyleSingle
      .LineWidth = wdLineWidth050pt
      .Color = wdColorAutomatic
    End With
    With .Borders(wdBorderBottom)
      .LineStyle = wdLineStyleSingle
      .LineWidth = wdLineWidth050pt
      .Color = wdColorAutomatic
    End With
    With .Borders
      .DistanceFromTop = 1
      .DistanceFromLeft = 4
      .DistanceFromBottom = 1
      .DistanceFromRight = 4
      .Shadow = False
    End With
  End With
  With Options
    .DefaultBorderLineStyle = wdLineStyleSingle
    .DefaultBorderLineWidth = wdLineWidth050pt
    .DefaultBorderColor = wdColorAutomatic
  End With
End Sub
```

Figure 3.20 *Macro code for adding a box to the paragraph in which the cursor is positioned*

Activity 3.34

Look now at some other applications software, e.g. a spreadsheet. You should find that the software includes many 'supplied macros'. Look at the code for these.

```
'
' red Macro
' Macro recorded 11/04/00 by First Class
'
'
Sub red()
   With Selection.Interior
      .ColorIndex = 3
      .Pattern = xlSolid
      .PatternColorIndex = xlAutomatic
   End With
End Sub
```

3 means 'red'

Figure 3.21 *A macro created within Microsoft Excel – to paint a cell red*

Figure 3.21 shows the code generated within Microsoft Excel spreadsheet software for a macro that changes the colour of a cell to red.

Activity 3.35

The Microsoft Excel macro includes the line .ColorIndex = 3. Editing this line of code to read .ColorIndex = 5 has the effect of painting a cell blue.

- ★ **Create a macro within your spreadsheet software to change the format of a cell. You could change the format to currency, or add a border.**
- ★ **Look at the code it produces. Change a parameter and see what effect it has.**

Most software applications offer macro support, and once you have mastered the sequence of recording macros you can use them in a variety of situations:

- To insert graphics, text, tables, lines and borders
- To adjust the page layout (margins, columns, headers, footers)
- To call or create a new template
- To modify application software configuration (set options, customise)

Activity 3.36

★ Choose one of the situations listed above and, with a particular user in mind, create a macro to meet the needs of that user.

★ Produce screen prints and printouts to show how your macro works.

★ Annotate your printouts accurately and clearly to show the purpose of your macro and how it works.

★ Decide how you could amend your macro code to produce a new macro. Annotate copies of the code before and after editing, to prove that you have edited the code to modify the macro.

★ Explain how your macro improves the efficiency and effectiveness of the user and the quality of the output.

Revision Questions

1. Name two input devices that can be used to transfer photos to a computer.
2. Explain the difference between memory and storage. Name two storage devices, and two types of memory.
3. Name two output devices that produce hardcopy.
4. Explain these terms: resolution, refresh rate, impact printer, BIOS.
5. What device is needed to connect a computer to the Internet via a telephone line?
6. What is the main difference between an operating system and applications software?
7. Name four examples of applications software, and for each write down its main purpose.
8. List four purposes of an operating system.
9. What is meant by the term 'default setting'?
10. Explain the difference between a spellchecker and a grammar checker.
11. What is meant by ergonomics?
12. What steps can be taken to keep data confidential? What steps can be taken to protect data from accidental loss, e.g. in a fire?
13. What is a virus? What can be done to avoid virus infection?
14. What is HTML? Explain its purpose.
15. Explain what a macro is, and give examples of macros that you have used and created.

Good Working Practice Guide

Before ICT systems, computers and word processing packages were invented typists had to type very carefully. If they made a mistake, they would have to retype a letter all over again.

With a word processing package you can **edit** your document. What does this mean?

- **You can change your mind about what you want to say**
- **You can think of a better way of saying something**
- **You can correct any keying errors**
- **You can check your spelling**
- **You can make sure the finished document is perfect, before printing the copy on paper**

It was thought that the introduction of word processing packages would create the **paperless office**. Instead users tend to print out many draft copies before they are satisfied with the finished document. The end result may be better, but a lot of paper is used in the process.

The type of information kept on an ICT system and possibly transmitted to other users is subject to laws, for instance the control of pornography. Unfortunately, computers make the spread of this information easier and detection quite difficult. Also, information may be sensitive, e.g. medical records or financial details. If hackers gain access to computer files through a network confidentiality may be lost. Commerce on the Internet has already introduced some questions that need to be resolved: which countries' trading

standards should apply if you buy something over the Internet? How safe is it to pay for goods using a credit card?

Many laws have been introduced, not least to try to combat computer-based crime:

- **Computer Misuse Act 1990**
- **Copyright, Designs and Patents Act 1998**
- **Obscene Publications Act 1990**

Although you do not need to learn about all these laws for the compulsory units, you should be aware of two important pieces of legislation:

- Health and Safety issues (see page 233)
- the Data Protection Act (see page 236)

and other good working practice expected of you during your practical work.

For your work to progress smoothly, you can help yourself by adopting standard ways of working. This can also help you to work well with others. In several units, standard ways of working are listed, e.g. in Unit 1: Presenting Information. You must apply these techniques to *all* of your ICT work.

Standard ways of working

Many organisations have rules and guidelines to help people to work effectively and to avoid problems. These 'standard ways of working' are particularly important for people working with information technology, and there are many reasons for having them. The most important is that information in ICT systems can be easily lost or misused:

- **Unauthorised persons may gain access to confidential information**
- **People may copy original work and present it as their own**
- **Information presented professionally may be believed, even though it may be inaccurate**

Often, things go wrong:

- **The computer crashes when you are halfway through keying in some new text**
- **A floppy disk is corrupted so you cannot access any of the files on that disk**
- **Paper files can be mislaid**
- **The operator miskeys while keying**
- **The wrong disk or tape is used**
- **The hardware malfunctions**
- **The power fails**

Equipment faults can happen with the hardware (e.g. the screen) or with the medium (e.g. the disk or tape). It is important to keep equipment and surfaces free of dust, and to store tapes and disks in sleeves or covers. Loss of information can be damaging for the user. They can be embarrassed and might lose customers. At worst, a business may fail. It is important to store consumables in a cool, dry and dust-free environment, and to replace them correctly. A paper jam when your deadline is fast approaching will not help! By adopting good working practices, you can minimise the disruptions these sorts of problems cause.

Most good working practices are based on common sense. Others show that you have thought about the possible consequences of your actions. The ones most people remember are the ones they learnt when things went wrong!

- If you print before you save a document, and the computer crashes due to some memory problem while printing, you will have lost any changes you made to the file since you last saved it. The sensible thing is always to save a document before printing!
- If you set up headers or footers to show the path name of the document, at a later date, you'll be able to find the file again
- If you number the pages of a document which has more than a couple of pages, there will be no chance of confusion, e.g. if the document is dropped and the pages scatter
- If you take a backup copy of your files, when one floppy disk lets you down, you have a backup copy you can use instead

Often, there is no single 'right' way of doing something. To select a function, e.g. 'copy', you could move the cursor to a toolbar and click on the 'copy' icon, or you could use a right click followed by selecting on the special menu which appears for you. Which method you use depends on how confident you are in using the software.

You should take time to learn how to use the mouse – some short cuts are available if only you know about them. For example, the mouse pointer changes shape depending on what you are pointing to or the task you are doing.

- If what you see is the I-beam pointer, a left click repositions the cursor at this point of the screen. A right click results in a menu – what appears on that menu depends on the type of text nearby.
- If what you see is an arrow pointing to the left, you may be within the menu area, an inactive window, a scroll bar, a toolbar or a ruler. Depending on which area you are in, clicking the mouse could choose a command or click a button.

You can also become better at using the software if you take the time to read through the help notes. Online help often also includes demonstrations. These may take a short time to follow through, but you may learn useful 'tricks' which will save you time later. Rather than limiting yourself to the few things you have learnt already and use regularly, take time to explore what other facilities the software offers. In the long run, this can save you a lot of time.

Sometimes a quick way of doing something is more 'dangerous' than a slower method. For example, if you want to move a paragraph from one place in your document to another, there are at least two ways you can do this:

- Highlight the paragraph, select copy, move the cursor to the new position, select paste. Then, return to the original position and delete the paragraph.

- **Highlight the paragraph, select cut, move the cursor to the new position, select paste**

The first way takes longer but there is no risk of 'losing' the paragraph. You may be able to think of other examples where you have choices about how to achieve an effect.

If you are not sure about how successful your next move will be, save your document before you attempt to make difficult changes. Then, if need be, you can retrieve the previous version of the document. Alternatively, remember that the undo button will reverse your previous actions.

As you become more confident in using a software application, you can take the quicker routes. While you are still learning, it is a good idea to think carefully about your working practices. Then, later, these good working practices will become second nature to you.

Most of the things that go wrong while working on a computer are your own fault:

- **Overwriting a document by accident**
- **Deleting a file or some text by accident**

One obvious statement: it is important to think before doing anything! The undo button cannot undo everything you do. For example, the undo button cannot undo the overwriting of a document.

You should know the different effects of the 'Save' and 'Save as' commands.

- **Save saves with the same name**
- **Save as prompts you to choose a different name**

If you select a name which is already in use, the operating software will warn you: Do you want to replace the existing 'xxx.doc'? Probably, your answer to this is 'No'!

Taking advice from others

It is very difficult to find everything out for yourself, without the help of others. Your teacher will provide a lot of help and information about how to do things on your ICT system, and using the software available to you. In addition to this, you can use other sources of information:

- **Manuals**
- **Online help**
- **Magazine articles from the computer press**
- **Television programmes about using ICT**
- **CD-Roms in your library**
- **Information on the Internet**

It is important that you know how to use online help. Often you need to know something in the middle of preparing a document while at a workstation. If you can use the online help, you can usually find the answer to your problem very quickly, and without interrupting anyone else.

Proofreading

Organisations may produce hundreds of letters or reports each day. Many of the staff will spend nearly all of their working day preparing documents. A major part of their work may be in proofreading drafts of documents.

So that people can work together on documents, it is important to understand and use a standard convention for the proofreading symbols for omissions and corrections. BS 5261 Part 2 1976 is the standard that most publishers and typesetters use.

Copies of the standard can be obtained by post from BSI Sales, Linford Wood, Milton Keynes MK14 6LE, Telefax 01908 320856.

Filenames

When you create a document, you must invent a name for it for storage purposes. Then, next time you need the document, you ask for the file by name.

There are restrictions on the names that you can use, and it is advisable to think carefully before choosing a name. There may also be a limit on the number of characters that you can use.

Choosing filenames is not a bit like choosing passwords! Passwords have to be kept secret so you try to think of a word which you can remember, which is special to you *and* that no one else might guess. Filenames are no secret, but you must be able to remember what you called your document. Otherwise you might never find it again!

Choose names that make sense. Meaningful file names which make the file contents obvious are best.

Managing your work

The way you manage your ICT work is important. Here are some of the things that you should do to manage your work:

- **Plan your work to produce what is required to given deadlines**
- **Use standard formats**
- **Enter information so that you can easily make changes, e.g. using spaces, tabs and indents correctly to ensure consistent layout**
- **Edit and save work regularly**
- **Make dated back-up copies of your work giving an idea of sequence**
- **When you are using any information that has been collected using secondary research, check it for validity and cross reference with other books to ensure that it is correct**
- **Keep a log of your work, especially any ICT problems you meet and how you solve them**

Keeping information secure

Protecting information from loss or misuse is essential in ICT. You must learn the particular importance of keeping information secure (e.g. from theft, loss, viruses and fire), protecting confidentiality, and respecting copyright.

Security of data

Having data on an ICT system rather than in paper files has advantages and disadvantages.

- **Lots of data can be stored on a single floppy disk**
- **The data is more easily moved and removed (e.g. stolen)**
- **If linked via networks, access is quite easy**

To improve security, two types of control can be used: **physical controls** and **logical controls**. Physical control includes locking doors, storing data in safes and issuing ID cards to users. Logical control includes using a password system and setting different access levels for different members of staff.

Protection from viruses

Viruses can damage the files on an ICT system. To avoid introducing viruses, some simple precautions can be taken:

- **Install virus checking software on the system which checks all files as they are opened**
- **Do not open files from sources that are unknown to you, e.g. sent over the Internet as attached files**

Protection from fire

Fires can start from cables and connectors that are not electrically sound. It is also unwise to overload sockets.

Protecting confidentiality

People or companies may wish to keep information confidential so that others do not know about it. You must learn to keep this type of information secure and not pass it on to others (e.g. prevent illegal access to medical or criminal records).

Password systems aim to restrict access to data, and these systems are fine, as long as you keep your password secret. Surveys on choices of passwords show that most people choose obvious ones, which are easy for friends to guess: the name of their pet, or a favourite place.

With more and more people using Internet cafés, it is quite easy to watch someone entering a password, and then to use this to gain access to files and information which is private to that person. One way to avoid this problem is to change your password regularly. Then you have to remember what the current one is!

Respecting copyright laws

A computer program, words, pictures and graphic images may belong to other people. The people who created or own this material have copyright and you must not use their work without their permission. If you do, you are breaking the law. You must understand and respect copyright law. Where you do use information created by others, and have obtained their permission, it is important that you acknowledge the source, by using an appropriate reference or listing it in a bibliography.

Security procedures

If work stored on an ICT system is lost, it is important that there is another file that can be used in its place. You will need to understand and use suitable security procedures when using ICT systems:

- **Making backup copies of your work**
- **Keeping dated backup copies of files on another disk and in another location**
- **Saving work regularly, and using different filenames**

Backing up data involves saving a copy of the data to a safe place. This should be done regularly, e.g. daily, so that, if there is any problem, you can retrieve your data from the backup copy. To avoid loss by fire or theft, backup copies are usually stored away from the ICT system, e.g. in a fire-proof safe or in another building.

Working safely

The ICT working environment is relatively safe. However, there are risks that should be minimised and hazards that can, and should, be avoided.

- **Obstacles, e.g. in doorways, which people may trip over or bump into and be bruised**
- **Obstacles on fire exit routes, which may prevent people escaping if there were a fire**

Most computers are powered by mains electricity, which introduces more potential hazards:

- Tripping over cables
- Static electricity build up
- Screen glare

Hazards exist only because not enough care is taken to keep the workplace safe. They must be prevented, though, under the Health and Safety at Work Act.

Risks usually result in stress on the worker. In time, this could mean they need time off work to recover, or that they can no longer do the job properly. Risks cannot always be eliminated, but they can, and should, be reduced.

The user, i.e. the operator, must be protected from potential danger. Seating is very important. Poor seating can result in poor posture and cause back problems, and many more working hours are lost due to illnesses such as RSI (repetitive strain injury). RSI is a painful complaint which can make continuing work impossible for sufferers. Usually it attacks the wrist or arm of people who have used a keyboard or mouse for a long time.

Ergonomics studies the relationship between people and their environment. Many different things can be adjusted to make the operator as comfortable as possible and many risks can be minimised by studying the ergonomics of the workplace. This means looking at many things which affect the worker:

- **How you are seated – the height of the seat and the desk, the angle of the seating, the height of your desk**

- How conveniently the desk is set up – whether you can reach everything you need without stretching too far, the keyboard and screen position
- Lighting – whether this is good enough for you to read without straining your eyes. Fitting anti-glare screens can prevent eye strain.
- Background noise – whether this allows you to think clearly while working

You should be aware that a comfortable working position is important to avoid physical stress, eye strain or safety hazards. This may include avoiding long periods of continuous VDU work by having brief rest periods and having a surrounding area that includes near and distant objects the eyes may focus on.

Do's and don'ts

- ***Do*** plan your work to produce what is required to given deadlines
- ***Do*** take a backup of your work. Label your backup with the date.
- ***Do*** keep backup copies of files on another disk and in another location
- ***Do*** keep previous drafts of documents, filed in date order and giving an idea of sequence. Then you can always look back if you need to.

- ***Do*** keep a log to provide a record of what has happened, especially what has gone wrong
- ***Do*** proof-read your database and spreadsheet information to ensure accuracy
- ***Do*** save work regularly using different filenames
- ***Do*** proof-read all documents before printing out the final copy
- ***Do*** evaluate your work and suggest how it might be improved
- ***Do*** keep information free from viruses
- ***Do*** respect confidentiality
- ***Do*** respect copyright
- ***Don't*** disconnect or connect equipment without first isolating the power source
- ***Don't*** eat or drink while working at a PC. Wash your hands after eating sticky or greasy foods – the remains of a jam doughnut can glue up a keyboard!

Health and Safety at Work etc. Act (1974)

The basis of health and safety law in Britain is covered by the Health and Safety at Work etc. Act 1974. The Act sets out the general duties which employers have towards employees and members of the public. It also explains the duties that employees have to themselves and to each other.

These duties are qualified by the principle of 'so far as is reasonably practicable'. In other words, the degree of risk needs to be balanced against the time, trouble, cost and physical difficulty of taking measures to avoid or reduce the risk. What is needed is good management and common sense: to look at what the risks are and take sensible measures to tackle them.

Risk assessment

The main requirement on employers is to carry out a risk assessment. Employers with five or more employees have to record the significant findings of the risk assessment. Risk assessment should be straightforward in a simple workplace such as a typical office. It should only be complicated if it deals with serious hazards such as those on a nuclear power station, a chemical plant, laboratory or an oil rig.

Besides carrying out a risk assessment, employers have other responsibilities:

- **To make arrangements for implementing the health and safety measures identified as necessary by the risk assessment**
- **To appoint competent people (often themselves or company colleagues) to help them to implement the arrangements**
- **To set up emergency procedures**
- **To provide clear information and training to employees**
- **To work together with other employers sharing the same workplace**

Guidance, ACOPs and Regulations

The Health and Safety Commission (HSC) produces guidance, Approved Codes of Practice (ACOPs) and regulations.

The HSC publishes guidance on a range of subjects, specific to the health and safety problems of an industry or of a particular process used in a number of industries for three main reasons:

- **To interpret – helping people to understand what the law says – including, for example, how requirements based on EC Directives fit with those under the Health and Safety at Work Act**
- **To help people comply with the law**
- **To give technical advice**

Following guidance is not compulsory and employers are free to take other action. However, if they do follow guidance, they will normally be doing enough to comply with the law. The HSC aims to keep guidance up to date, because as technologies change, risks – and the measures needed to address them – change too.

ACOPs offer practical examples of good practice. They give advice on how to comply with the law by, for example, providing a guide to what is 'reasonably practicable'. If regulations use words like 'suitable and sufficient', an ACOP can illustrate what this requires in particular circumstances. ACOPs have a special legal status. If employers are prosecuted for a breach of health and safety law, and it is proved that they have not followed the relevant provisions of the ACOP, a court can find them at fault unless they can show that they have complied with the law in some other way.

Regulations are law, approved by Parliament. These are usually made under the Health and Safety at Work Act, following proposals from the HSC. The Health and Safety at Work Act, and general duties in the Management Regulations, are goal-setting and leave employers freedom to decide how to control risks which they identify. Guidance and ACOPs give advice, but employers are free to take other measures provided they do what is reasonably practicable. However, some risks are so great, or the proper control measures so costly, that it would not be appropriate to leave employers discretion in deciding what to do about them. Regulations identify these risks and set out specific action that must be taken. Often these requirements are absolute – to do something without qualification by whether it is reasonably practicable.

Some regulations apply across *all* companies e.g. the Display Screen Equipment Regulations apply wherever VDUs are used. Other regulations apply to hazards unique to specific industries, such as mining or nuclear safety law. Besides the Health and Safety at Work Act itself, these regulations apply across the full range of workplaces.

For your own safety, and that of others around you, you should make sure you follow all safety procedures adopted by your employer, your college or school. Visit the website at http://www.hse.gov.uk. for more information – many documents are available for downloading as Adobe Acrobat files.

Data Protection Act (DPA)

Computers are in use throughout society: collecting, storing and distributing information (processing). Much of that information is about living people (personal data). The DPA places obligations on those who record and use personal data (data users). They must be open about the use (through the data protection register) and follow sound and proper practices (the Data Protection Principles).

The DPA also gives rights to individuals about whom information is recorded (data subjects). They may find out information about themselves, challenge it, have it corrected or erased if appropriate, and claim compensation in certain circumstances. When it was first passed in 1984, the DPA also allowed the UK to ratify the Council of Europe Convention on Data Protection, allowing information to flow freely between the UK and other European countries with similar laws.

The Data Protection Registrar

The Registrar, an independent officer appointed by Her Majesty the Queen and reporting directly to Parliament, has many duties:

- **Establishing and maintaining a register of data users and computer bureaux and making it publicly available**
- **Promoting compliance with the Data Protection Principles**
- **Encouraging, where appropriate, the development of Codes of Practice to help data users comply with the Principles**
- **Considering complaints about breaches of the Principles of the Act and, where appropriate, prosecuting offenders or serving notices**

What the DPA covers

The DPA only applies to automatically processed information. It does not cover information which is held and processed manually, for example in ordinary paper files. Not all computerised information is covered by the DPA, only that which relates to living individuals. So, for example, it does not cover information which relates only to a company or organisation.

Registration

Did You Know?

People or organisations who have personal data processed by a computer bureau, are still data users even if they do not have their own computer. A **computer bureau**, in broad terms, means anyone processing personal data on someone else's behalf.

The term 'computer' is never used in the DPA. Instead, it uses the terms data and data user. Anyone who holds personal information about living individuals on computer must register unless covered by one of the exemptions provided by the DPA.

To register as a data user, information has to be supplied for inclusion in the register:

- **The name and address of the data user**
- **A description of the purposes for which personal data are used**
- **The type of personal data held**
- **Where the personal data are obtained**
- **To whom they will be disclosed**
- **A list of any countries outside the UK to which they may be transferred**

Once a data user has registered, they must only act within the terms of their register entry. Not to do so is an offence. A data user can apply to the Registrar to alter their register entry at any time. It is an offence to fail to register or to provide false information to the Registrar.

The Data Protection Principles

Once registered, data users must comply with the Principles in relation to the personal data held:

- **Personal data shall be collected and processed fairly and lawfully**
- **Personal data shall be held only for specified and lawful purposes**
- **Personal data shall be used only for those purposes and only disclosed to those people described in the register entry**
- **Personal data shall be adequate, relevant and not excessive in relation to the purposes for which they are held**
- **Personal data shall be accurate and, where necessary, kept up to date**

- Personal data shall be held no longer than is necessary for the registered purpose
- Personal data shall be protected by proper security

However, the Registrar cannot enforce the Principles against unregistered data users.

The Principles also provide for individuals to have access to data held about themselves and, where appropriate, to have the data corrected or deleted.

The rights of the individual

An individual is entitled to be supplied by a data user with a copy of any personal data held about him or her – the 'subject access' right. Individuals may write direct to the user for their data, or they may consult the register to obtain more details about the user.

Data users may charge up to £10 for meeting each request but some may decide to charge less, or nothing at all. They have up to 40 days in which to provide the data from the date of receiving adequate information to help them locate the data or identify the individual making the request. If the data are not provided within the 40 days, the individual concerned can complain to the Registrar or apply to the courts for an order that the data user should provide access.

Exemptions from the DPA

There are several exemptions. Manually held information, e.g. in card indexes or paper files, is not covered by the DPA. Otherwise the exemptions from the need to register are extremely narrow. They cover only the simplest tasks in the following areas: calculating pay and pensions; keeping accounts or records of purchases or sales; distributing articles or information (mailing lists); and preparing text documents. Most businesses find it difficult to meet and stay within the limits imposed by these exemptions and find it safer to register.

So, people and organisations who hold personal information about living individuals on computer or have such information processed on a computer by others (e.g. by a computer bureau or an accountant) probably need to register under the DPA. No matter how unimportant this information may appear (and it may be as little as a name and address), the fact that it is on computer almost certainly makes the data user liable for registration.

Where personal data are exempt from the whole of the DPA, those data need not be registered, there is no right of subject access and the Registrar and courts have no powers regarding this personal data. Some exemptions are unconditional, for example where national security is involved, or where an individual holds personal data for recreational purposes or for managing his own personal, family or household affairs. Other exemptions have conditions which must be complied with before the data can be deemed exempt: for example, where data are held for payroll, pensions and accounts, they are exempt unless they are also held for other purposes. Other conditional exemptions exist for unincorporated members' clubs and mailing lists. In the case of all the conditional exemptions, the data may not be disclosed without the consent of the individual to whom the data relate. Limited disclosures are permitted for the payroll, pensions and accounts exemptions without the consent of the individual.

There are also a number of exemptions from the need to provide information under the subject access provisions of the DPA. Some examples of where personal information may be withheld are where this would be likely to prejudice the prevention or detection of crime; the apprehension or prosecution of offenders; or the assessment or collection of any tax or duty. Decisions to withhold information under these exemptions can be challenged by the Registrar on receipt of a complaint from a member of the public.

More detailed information on all aspects of the Data Protection Act is contained within 'The Guidelines', a free publication available from the Registrar's Office. For full details of the Data Protection Act and how it is enforced in particular circumstances, visit the website http://www.hmso.gov.uk For details of the functions and activities of the Data Protection Registrar, visit the website http://www.dataprotection.gov.uk You may also be interested to visit http://www.europe.eu.int/comm/internal_market/en/media/ which lists the EU directives and proposals relating to a range of e-commerce issues including data protection. For the full text and an analysis of the EU's data-protection directive (issued in 1995) visit http://www.privacy.org

Portfolio Guide

Your portfolio should contain all the evidence collected as you work through the units. For some units, assessment is by external testing, but material in your portfolio may well be needed to show your achievement in Key Skills. It therefore makes sense to keep a portfolio of all your work for all your units, even those which are not portfolio assessed.

To decide what material you need to produce and put in your portfolio, you need to look at the assessment grid at the end of each unit specification. Your portfolio must contain at least the minimum stated in the first column of the Assessment Evidence section of each unit.

The Assessment Evidence section tells you exactly what type of evidence you need to produce – like list, notes, records and summary – to show what depth of work is needed, and you need to check you have met this level of presentation.

- **Lists** are simply a series of brief comments on the main points
- **Notes** are more than just a list. For each item, you may write a paragraph of information. You may write notes when preparing for a task. They may include draft ideas, initial plans and drawings, and so on.
- A **record** is an account of the activity which is being assessed. It could be a written record, including tables of data, a check-list of activities, and so on. You decide exactly what to include, after discussion with your teacher.
- A **report** is a finished piece of work which brings together lots of ideas and information

- **A summary is a short account, similar to a record but should not include all your working papers**

For some activities your teacher will watch you working, and then write an assessment of your performance. In some situations, another person, e.g. your supervisor in a work placement, may observe you.

With a presentation, you will present your finished work to an audience (maybe only to your teacher), but your portfolio evidence might include a taped recording or a video together with the material (e.g. OHTs or slides) that you used. Your teacher will be responsible for agreeing that you used a good standard of English during your presentation, and that your manner and tone were suitable for your audience.

For the tested units , the assessment grid does say what you have to produce, but your awarding body will specify the precise requirement in pre-release material given to you some time before the examination. See the Examination Guide on page 257.

Performance when doing assignments

Teachers can most easily assess the quality of your work by watching you when you do assignments, and by looking at what you produce for your portfolio.

When you prepare for a task and are identifying sources of information, your teacher may consider these questions:

- **Were you usually told which tasks needed to be done and then had to be guided through them?**
- **Were you able to decide what steps you needed to take, and did you arrange the tasks into a sensible order, setting your own time scale?**
- **Did you use sources of information suggested by your teacher, and were you able to select and use the relevant information from these sources?**
- **Were you able to understand what the task involved without any guidance from your teacher?**
- **Did you understand what information was required and did you look for extra sources of information, as well as investigating those suggested by your teacher?**

The more independent you are, the higher your grade should be. Similarly, the more care you take over planning and monitoring your work, the more likely you are to be successful, and the higher your grade should be. During every task, you should be checking that your original plan is working, by monitoring and reviewing your progress. You should recognise that the planning may need changing. Sometimes, through no fault of your own, the plan does not work:

- **Computers crash**
- **Books and other sources may not be available**
- **People that you have arranged to meet may fall ill and have to postpone your appointment**

Even if things do not go wrong, you should be able to demonstrate that you have regularly checked progress against the original plan.

The quality of your work is also very important.

- **At pass level, you should be able to demonstrate a basic understanding of the knowledge and skills required, but you may not be able to make connections between different aspects of your work. You should be able to use the normal ICT terminology but may need some help from your teacher.**
- **At merit level, you should be able to make connections between different aspects of your work and demonstrate a clear understanding. Your use of ICT terminology should be accurate, and your written work should show confidence in the expression of your ideas.**
- **At distinction level, you will have a clear understanding of the knowledge, skills and understanding required. You will draw on your personal experience to draw conclusions or suggest alternative courses of action.**

At the end of each assignment, all students are expected to be able to describe what they felt went well, and what went badly. Evaluating your work is an important part of improving your own performance – as is one of the six Key Skills.

- **Distinction level students are able to learn from what they have done to date. They learn from any mistakes and build on success.**
- **Pass level students will be saying – oh, that went wrong last time!**

So, while doing practice or real assignments, remember that if you perform well, you may be awarded a higher grade for this work. Here are some of the things your teacher will be checking when awarding a grade.

- **Have you shown independence in your approach to your work?**
- **Have you completed the work to given deadlines?**
- **Have you planned your work effectively?**
- **Have you selected and used relevant information to help you meet your purposes?**
- **Have you used technical language correctly?**
- **Have you reviewed your work?**

When assessing your portfolio, your teacher is looking for the right quality and quantity of work. He or she will first look to see that you have covered everything by checking that you have covered all items listed in the various columns of the Assessment Evidence chart. Work of a high quality may earn you a higher grade, so your teacher will be looking at all the columns of the chart.

What are the general 'rules' that allow your teacher to decide on your grade? This depends on the unit, and is detailed in the section called Assessment Strategies. Although this section is written for your teacher, you should read it carefully. Then you'll know how your work will be viewed by your teacher.

Generally speaking, the teacher will try to distinguish between students and award grades so that the higher grades are given to students who perform best. These are the qualities that your teacher will be looking for:

- **Increasing depth and breadth of understanding**
- **Increasing coherence, evaluation and analysis**
- **Increasing independence and originality**
- **Increasing objectivity and critical understanding**

Presenting information within a portfolio

It will help your teacher, and give extra information about your performance overall, if your portfolio is well presented. Chapter 1 of this book covers Unit 1: Presenting Information. As a student on the Intermediate GNVQ ICT course, you must be able to demonstrate that you can do this well!

You can handwrite your assignments, or you could use a word processor. If you handwrite your work, you will have to be very neat. If you make a mistake in your 'final' version, it will show and you may feel you have to write out a whole sheet again.

If you use a word processor, apart from showing ICT Key Skills, you will have the benefits of using ICT:

- **You can edit your work until you are happy with it**
- **You can choose a style which reflects your own personality. You can choose a point size and a font that you like**
- **You can include clip art or other graphics, e.g. using WordArt, to improve the appearance of your portfolio material**

For some assignments, you will have to use a computer. When doing assignments, most of your material will be produced on the computer.

The structure of your portfolio

There are a number of sections which your portfolio should include. This will demonstrate that you can structure material and present it in a sensible way.

The main sections are listed here, but you can choose your own sections if you prefer.

- Front cover
- Contents list
- Assignment material
- Appendices

You may also have checklist sheets supplied by your teacher. These may be used to refer to where Key Skills are demonstrated. In addition, you may have material which confirms that your teacher saw you present some information, or has discussed your material with you.

Your name (and centre details) should appear at least once on the portfolio. For safety's sake, it would be good practice to include this information on every page. If you are using software, this is easily achieved by including this information in a header or footer.

It will be important that your contents list matches whatever you have included in the rest of your portfolio. Although it appears at the very start of your portfolio, it is one of the last pages you can complete. However, if you produce it using a word processor you can prepare a contents page at the very beginning and update it every time you add some material to your portfolio. Then it will be one less job to do when you are rushing to meet the final deadline.

In this book, the pages run from 1 to 268, and the contents page (on page v) shows the starting page numbers for each chapter. For your portfolio, it may be easier to number the sections and then, within each section, number the pages by section. This numbering method is often used in manuals and means that extra sections can be added at any time, without it upsetting the page numbering too much.

For the material produced when doing assignments, plus any material produced when doing activities, it probably makes sense to present the material in the same order as you completed the work. For each assignment, make sure you show clearly what the assignment is called, and what it covers. It may be possible to use material produced in another course as evidence of your ICT skills. It will help your teacher if you write clearly on each assignment, which unit (and course) the assignment refers to.

Sometimes it makes sense to move some material to an appendix. This shortens a section, and yet the material is available if the reader wants to look at it. So, for example, lengthy tables or diagrams or copies of original source materials may be put into an appendix.

You can also list your references within an appendix. It is important to include all your references: the books, magazines and CD-ROMs you used to find information for your assignments.

While building your portfolio, leave yourself messages about things you still have to include. You could write these notes on your plan (which will provide evidence of the fact that you have been reviewing and monitoring your plan), or put post-it notes on pages that still have work to be done, or write yourself a checklist, which you can then tick off as you complete the work.

Moderation and Internal Assessment

Your portfolio material is first marked by a teacher and marking is then internally standardised by other specially trained staff at your school or college. The teacher who marks your portfolio and the staff who carry out internal assessment of all the portfolio material use the unit assessment grids in accordance with their awarding body's procedures. The awarding body provides Centres with forms on which to record these assessments.

The teachers must be able to verify that the work submitted by you is your own work. This does not prevent groups of students working together in the initial stages, but it is important to ensure your individual contribution is clearly identified separately from that of any group in which you work.

When all portfolios have been internally standardised data about your portfolio (and the portfolios of all other students on your course) is then submitted to the awarding body by a specified date, after which postal moderation takes place in accordance with the awarding body's procedures and the Code of Practice. Detailed arrangements for moderation is forwarded to all schools and colleges before the start of the course, so your teacher should be able to tell you when your deadlines will be.

Key Skills Guide

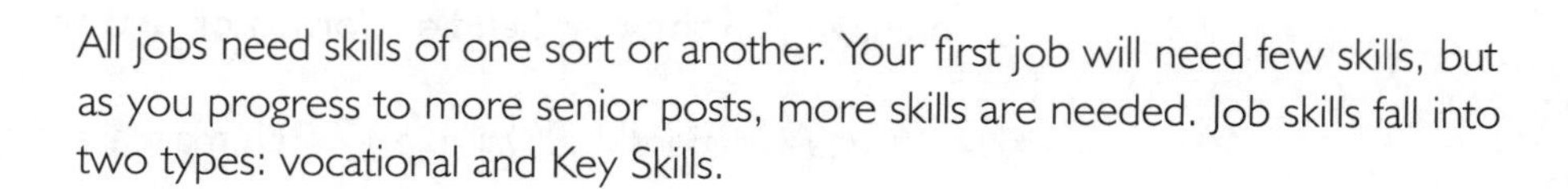

All jobs need skills of one sort or another. Your first job will need few skills, but as you progress to more senior posts, more skills are needed. Job skills fall into two types: vocational and Key Skills.

Vocational skills are the skills that are linked to the actual job.

- The ability to use a keyboard or mouse
- The experience of using a word-processing package
- The experience of using a DTP (desktop publishing) package
- The ability to install software and to customise application programs

You will learn vocational skills while following this course, and in doing so will need to use Key Skills.

Key Skills are not specific to a subject like ICT. Instead they are useful for most jobs and include these abilities:

- To think for yourself
- To work without supervision
- To work in a team
- To work with numbers
- To solve problems
- To communicate your ideas to others

- **To remember names and other important facts**
- **To work to a deadline**

So, Key Skills can help you to improve your own learning and performance in education and training, work and life in general.

- **In your learning, Key Skills help you to focus on what and how you are learning. In this way, while reviewing your progress, you can get better results.**
- **In your career, Key Skills enable you to be flexible in whatever kind of work you do. Employers look for Key Skills when recruiting and promoting people. In particular, your ability to work well in a team, and your motivation to learn, will be of interest to your interviewer. These skills are relevant to all levels of an organisation, including self-employment.**
- **In your personal life, Key Skills can help you to organise yourself, manage your money, handle information and get on with others**

Key Skills qualifications are available in three main areas:

- **Communication**
- **Application of number**
- **Information technology**

The broad aim of these three Key Skills units is to develop and recognise these skills:

- **To obtain and interpret different types of information: written, numerical and electronic**
- **To use, develop and communicate different types of information**
- **To effectively present the results of your work so as to meet the purpose of your studies, work or other activities**

There are then three other Key Skills areas – the 'wider' Key Skills:

- **Working with others**
- **Improving own learning and performance**
- **Problem solving**

These three Key Skills will become essential for success in your course. Many activities are based on teamwork, and employers are particularly interested in your ability to work well within a team. The 'Working with Others' key skills specification also includes working on your own though! Employers are also looking for staff who can work unsupervised and who are motivated – not only to get a job – but to improve their own learning by attending courses and learning as much as possible while working.

Key Skills awards are available in each of these six areas at levels 1, 2, 3 and 4. At level 5, a single unit combines communication skills with the skills of working with others, improving own learning and performance, and problem solving.

As you move up the levels, you are expected to take more responsibility for decisions on how you use your skills to suit different tasks, problems and situations. Students working at levels 1 and 2 work with straightforward subjects and materials, in routine situations. Students at higher levels deal with complex subjects and activities that are more demanding. At the higher levels, planning is very important. Students at levels 3 and 4 need to think about how to tackle tasks, what resources they will need and how to check their own work.

To achieve this qualification, you must demonstrate your skills through a portfolio of evidence. This evidence should not involve you in a lot of extra work. Instead, you should be able to collect evidence from your day-to-day studies, work or other activities and an appropriate form of independent assessment. As well as producing a portfolio of evidence, you also have to pass an externally set test.

Key Skills signposting

Within the Intermediate GNVQ course, you have the opportunity to learn, practice and gather evidence of all six Key Skills.

Within each unit of the specification for the Intermediate GNVQ in ICT, there is a section called Guidance on Key Skills. This highlights the most relevant Key Skills opportunities available for that particular unit. The Key Skills guidance has been designed to support the teaching, learning and assessment of the vocational content, as well as the teaching, learning and assessment of the Key Skills.

Key Skills and vocational achievement are interdependent, and the guidance section shows how vocational and Key Skills achievement can be successfully combined. Guidance is referenced in two ways: keys to attainment and signposts. The two sections should be used together – they are intended to complement each other.

- **Keys to attainment** are Key Skills (or aspects of Key Skills) which you should achieve at the same time as you meet the vocational requirements of the unit. They are central to your vocational achievement – they really are the 'key skills' needed to ensure your success.

- **Signposting** shows opportunities that can be incorporated into the learning process, without necessarily being achieved at the same time as producing evidence of your vocational skills. These signposts point to naturally occurring opportunities for the development of key skills so it may make sense to go a bit further in your studies to produce evidence which meets key skills requirements, on top of your vocational evidence.

The Guidance on Key Skills section of each unit contains suggestions only. Since the units tend to expect you to produce similar material – although on different topics – opportunities to meet Key Skills seem to appear almost the same in every unit. For some aspects of Key Skills, this is very helpful, because you need to produce more than one example as evidence. However, don't be fooled by the apparent repetitiveness of the Key Skills guidance sections. This is not actually the case; and it is important to concentrate on the keys to attainment, because these offer the best opportunities to achieve Key Skills within your vocational work.

The compulsory units should provide you with all the opportunities you need, but there are also opportunities within the optional units. In choosing your mix of units, you will need to ensure that Key Skills evidence can also be produced, without having to do lots of extra work.

To help you, the three awarding bodies include grids in their respective specifications, showing which Key Skills match which of their units. In this book, each Activity includes an indication of what Key Skills may be useful, and this may also help you to decide where your evidence of Key Skills will naturally arise.

Communication

Application of number

Working with others

Problem solving

Improving own learning and performance

You (with the help of your teacher) will then need to decide how and when you will produce all the evidence required to meet the Key Skills specifications. It is quite possible that you may need to develop additional evidence elsewhere – even on another course – to meet fully the requirements of the Key Skills specifications.

Note that, not surprisingly, Information Technology Key Skills (level 2) are automatically included in the units covered for Intermediate GNVQ ICT. So you do not need anything extra to achieve Key Skills in ICT, unless you are aiming for Key Skills at level 3 or higher. You do, however, have to take the external assessment test!

Key Skills terms

The Key Skills specifications use special terms in a special way:

- **Evidence** is what you produce to prove you have the Key Skills required. Examples may include things you have made, written work, artwork and diagrams, photos, audio/video recordings, print-outs, together with records from your assessor and others who have seen your work.
- **Portfolio** is where you collect and organise evidence for assessment: in a file or a folder large enough to carry everything you have produced. Your portfolio should include a contents page to show where evidence for each part of the unit(s) can be found. For more details on how to prepare your portfolio, see the Portfolio Guide on page 241.

It is possible, and it makes sense, to use some evidence for more than one Key Skill, e.g. a print-out of text and images, such as graphs and charts may provide evidence of written communication skills as well as presenting findings in application of number and ICT. The subject content and the material you use and produce are described either as straightforward or as complex.

- **Straightforward** subjects and materials are the ones that you meet most often in your work, studies or other activities. Content is presented in a direct way so that it easy to identify the main points. The sentence structures are simple and the vocabulary will be familiar to you.
- **Complex** subjects and materials present a number of ideas: some abstract ideas, some very detailed concepts and some requiring you to deal with sensitive issues. The relationship between ideas

and any lines of reasoning may not be immediately clear. You may need to understand specialised vocabulary, and complicated sentence structures may be used.

During your Intermediate GNVQ ICT course, you may use and prepare **extended documents**. These include text books like this one, newspaper reports, articles on the Internet and essays that you write – anything that has more than three pages. Such documents may relate to straightforward or complex subjects. They may include images such as diagrams, pictures and charts.

Any activity that includes a number of related tasks, where the results of one task then affects how you carry out the remaining tasks, is called a **substantial activity**. For the Key Skill Application of Number, a substantial activity may involve obtaining and interpreting information, using this information to carry out calculations and then explaining how the results of your calculations meet the purpose of the activity.

How to read a Key Skills unit

Each Key Skills specification document is four sides of A4 presented as a folded sheet of A3 paper. It covers one level of one Key Skill area, e.g. Application of Number, level 2.

It is important to read the whole specification, not just a single part of it, because all four pages present a different view of the Key Skill – and you need to see it from all angles.

What is this unit about? On the front cover, the first section gives an outline of the unit. Check that you have the correct Key Skills specification, at the right level. The specification documents look very similar, so it is easy to be looking at the wrong level.

How do I use the information in this unit? A second section on the front cover shows the other three pages – parts A, B and C of the specification – and explains the purpose of each section.

Part A: What You Need To Know lists what you need to learn and practise to feel confident about applying the Key Skill in your studies, work or other aspects of your life. You should check whether you know how to do these things and think about the opportunities you might have for showing these skills. Some topics may be familiar to you, and you may feel confident you can produce evidence to prove this. For other topics, you may have some learning to do and you may need practise before you are ready for assessment.

Part B: What You Must Do has a numbered list of the Key Skills you must show. The numbers used are then used as signposts in other examination specifications. For each numbered item, there is then a bullet list of evidence that you must produce. All your work for this section has to be assessed. You must have evidence that you can do *all* the things listed in the bullet points.

Part C: Guidance describes some activities you might like to use to develop and show your Key Skill and some ideas on the sort of activities that could be suitable. It also contains examples of the sort of evidence you could produce to prove you have the skills required.

Examination of Key Skills

External moderation will be used to check how well you demonstrate your Key Skills within your portfolio material. More details on how to present your portfolio are given in the Portfolio Guide on page 241.

Tests for Key Skills are being developed while this book is being written, so it is not possible to say, at this moment in time, exactly what form the examinations will take. However, material will be made available later this year (2000) and teachers and students alike will then be able to access this information from the Internet.

Examination Guide

For the Intermediate GNVQ course in Information and Communication Technology, there are three **compulsory units**:

1: Presenting Information

2: Handling Information

3: Hardware and Software

There are two different awards available:

- For the 3-unit award, the Part One Intermediate GNVQ award, you study only the three compulsory units
- For the 6-unit award, the Intermediate GNVQ award, you study six units: the three compulsory units plus any three others chosen from optional units

For some of the units, you will demonstrate your understanding by your portfolio material; for other units, you will externally assessed. However, the balance of portfolio to externally assessed units means that most of your work will be assessed as you work through the course (continuous assessment).

Each unit, whether assessed by portfolio or external assessment, is individually graded and points for each unit will be awarded on a scale of 0–16:

0–6 below pass

7–9 pass

10–12 merit

13–15 distinction

For tested units, your grade will reflect how many marks you earned in the test. For portfolio assessed material, the mark awarded will take into account the extent to which the evidence matches both the unit pass standards, represented by the set of criteria in the pass column of the grid, and the grading standards, represented progressively by the criteria in the merit and distinction columns.

Then, a single grade (pass, merit or distinction) is decided on a points basis, to reflect your performance over all your units; this single grade is then your 'final' grade for the Intermediate GNVQ (as with GCSEs) and can be used for entry to higher education on the usual points basis.

When you have completed the work for a single unit, you should be ready to sit the external test.

Tests and assignments are scheduled to take place at set times of the year, after you have worked on a particular unit. It does not matter what order you take the external tests, because each unit is available for assessment in both testing sessions: January and June. The important thing is to make sure you are confident that you have covered all the material for the unit, *before* you sit the test.

According to the unit, and your awarding body, you may be expected to do an assignment, or perhaps some preparatory work before sitting the written test.

Although your choice of units may result in more externally tested units, there is a minimum number of externally assessed units for Intermediate GNVQ:

- **1 unit for the 3-unit Part One Intermediate GNVQ award**
- **2 units for the 6-unit Intermediate GNVQ award**

The written tests, one per tested unit, last 90 minutes each, in which you write your answers within a booklet in the spaces provided.

Sample papers which you can use as 'mock' examinations for the tests are available on the web. The revision questions given at the end of each chapter will also provide you with some practice.

Which units are externally tested?

This grid shows for each chapter in this book (and the accompanying *Intermediate GNVQ Information and Communication Technology Options* book), which units are covered for each awarding body. The unit numbers for those units that are externally assessed by the three awarding bodies are shown in bold.

Chapter	*Title*	*OCR*	*AQA*	*EdExcel*
1	Presenting Information	1	1	**1**
2	Handling Information	2	2	2
3	Hardware and Software	**3**	**3**	3

The *Options* book:

Chapter	*Title*	*OCR*	*AQA*	*EdExcel*
1	Design Project	4	4	4
2	Information Resources	–	–	**5**
3	Communicating with Multimedia	5	5	7
4	Graphics and DTP	**6**	**6**	6
5	CAD	–	–	**12**
6	Numerical Modelling using Spreadsheets	7	7	9
7	Databases	8	8	10
8	Monitoring and Control Systems	**9**	**9**	–
9	Data and Communications	10	10	8
10	Programming	11	11	11
11	Impact of ICT on Society	12	12	–

Abbreviations

ATM	automatic teller machine
BACS	bankers automated clearing services
BIOS	basic input/output system
bits	binary digits
bps	bits per second
BMS	building management system
CAD	computer aided design
CD-Rom	compact disc, read only memory
CTRL	control (key)
CPU	central processing unit
CV	curriculum vitae
DOS	disk operating system
DRAM	dynamic random access memory
DTP	desktop publishing
E&EO	errors and omissions expected
EFT	electronic funds transfer
EFTPOS	electronic funds transfer at point of sale
ESC	escape (key)
fax	facsimile
Gb	gigabyte
GCSE	General Certificate of Secondary Education
GNVQ	General National Vocational Qualification
GPS	global positioning system
GUI	graphical user interface

HTML	hypertext mark-up language
IAS	immediate access store
ID	identity number
ICT	information and communication technology
ISDN	integrated services digital network (telephone line)
IT	information technology
ITU	International Telecommunications Union
Kb	kilobyte
LAN	local area network
LCD	liquid crystal display
Mb	megabyte
MICR	magnetic ink character recognition
NI	National Insurance number
NLQ	near letter quality
NRA	National Record of Achievement
OCR	optical character recognition
OMR	optical mark reader
PAYE	pay as you earn
PROM	programmable read only memory
pt	point size
RAM	random access memory
ROM	read only memory
RSA	Royal Society of Arts
SVGA	super video graphics array
tab	tabulation
Tb	terabyte
TP	twisted pair (cable)
TV	television
UK	United Kingdom
UTP	unshielded twisted pair (cables)
VAT	value added tax
VDU	visual display unit
VGA	video graphics array
WIMP	window, icon, mouse, pointer
WORM	write-once, read-many
WYSIWYG	what you see is what you get

Index

absolute cell referencing 138
access controls 228
access types 184, 185
accessing information 86
accuracy 56, 65
see also proofreading, spell checkers, validation, verification
active devices 170
actuator 181
agendas 45
alignment 133
analogue devices 170
anti-virus checks 198, 203
any other business (AOB) 46
apologies 46
appendices 43
applications software 193, 203
archiving 172, 207
ascending order 93
attribute, font 13
AUDIT option 138
AUTOEXEC.BAT file 194
automatic data entry 163
automatic input devices 157
autosave 207
AVERAGE function 138

backing store 183
backup 90, 183, 206
banner headline 35
barcode reader 164
batch file 194
bibliography 43
BIOS 193, 194
bits 183
blank cells 129
bold highlighting 69
booking form 19
boot-strapping 194
break-even point 146
browser software 212
bubble jet printers 177
bullet points 70
business cards/letters 7, 13, 14
bytes 183

cabling 191
cache memory 184
calculation(s) 126, 136
'calling' a macro 216
camera, digital 171
CD-Rom 82, 186
cells 81, 129
cell formats 133
cell referencing 127, 138
range of cells 137
central processing unit (CPU) 188, 189
centring 68
character format 129
charts 125, 143, 144
clicking (left, right, double) 160–1
coaxial cable 191
colour monitor 174
columns 81, 127
column title(s) 132, 135
column width 128
command-driven operating systems 195
communications
communications software 203
external communications 7, 43

informal communications 21
internal communications 20, 43
computer language 202
Computer Misuse Act (1990) 222
computer programming 209
concept keyboards 159
conditions 97
CONFIG.SYS file 194
configuration 197
contact sensors 167
contents list 43, 95
control(s) 121, 214
control signals 190
controlled devices 181
copper cables 191
Copyright, Designs and Patents Act (1998) 222, 229
CTRL key 157
cue card(s) 110
currency format 129
customising 197, 198, 205
cut and paste 71

data 80
data capture 170, 171
data collection errors 60
data display 172
data entry 86
automatic data entry 163
manual data entry 157
data logging device 171
data processing 187
Data Protection Act 236
data security 227
data transfer 60
data types 106
numeric data 129, 135
databases
database facilities 109
database methods 103
database software 203
flatfile databases 103, 109
hierarchical database 109
hypertext database 82, 213
number-structured databases 81
record-structured databases 81
relational database(s) 81, 103
date(s) 126, 129, 135
defaults
file location 207
language 206
templates 205
values 197
width 127
delivery notes 15, 20
descending order 93
desktop appearance 199
devices 186
active/passive 170
analogue/digital 170
automatic/manual input devices 157
controlled devices 181
data capture devices 171
data logging device 171
input/output devices 182
output devices 156, 172
peripheral devices 190
pointing devices 160
dictionary 60
digital devices 170–1
direct (random) access 185
directories 90, 199
disk/diskette 185, 186, 187
display parameters 207
documents
documentation 58
formal documents 43
source document 85
domain name 23
DOS-based systems 126, 194
dot matrix printers 177
drafts 40
drag-and-drop editing 161
drivers 191, 207
drives 186
DTP 7, 37, 203
dynamic RAM 184

E&OE 17
e-commerce 6, 89
editing
documents 221
drag-and-drop 161
e-mail 20, 21
e-mail addresses 23
e-mail software 203
emboldening/enhancing text 69
entity 110
envelopes 10, 17
equipment faults 223
ergonomics 220, 230
errors
data collection 60
transcription 65
ESC key 157
exporting files 91
external communications 7, 43

faults, equipment 223
faxes 20
fax-back facility 29
fax machines 26
fibre optic cable 191
fields 103, 104
field length 107
field name 105
field title 98
file extension 57, 66, 91

file names 91, 226
find function 95, 143
fire risks 228
flags 41
flatfile databases 103, 109
floppy disk 186, 187
flyers 29
font(s) 13, 68
footers 43, 122
foreign key 107
formal documents 43
formats
  cell formats 133
  character format 129
  currency format 129
formulae 125, 129, 136
full justification 68
function keys 157, 204
functions 125
  AVERAGE function 138
  find function 95, 143
  IF function 138
  SUM function 137

gigabytes 183
global positioning system (GPS) 169
graphic user interface (GUI) 195
graphics software 203
graphs 125, 143, 144
group header/footer 122

hanging indents 69
hard copy 172, 176
hard disk 186
hard page break 69
hard space 68
hardware 155, 156
headers 43, 122
heading levels 45
health and safety issues 233
heat sensors 166
help, on-screen 205
hierarchical database 109
highlighting 69
hit 210
home page 5, 210
hot link(s) 82, 203, 209
hot spot 209
HTML programs 209
hypertext database 82, 213

icons 204
identifier 216
IF function 138
illuminance 166
immediate access store (IAS) 183
impact printers 177
importing files 57, 91
indentation 69
index files 93
indexes 95
informal communications 20
information 80
  accessing information 86
  information handling 79, 80, 85, 100
  sources 82
ink jet printers 177
input
  input devices 156, 157
  input/output devices 182
  primary input 157
  secondary input 156
insert mode 87
insertion point 160
interaction 172
internal communications 20, 43
interrogation 86, 143
interviewing 84
invoices 15, 17
ISDN 26
italics 69
item(s) 126, 135
itineraries 50
ITU 28

joy stick 162
justification 68, 133

key
  CTRL key 157
  ESC key 157
  function keys 157, 205
  key strokes, multiple 204, 216
  toggle key 87
key field(s) 93, 97
  primary/foreign key 106
key skills 249
keyboard 157
  concept keyboards 159
  keypad 158
kilobytes 183

landscape orientation 12, 67
language
  computer language 202
  default language 206
laser printers 177
layout
  page 68
  spreadsheet 127
LCD (liquid crystal display) 175
left click 160
left justification 68
legislation 222, 229, 236
levels of heading 45
light sensors 166
line spacing 40
liquid crystal display (LCD) 175

logical access controls 228
logical operators 97
lookup table 115
loudspeaker 180
lower case 71

macro(s) 67, 73, 203, 207, 216
magnetic disk 185
magnetic ink character recognition (MICR) 166
main memory 183
main processing unit 156, 187
main title 132
manual data entry 157
manual input devices 157
many-to-many/many-to-one relationships 114
mark sense reader 164
match, search on a 98
matters arising 46
medium 186
megabytes 183
memorandum 20, 21
memory
  cache memory 184
  main memory 183
  memory devices 156, 182, 189
  permanent memory 184
  primary memory 183
  volatile/non-volatile 184
  see also storage
memos 20, 21
menu driven software 204
  menus 172
messages 172
MICR 166
microphones 167
microprocessor 190
minutes 45, 46, 48
mistakes 59
model 146
modelling software 204
monitors 173–4
motherboard 189
mouse 160
  mouse events 161
  mouse settings 199
multimedia software 204
multiple key strokes 204

newsletters 33, 36
non-volatile memory 184
number-structured databases 81
numeric data 129, 135
numeric keypad 157

Obscene Publications Act (1990) 222
observation 83, 84
occasion 53
OCR 166
OMR 164
on-screen help 204
one-to-one/one-to-many relationships 114
operating systems 193, 195
operators, logical/relational 97
optical character recognition (OCR) 166
optical mark reader (OMR) 164
order
  ascending/descending 93
  sales/purchase 15, 18
organisations 72
orientation 12, 67
orphan 69
outline 44, 45
output
  output devices 156, 172
  printed output 143, 172, 176
  overtype mode 87

package, software 204
page break, hard/soft 69
page header/footer 122
page layout 68
pagination 69
paper size 12, 21, 66
paperless office 41, 221
parallel cables 191
passive devices 170
password 198
pathname 91
peripheral devices 190
permanent memory 184
photo cell 170
physical access controls 228
pitch 13
pixels 174
Plain English Society 58
platforms 203
plotter 176
point size 13
pointing devices 160–1
portability 172, 183
portrait orientation 12
ports 189, 190, 191
presentation 66
  presentation techniques 3, 125
  presenting information 1
  presenting results 86
primary input 157
primary key field 106
primary memory 183
primary sort field 97
printed output 143, 172, 176
printer driver(s) 191, 207
printer port 191

printers 176–7
programmes 50–1
programming 209
  HTML programs 209
  languages 193, 202, 203
  macro programs 216
prompt 174
PROMs (programmable ROMs) 185
proofreading 60, 62, 65, 226
proximity sensors 167
publicity flyers 29
pulsed signals 190
punctuation 60
purchase order 18

QBE 118
queries 118
questionnaires 83, 84
QWERTY keyboard 157

random access memory (RAM) 184, 185, 189
range
  cell range 137
  searching within a range 98
read-only memory (ROM) 185, 189
readability 56
readers 52
reading age 53
receipts 18
record(s) 81, 103
record-structured databases 81
relational database(s) 81, 103
relational operator(s) 97
relationships 81, 113–14
relative cell referencing 138
relay 181
replacing multiple key stokes 216
replication 138, 139
reports 42, 112, 118
resolution 174, 178
restoring backups 207
right click 160
right justification 68
ROM (read-only memory) 185, 189
root directory 199
rows 87, 127
  row title(s) 132, 135
ruler 69

safety hazards 229
sales order 18
sampling 170
sans serif font 13
scanner 163
screens 173
  on-screen help 204
  screen verification 172
  touch screen 162
scrollbar 161
searching 92, 95, 98
  wildcard search 99
secondary input 156
secondary sort field 97
secondary storage 183
security
  of data 227
  passwords 198
  procedures 229
selection
  selected records 98
  using a mouse 160
sensors 166–7
serial access 185
serial cables 191
serif font 13
setting/modifying default templates 205, 206
signals 190
size of screen 173
soft page break 69
soft space 68
software 155, 193
  applications software 193, 203
  browser software 212
  communications software 203
  database software 203
  e-mail software 203
  graphics software 203
  HTML programs 209
  menu driven software 204
  modelling software 204
  multimedia software 204
  software package 204
  software utilities 191, 203
  user friendly software 204
  word processing software 203
  see also graphic user interface, operating systems
sorting 92
  sort field 97
sound card 180
sound recognition 167
source document 85
sources of information 82
space
  hard/soft 68
  white space 67
spellcheckers 60, 65
spreadsheets
facilities 143
layout 127
methods 125
software 203
SQL 118
standard documents 3, 5
static RAM 184
storage

backing store 183
immediate access store (IAS) 183
secondary storage 183
storage devices 156, 182
temporary storage 184
see also memory
structure
directory structures 199
information structure 85
structured documents 43
styles of writing 3, 52
sub-editor 37
subdirectories 199
subscripts 77
SUM function 137
superscripts 71
SVGA 174

tables 81, 110, 114
tabulation 69
tags 210
tax point 15
templates 66, 73, 205
temporary storage 184
terabytes 183
thermistor 170
thesaurus 55
title(s) 46, 98, 132, 135
toggle key 87
total(s) 126, 136
touch screen 162
trackerball 161
transcription errors 65
transducer 170
trial and improvement 143
truncation 128
twisted pair (TP) cable 191
type/ typeface 13

underlining 69
unshielded twisted pair (UTP) 191
upper case 71
user friendly software 204
user ID 198
utilities 191, 203

validation 60, 65, 89
VAT 16
VDU (visual display unit) 162, 173
venue 46
verification 60, 65, 89, 172
vertical refresh rate 174
VGA 174
viruses 198, 203, 228
visual display unit (VDU) 162, 173
volatile memory 184

wand 164
web page 5
'what if?' query 126, 143, 146
white space 67
widow 69
width 127, 128
wildcard search 99
WIMP environment 195
window envelopes 17
Windows-based system 126
wizard(s) 203
word-processing software 203
write-once, read-many (WORM) 185
writing style 3, 52
Plain English Society 58